COMPLETE GUIDE FOR SAME-SEX FAMILIES

by Shana Priwer and Cynthia Phillips, Ph.D.

New Horizon Press
Far Hills, New Jersey

Requests for permission should be addressed to:

New Horizon Press
PO Box 669
Far Hills, NJ 07931

Shana Priwer and Cynthia Phillips
Gay and Lesbian Parenting
Complete Guide for Same-Sex Families

Cover Design: Wendy Bass
Interior Design: Susan Sanderson

Library of Congress Control Number: 2005924254

ISBN 10: 0-88282-271-3
ISBN 13: 978-0-88282-271-6
New Horizon Press

New Horizon Press books may be purchased in bulk quantities for educational, business, or sales promotional use. For information please write New Horizon Press, Special Sales Department, PO Box 669, Far Hills, NJ 07931 or call 800-533-7978
e-mail: nhp@newhorizonpressbooks.com

Visit Us on the Web: www.newhorizonpressbooks.com

Manufactured in the USA

TABLE OF CONTENTS

AUTHORS' NOTE:

Due to privacy concerns, the names and personal information for all individuals mentioned in this book have been changed, and some characters are composites.

DEDICATION:

This book is dedicated to our three children (Zoecyn, Elijah and Benjamin) who have enriched our lives and taught us the most important elements of parenting first-hand.

ACKNOWLEDGEMENTS:
The authors would like to thank the gay parenting groups in the San Francisco Bay Area who contributed their knowledge and expertise, as well as the many people whose stories are shared in this book. They also would like to thank the mothers of the MOMS e-mail list, hosted by Queernet.org, for their wisdom over the years. Special thanks to Dr. Marshall Gilula for his continued love and support.

chapter one

CHOOSING A FAMILY

The decision to raise a child is, without a doubt, the most consequential one you will ever make, simply meaning that this choice is full of consequences! It is also full of love, energy, happiness, sadness, sickness and health.

Gays and lesbians arrive at the decision to become parents through many different courses, all of them involving soul-searching and in most cases research. Gay families will encounter issues that straight families generally do not consider. The road is not always easy, but the end of the journey is, in our opinion and the opinions of those we've interviewed, worth every moment of stress and contemplation. The goal of this chapter will be to explain some of the "generic" issues crucial to any family on the brink of parenthood, and will pay special attention to ones that gay and lesbian parents need to be aware of.

Gay families often consist of two mothers or two fathers; single gays and lesbians, as well as bisexual and transgender individuals, can, of course, start their own families as well. A note on terminology: we will often use the shorthand "gay family" or "lesbian family" to actually mean "gay or lesbian parented family." In most cases of a gay or lesbian couple with children, it is the parents who are lesbian or gay, not necessarily the children!

Extended family can be one major source of either bliss or contention in a gay family's life. Factors that may affect the role that the extended family plays in your child's life are the quality of your relationships with your in-laws and your own relatives' degree of acceptance of your sexuality. These are topics to think about as you consider what role your child's grandparents will play in his or her life. Oftentimes the lure of grandchildren can be enough to change a parent's acceptance level, but other times it can go in the opposite direction. Depending on how important it is to secure the approval of the future grandparents, a gay or lesbian family may want to deal with these issues before heading down the road to parenthood.

ARE YOU SURE NOW'S THE TIME?

While deciding to become a parent can be a decision that couples belabor for months or even years, the desire can also be sparked very quickly. While some gay or lesbian couples consider parenthood for an extended period, one partner may wake up one morning and feel the time is right. Especially for lesbian couples, one woman's biological clock (or both!) may have been ticking away for years, and finally gotten to the point where the decision to parent can no longer be ignored if the person is to give birth to a child

Marty and Chris are one such couple. When they first met, both women talked about wanting children one day, but neither felt ready to take on the responsibility at that point. As their relationship became more serious, their talks of becoming parents became more frequent, but always ended in, "We'll do it some day."

They'd been together for about five years when Marty decided it was time to start a family. "I was finishing up a graduate degree," Chris comments, "when Marty said that she made an appointment with an infertility doctor. I thought, 'WHAT? Now?'" After weeks of debate and discussion, Chris realized that the choice simply wasn't hers to make alone. "Marty felt with every inch of her being that it was time to get pregnant. I knew there was no talking her out of it, and it wouldn't have been fair to try." One partner's feeling that the time has come to bear children may make little or no sense to the other partner, but that doesn't make the urge any less real.

The desire for a child is not always a rational decision. While some parents may want to wait until they are financially secure and have jobs that can easily accommodate being a parent, others simply cannot wait. The notion of the biological clock is the subject of some scientific debate, but it's undeniable that hormones play a major role in the way we live our daily lives. Biological timers help our bodies adjust to daily fluctuations, such as waking up as the sun rises and getting sleepy as the sun sets. While humans certainly can (and do) override these natural preferences, there's little doubt that the body and nature have been designed to work together in a complementary fashion. Parenthood is one of those decisions that can come on a gut, instinctual level rather than being an intellectual decision. Parenting involves many losses of control, and the decision to become a parent is often the first of those seemingly irrational decisions!

One of the first facts to become immediately obvious to a gay or lesbian couple is that their parenting experience will be a very different proposition from what is experienced by a heterosexual couple. A major difference is that, for gay and lesbian couples, parenthood is usually a conscious decision. There tend to be very few unplanned gay pregnancies or adoptions. Because of this reality, gay and lesbian couples often tend to be older than their heterosexual counterparts before parenting their first child. Gay couples will often go back and forth for years before succeeding in their dream to become parents.

DON'T WAIT FOREVER

While it's always wise to study the available options before making an informed decision, it is important not to wait too long. Once you've committed yourselves to becoming a family, let the debates and indecision cease.

Remember that there's no perfect time to become a parent. Abhi and Jose, a gay male couple from Oregon, had the "Are we ready?" discussion for several years before deciding that they simply wanted to be parents. Abhi recalls, "You can always have more money or a better job. You can always live in a better house. So at some point, you just have to stop worrying and do it."

Money and material possessions won't make you a better parent and it is important eventually to come to terms with the idea that you cannot prepare yourselves for parenthood one hundred percent. Jose and Abhi knew that the right time to have a child was when they both decided that they were ready. "Eventually, we knew that all these external factors just didn't matter that much," Abhi says. "We both had well-paying jobs, and we figured that that was enough."

There are several actual reasons not to put off the parenting decision indefinitely. Raising young children is exhausting, and people in their twenties and thirties have more energy (and usually better health) than those in their forties or fifties.

In addition, waiting too long could actually make it much more difficult to become parents. Women's fertility begins to decline dramatically after age thirty-five so lesbian couples, like all women, have a built-in timeline for achieving pregnancy. For men considering using a surrogate, the age of the surrogate (or egg donor) is more of an issue than the age of the sperm source, though sperm count and motility do start to decline later in life. Also, most international adoption agencies require younger parents to adopt babies and toddlers. People in their fifties will only be allowed to adopt older children. If you and your partner are on the outer limits of the optimal age period set by agencies, don't wait another five years! There is also a lower age limit to be considered: many countries will not allow people under thirty to adopt.

Of course, older parenthood comes with its own set of perks – older parents are often more mature, more settled in their jobs and careers, more financially secure and more knowledgeable in general. The tradeoffs are important to consider when thinking about starting a family – one interesting data point is to think about how old you will be when your youngest child graduates from high school or college. For parents of a newborn who are in their forties, college expenses can be formidable at a time when they may be living on a retirement budget. Of course, this situation can be surmounted with a bit of planning, but it's certainly worth taking into account.

WE THINK WE'RE READY… ARE WE?

While there is never any perfect time to become a parent, some times are better than others. Harbor no misconceptions that having a child is inexpensive or fast. If you and your partner are currently buried under a mountain of debt, you may want to at least try to get your finances in order before taking on the responsibility of raising a child. Also, bear in mind that the cost of acquiring a child varies drastically. The bare minimum costs may be incurred by a lesbian couple attempting to get pregnant using fresh sperm from a known donor; if everyone is healthy and fertile, this process may cost as little as the price of the syringes. At the other end of the spectrum, international adoption or in vitro fertilization can easily rack up tens of thousands of dollars of bills. Be realistic about both what your family can afford, and what kind of debt you're willing to take on in order to have a family.

Also, the expense of a child certainly does not end with the acquisition of said child. Jose was shocked at how much it cost to raise a child. "The adoption itself wasn't too bad, but my lord! The diapers, the formula, the bottles, the baby food, clothes… And he's only two years old!" The expenses grow with your children; eventually they'll want bikes, the latest electronic gear and summer camps. And this doesn't even take college into account! While it's possible to raise a child as extravagantly (or not) as possible, a newborn will sleep as soundly in a basic bassinette as she will in a top-of-the-line crib.

Unfortunately, not all expenses can be foreseen or avoided. Consider that your child might have a major medical problem that isn't covered by insurance; the bill will eventually fall to the parents. Also consider that you might have a teenager who needs major orthodontia, most of which likely won't be covered by dental insurance. It is always best to have some savings as a buffer against these sorts of unforeseen expenditures.

In the case of Marty and Chris, both women were young and for them, starting early ended up working to their benefit. "We'd always talked about having a big family… I wanted two kids, she wanted three," says Chris. "Even though we debated a bit before getting started, it ended up being a good thing that we started young."

WHERE DO BABIES COME FROM?

Most gay or lesbian couples have to come terms with the fact that, while cutting-edge reproductive technologies are becoming more prevalent, it is next to impossible for a gay or lesbian couple to be the sole genetic contributors to a child. While heterosexual couples can certainly have serious problems with infertility, most couples composed of a male and a female member expect that they will be biologically related to their offspring. For gays and lesbians, this is usually not the case.

For example, a gay couple using a surrogate to carry a child to term will have to choose the sperm of one of the men. In some cases, the two men may choose to mix their sperm so that they don't know which one is the biological father; however, the egg will ultimately only be fertilized with the sperm of one man. And just a warning on the subject: this practice might reduce the chances of conception because of antibodies which could cause problems for normal sperm function.

In the case of a lesbian couple that decides to have a baby, one of the big decisions will be which woman should carry the child. For some couples, one woman may really want to be pregnant while the other does not necessarily want to give birth herself. Marty and Chris had this "dilemma," but were able to work it out since Chris had no interest, at the time, in getting pregnant. "For us, the decision was easy. I really wanted to get pregnant, and she didn't!"

However, in other lesbian couples, both women may have intense desires to be birthmothers, and in these cases the decisions will be much more difficult.

Options to circumvent this situation include both women attempting to get pregnant at the same time or implanting the eggs of one woman into the uterus of the other.

The issue, though, remains a major one: only one member of the couple usually will have a primary biological relationship to the baby. Some lesbian couples may choose to use a sperm donor who is a relative of the non-carrying partner; that way, both families' blood lines will be present in their offspring. However, this solution to fathering the child relies on the availability and willingness of a male relative.

Do not discount the emotional impact of these decisions. It is important for gay and lesbian couples considering parenthood to discuss their roles in the family that they will create. One satisfying approach to give both parents equal status is for the child to assume the last name of the partner who is not biologically related. That way, both parents can assert their relationship to the child without rendering anyone unequal.

Of course, equal parenthood isn't always a necessity. In some cases, one member of a couple may really want a child while the other member is less interested in the entire process. They may decide to configure their family so that the biologically-related partner is the primary parent, and the other partner has a role more like that of an aunt or uncle. While less common, this method can give each parent the roles desired. Beware, though, that once the theoretical child actually exists, all bets are off: hormones kick in and roles may change. Be prepared to be flexible. However, in a gay or lesbian couple starting a family there are no fixed roles for each parent, as there are in a heterosexual family. Without predetermined gender roles, each member of a couple can instead choose the role that fits that person the best: equal parents, mommy and auntie or daddy and his partner.

OUT AND ABOUT

Another important issue for partially-or completely-closeted gay and lesbian parents is the fact that, by virtue of having a child, not disclosing one's sexual orientation becomes much more difficult. Many gay people are only comfortable being conservative in their display of their sexuality.

Abhi and Jose learned first-hand that one can't maintain that level of privacy with a family. "When it was just the two of us, we were pretty careful not to look 'too gay,'" Jose says. "We both had some bad experiences in college, and just wanted to be ourselves without being harassed. But after we adopted

Kenny, we ended up all walking down the street holding hands together. It's just what you do as a parent – you stop worrying about what other people think."

Having a child call both parents "Mommy" or "Daddy" in public will make your family structure clear and apparent to all but the most oblivious observer. Once your child is older, she will talk about her family with friends, neighbors, teachers, the lady at the grocery store and anyone else she meets or comes into contact with. Expect to be "outed" in the most mundane of situations. Don't expect your children to respect your desire to hide your lifestyle. If you can't handle this sort of exposure, gay parenting may not be for you.

Children are not known for their subtlety and will probably fail if asked to keep the "family secret." In fact, it is far preferable to teach children to be open and proud of their family structure. Keeping secrets will teach them that there's something wrong with their family, and that is not a good thing with which to burden a child.

If you and your partner are not comfortable being out in everyday situations, it may be a good idea to practice before the child is old enough to understand what you're saying. For example, if you're sitting at a park with your infant and the mom on the next bench asks what your husband does for a living, it's a good idea to practice saying something like, "my partner is an architect – she works up in the city." While it may seem difficult or uncomfortable at first, remember that talking about your family structure will get easier in time.

FEAR NOT STRAIGHT STRANGERS

Gay families may encounter some confusion, hostility or outright homophobia from heterosexuals. Be prepared to deal effectively with these situations, especially in front of your children. If your children are verbal, express matter-of-fact pride in your family structure. If you are asked any sort of intrusive questions, such as how your children were conceived or adopted, feel free to brush them off if you are uncomfortable answering. If you feel the person is asking out of genuine interest instead of prurient curiosity, but don't want to discuss the details of picking a sperm donor in front of your children, it can be best to have a prepared answer along the lines of, "Those are personal details that are just for our family, but if you want to give me a call later I can give you some more general information."

Don't assume the worst, however. You'll probably find that you'll bond just fine with the other parents at your child's baby gymnastics class over the mundane details of parenting. Every parent has to deal with issues like diaper rash and reflux! An interesting facet of becoming a parent is that you may find yourself having much more in common with the straight couple down the street than you did before you had kids. In fact, you will probably have much LESS in common with your gay friends who have chosen not to be parents.

To this extent, parenting is a great equalizer. You may find that you mesh into "straight culture" more than you ever dreamed (or wanted!) and that, conversely, the bar scene doesn't hold the appeal that it did before the 3:00 a.m. feedings and diaper changes. Perhaps the best way around this situation is to connect with other gay and lesbian families in your area. Don't be surprised if you find yourself acquiring a number of straight friends as well, especially ones with children the same ages as yours.

Keeping your existing circle of friends is not impossible. Many of your gay and lesbian friends, while they might decide not to become parents themselves, may make excellent honorary aunts and uncles to your children. Don't discount any offers of free babysitting! What's important to remember is that, even as your primary function is now that of a parent, you are still the same person you were before you had children, and you still have your own intellectual and emotional needs. Try not to isolate friends just because they don't have children. Incorporate them into your life to the extent that they are willing. Especially if your household includes a stay-at-home parent, childless friends can be a lifeline back to the adult world where conversations rarely involve what shade the baby's poop is.

You may, of course, find that in reality, once you have kids, you have little time for anyone else. If this is the case, don't be self-critical. For most of us, family comes first, and you have to accept that one of the prices of parenthood is making certain sacrifices.

CHOOSING TO BE A SINGLE PARENT

Single people, we believe, are capable of becoming excellent parents. The reality of single parenting, though, will be different from that of parenting as a couple.

People making a conscious decision to be single parents are becoming more and more common, and have certain advantages and disadvantages over parenting as part of a couple. On the plus side, the decision is all yours. When you decide the time to become a parent is right, you can begin to take action without further ado. As a single parent, you can have absolute consistency in your style of parenting. Your child will not need to adapt to two disparate sets of rules. For some, the most significant benefit is that you and your child can develop an exceptionally close relationship without having to make time for a spouse or partner.

On the other hand, single parenting is a lot of work. There will probably be times that you wish for someone (anyone!) to share your screaming baby at three in the morning. Single parents are on duty all the time. While some are lucky enough to have grandparents or close friends living nearby to help out, others do not have this sort of help available.

Single parents should know that they're not alone – statistics show that the majority of single parents are no longer teenagers. They're older women. There are even support groups for "single parents by choice" that include both heterosexual and gay or lesbian parents who have decided to share their lives with a child, with or without a partner.

CAN I AFFORD A BABY ALONE?

Before choosing to become a single parent, seriously consider the financial realities. As the only parent, you'll have to work full-time, unless you're independently wealthy. While working from home could be a fantastic way to cut down on daycare bills, full-time work-at-home jobs are few and far between. Even if such an opportunity presents itself, it can be difficult to put in a forty-hour work week while tending to a baby or toddler.

Daycare costs can eat up a large portion of your salary. The exception would be a fortuitous situation where you know someone who would watch your child for a reduced fee. Be advised, though, that this person should be a certified childcare worker and his or her home needs to be safe for children. This person could also be a close, trusted friend or relative, but he or she would need to understand the commitment that is required for watching a child five days a week. Try to figure out a plan for returning to work once your child has arrived and make sure that it will be feasible.

The options for having a child as a single parent are generally the same choices that a lesbian or gay couple would make. Insemination, surrogacy and adoption are the three primary options. The notable disadvantage is that, as a single person, you'd be responsible for the entire cost (as opposed to it being split between two partners) so finances could partially dictate the route you choose.

In some cases, it may actually be easier to adopt a child as a single parent than it would be as a couple. Your sexual orientation becomes much less of an issue as a single man or woman, particularly for international adoption.

However, conceiving and giving birth may be more difficult without the support of a partner. The decision is an individual one, but it should be considered from all these different angles.

CHALLENGES FROM WITHOUT: EXTENDED FAMILY

Are you expecting Grandma and Grandpa to welcome your child with open arms? Don't be shocked if they're not as pleased as you are with your new family. As a gay or lesbian couple, you may find that the level of acceptance you receive from your parents and other extended family members varies widely. This may depend on the relatives' ages, where in the country they live, whether they know any other gays or lesbians, whether any of their friends have gay or lesbian children, etc. Depending on how long you've been in your current relationship, you may find that parents especially regard your being gay as "just a phase" and think of your partner as "just a roommate" or a friend. They may go on in their denial for much longer than you would have thought possible.

The presence of a child in your lives, however, can be much harder for parents and other family members to ignore. While you and your partner may attend family holidays and other gatherings simply as "roommates" or friends, showing up with one partner holding a baby and the other partner holding a diaper bag makes the relationship much more obvious. Even if you feel as though you laid the groundwork years or even decades ago and have been out to your parents forever, be prepared for the fact that becoming parents is often what finally forces your own parents to consider you and your partner as lovers, partners and spouses.

If having a child doesn't turn your parents into true believers, don't despair. Often it's just a matter of time before parents can finally accept and acknowledge their child's homosexuality. In many cases, parents will come to a gradual realization that homosexual relationships are, in fact, relationships. They may meet other gay couples in other situations, and may realize that their friends also have gay children. They may see others in their day-to-day lives, from plumbers to store owners, who are out and gay; eventually, these casual relationships may positively affect their relationships with their own children.

On the other hand, don't be shocked if parents who have shunned you for years for being homosexual suddenly welcome your new child with open arms! There is something about the lure of a grandchild that can make older or more conservative people more accepting. Especially if this is the first grandchild on either partner's side of the family, you may find that much is forgiven when grandma gets to hold a smiling bundle of joy for the first time. Allow grandma and grandpa the pleasure of experiencing their first grandchild and give them the benefit of the doubt. While all families may not come around just because a child has been born, you may be pleasantly surprised. At the very least, don't deny yourself the pleasure of finally being accepted, even if it had to come without direct action of your own.

You may also find that proud grandparents will naturally want to brag about their grandchild. They may want to show baby pictures to everyone they meet. This may actually force them to be much more open about your relationship than they would have been previously. Even if you've been out for years, don't be surprised if everyone in your hometown suddenly seems to know both that you're gay, and that you've had (or adopted) a child.

Once you've decided to try to become parents, you may want to tell your friends and acquaintances before the child is even conceived. However, rethink this. Both pregnancy and adoption can be long and bumpy roads, and if the people you tell are not supportive, their negative influence can add to your potential feelings of frustration. Reserve the announcement for the time when parenthood is imminent.

For example, if you're using a surrogate to achieve pregnancy, you may want to wait until the pregnancy is fairly well established (or even until the child is born, in cases where extended family is more estranged) before announcing the child. When considering adoption, you may want to wait until you're actually matched with a birth mother or receive a referral (for international adoption) before breaking the news to relatives.

On the other hand, some relatives may need quite a bit of time to get used to the idea of your becoming a parent. They could be better off with a slow approach, rather than a phone call saying, "Hey mom, we're pregnant!" In these cases, you may want to break the news more gradually, perhaps as a series of hypothetical statements, such as "gee mom, we're thinking of moving to a bigger house because we might start a family some day" or "how did you manage it when you had three small children at home?" Such questions will not only involve your parents by asking for their advice, they should give them some clue as to your plans.

You may also find that pregnancy and parenting a young child may bring you closer to both your parents and your partner's parents than before. Feel free to ask for stories about when your mother or mother-in-law was pregnant; ask for advice on a wide variety of topics. Taking the advice is completely optional!

The point is simply that starting a family can be a shared experience through which the entire family can bond.

For many, starting a family is a badge of true adulthood. Most gay and lesbian couples are not privy to weddings. The birth or adoption of a first child has a tendency to elevate a couple to adult status in the eyes of their other family members. Don't be surprised to be invited, as a couple, to family gatherings and events for the first time.

HEY, THAT'S NOT FAIR...

Be aware of the potential for difference in treatment of your children and other grandchildren. For example, your sister may be married with a few children of her own. Suppose you then adopt a child, or your partner gives birth to a child. Your parents may be wonderfully accepting of your children and may welcome them as grandchildren. However, they could instead treat only the children that they are biologically related to as "real grandchildren."

Unfortunately, the last scenario can be fairly common among gay couples and their extended families. If it happens to you, you'll need to explain that all of your children are full members of your family and, therefore, of theirs. The first and best option is to be forthright: speak to the offending grandparents and make it clear that this difference in treatment is unacceptable. If this approach doesn't work, it may be necessary to issue an "ultimatum" – treat all the grandchildren equally, at all times. Always remember what is most important: your children deserve to live in an environment where they are loved, respected and valued. These things are much more important than any supposed "rights" that extended family members may think they have. If you don't like the treatment that your child is getting, even from a close relative, the best choice may be simply to eliminate contact with that person.

It is well-documented that children thrive in an extended family environment. If neither partner is close to anyone in his or her own family, remember that this extended community doesn't have to be a biological one. If you experience hostile or unequal treatment from some or most family members, you can create a family of choice consisting of friends and supportive relatives. They can help provide a nurturing and caring environment that your children need and deserve. You can give them honorary titles of "Aunt," "Uncle" and "Grandma", and they can fulfill required roles at holidays, school plays and other celebrations.

Even if your family is supportive, they may live far away from you and your new family. In that case, a local family of choice can still be an excellent mechanism for support.

CONCLUDING ADVICE

We've discussed many things to think about as you start considering parenthood. The most important thing to ask yourself is, do you feel ready? If the answer is yes, then be confident in your decision to start a family. There will be bumps and potholes along the way, but your first day as a parent will be one of the happiest days of your life.

QUESTIONS FOR PROSPECTIVE PARENTS:

1. Are you prepared for a child, not just emotionally, but also financially?
2. Have you thought about how having a child will change your life?
3. Are you comfortable being "out"?
4. If you have a partner, does he or she feel the same way you do about starting a family?
5. Do you have any friends who are parents?
6. Have you spoken to your own parents about your desire to raise children?
7. Do they support you?
8. If you are single, do you have a good support network?

chapter two

FIRST THINGS FIRST: LEGAL ADVICE

While married heterosexual couples can assume that they will receive the rights and responsibilities that come with a marriage certificate, most gay and lesbian couples can make no such assumptions. It will take work on your part to obtain similar protections. As of this writing, only one state in the United States (Massachusetts) allows full legal marriage for homosexual couples. While other states have a variety of other protections (or none at all) for same sex couples, no other states give the full benefits of marriage and no same-sex marriages are recognized at a federal level. (See Appendix I for more information.) Ongoing litigation in several states is challenging the status quo. For the time being, though, it is critical for gay couples to do everything they can to protect their growing families.

Unfortunately, there isn't one single thing or one individual document that a same-sex couple can fill out to gain all of these protections. Gay and lesbian couples have to put together these protections in a piecemeal manner. The exact requirements vary depending on one's state of residence. Even if you live in a relatively liberal state, it is important to get the fullest possible legal protection in writing, just in case there is a medical or other emergency while you are traveling in a more conservative state or country.

It can be awkward to think about legal rights, because most are for worst-case scenarios such as serious illness or sudden death. In the first blush of a new relationship, this may be the last thing a couple wants to think about! With a more long-term established relationship, the partners may think these protections are unnecessary and should be taken for granted. However, never underestimate the greediness of distant relatives or the discrimination of our medical and legal system. Nobody wants to end up in the hospital, arguing with an emergency room physician over the right to visit a critically-ill partner. Even for couples who aren't planning on having children, and especially for couples who are considering starting a family, it's very important to have all legal rights and paperwork in order before proceeding.

WILLS AND TRUSTS

Planning for one's own death is rarely a cheery proposition. However, it's one of those "adult things" that has to be taken care of at some point, so why not sooner rather than later? If you were to die without a will or any sort of legal document indicating your wishes, your property would be distributed to your legal heirs (i.e. blood relatives) by the court system.

In most states, except for those with same-sex marriage, civil union or full domestic partnerships, your domestic partner will not be considered a legal heir for the purpose of inheriting. This can lead to an awkward situation; relatives of your partner, possibly people you've never met, may lay claim to the house you and your partner shared, your car and any other worldly possessions that you cannot prove were owned solely by you. Don't expect such individuals to respect your relationship when it comes to money. Even the best of intentions will often be forgotten when the law is not on your side.

JANE AND DEBORAH: A WARNING

Jane, who had been Deborah's partner for thirty years, died suddenly and without a will. The two women had a long, trusting relationship and never had much interest in paperwork. The deed to the house that they shared together was only in Jane's name; her surviving partner, Deborah, therefore had no legal ownership of it. Jane's name was also the only one on the car title, since in the beginning Deborah only used the car to go to the store and back. As they grew older, though, Deborah used the car more and more to shuttle Jane back and forth to medical offices and pharmacies.

After her death, Jane's blood relative (a nephew she barely knew) showed up to claim her body. He did not have any understanding of Jane's relationship with Deborah, and didn't particularly care to listen. He did not listen to Deborah's input for the funeral and, following the ceremony, he proceeded directly on to "his new" house. He emptied it of the priceless treasures and emotional keepsakes that Deborah had wanted to keep because, legally, the house belonged to his aunt and not to Deborah. Without legal standing, Deborah found herself homeless and was forced to move. Since the bank accounts were also only in Jane's name, she lost her share of their money and other investments.

BE CLEAR NOW, AVOID TROUBLE LATER

The importance of stating one's wishes in terms of property inheritance cannot be underestimated. By drafting a will, it is possible to designate exactly who should receive your property, as well as when they will receive it. You will also be able to name a person to be in charge of distributing your assets. This person is known as the "executor" of the will. His or her consent will need to be obtained first, since it's not the kind of thing someone would want to be surprised with! This person should be made aware of your will and its location, so that he or she can access it if it ever becomes necessary.

In a will, it is appropriate to make provisions for the type of funeral you want, including who will have control over its content and format. Other funeral arrangements can also be specified. You can state your wishes about whether you want to be cremated or buried, and whether you want a funeral service in a particular religious tradition or a non-traditional memorial service of some sort. It can be a comfort to your partner and other relatives to know that your wishes are being carried out after your life is over, and can remove a significant burden during a very difficult time.

If you have children, you can nominate a guardian for your children in your will. This doesn't have the legally binding nature of an adoption, but in most cases, depending on what state you live in, the court will respect a designated guardian if there are no other challengers. Again, be sure that you speak to any potential guardian ahead of time, obtain his or her consent, and if your children are old enough, discuss it with them.

Jing and his partner Mark adopted a baby boy, with Mark as the legal parent of record. Where they lived, domestic partner adoptions were not an option, so the two men created a guardianship agreement in which Mark specified that Jing should have legal guardianship of their son, should anything ever happen to him. Sadly, Mark was killed in a car accident; Jing had enough to worry about, without having to think about losing custody of their son.

Unfortunately, the story didn't end there. Mark's parents never approved of his relationship, and they didn't want their grandson being raised by a "stranger." They filed for adoption of the baby and won their petition in court. Jing's lawyer appealed the decision, and the case was resolved by the judge's decision that Jing should be allowed supervised visitation with his son. The solution here was far from optimal, to be sure, but without the guardianship agreement, Jing might not have won even that small victory.

In most cases of same-sex couples (with or without children), two contingencies need to be considered when drawing up wills. One is what happens if one partner dies before the other. The other is what will happen if both partners die at the same time (as in a car crash, etc.) In the first case, most partners would usually leave all or most shared asserts to the surviving partner. If you have any particular heirlooms from your family that you want to pass on to brothers, sisters or other immediate relatives, you should also indicate that.

In the second scenario, if you do have children or if you intend to have any in the near future, place the appropriate contingencies in your will. Example: say that John dies, leaving behind minor children. John wants them to inherit his possessions and assets. He may want to stipulate that his children's living expenses will be paid for, and that the rest should be held in trust until the children reach legal adulthood or enter college. The situation of parents dying and leaving behind minor children is of course a very difficult one to contemplate; it is, however, important to take care of these things. Knowing that your children will be taken care of were anything to happen can provide a sense of security.

LIVING TRUST

Depending on your state and particular distribution of assets, instead of a will you can choose to use a revocable living trust to indicate who will get your property in the event of your death. A living trust functions much like a will. The main difference is that a will must be settled by the court system, while a living trust can transfer property directly upon your death. The court probate process can sometimes take up to a year, especially if you have debts that must be settled first or if the will is challenged. Also, depending on your particular circumstances, sometimes using a living trust can keep your heirs from having to pay certain taxes on received property, so there may be financial benefits to going with this method.

A trust differs fundamentally from a will in that once a trust is executed, you actually legally transfer the ownership of your assets to the trust. You still will have complete control of your assets during your lifetime, but the trust will technically own your property. Because of some state and federal tax laws, in some cases property left by one partner to another in a will may be subject to much higher tax rates than a comparable situation in which a wife leaves property to her husband. For this reason, especially if you have sizeable assets, it may make sense to use a living trust instead. If you think this situation applies to you, always speak with an attorney who's familiar with the particular situation for same-sex couples in your state.

As of this writing, the states of California, Hawaii and Vermont allow same-sex partners to inherit without wills. Massachusetts also allows for this inheritance, but that is because same-sex couples can legally get married there.

To take advantage of these rights:

- In California, you need to be registered domestic partners.
- In Vermont, you need to have completed a civil union.
- In Hawaii, you need to be reciprocal beneficiaries.

There is a caveat, though. Even if you live in one of these states, your property may be distributed between your partner and any other legal living heirs if you didn't prepare a will. The bottom line: no matter where you live, write a will or living trust.

DURABLE POWER OF ATTORNEY FOR FINANCES

A Durable Power of Attorney for finances can be used to ensure that your partner has full control over joint assets should you be incapacitated. This document lets you give a particular person full access to your finances without relinquishing any of your own control. In such a situation, this person would be able to pay your bills, cash your checks or receive various other benefits in your name. Obviously, this sort of document gives another person serious control over your money. Remember that you're basically giving someone else the ability to empty out your bank accounts, sell off your assets and drain your 401k plan. Don't take this decision lightly!

To whom should you give this sort of power? If you and your partner already have mingled finances, a durable POA for finances can allow your partner to continue paying bills and have access to money that may be listed only in your name, but has become de facto joint property.

Mark and Jing, the couple we discussed earlier, never filed a Durable Power of Attorney and, as a result, Mark's parents claimed most of their joint assets upon their son's death. Jing says, "In retrospect, I can't believe we didn't deal with this years ago, but it never seems like you need to, you know? But then, if you don't deal with it, it may be too late."

If you don't want to give someone a complete Power of Attorney for finances, you can instead draw up a Limited Power of Attorney for finances. This version gives your designee the same powers, but only for a specific amount of time. For example, if you know that you'll be going into the hospital for scheduled surgery and will be recuperating and unable to manage your finances, it may make sense to give your partner control over your assets (and debts) for the duration of your absence. You can also limit the designee to specific functions; for example, you could allow this person to pay your bills, but not empty your bank account. It's something that would be taken for granted in a typical heterosexual marriage, but is an example of an extra precaution that gay and lesbian couples need to take in order to achieve the necessary protections.

The Power of Attorney for finances should be filed with your bank and any other financial institutions you might deal with (such as brokerage accounts or mortgage companies). Some banks will have their own versions of this form that you'll be required to use, so be sure to check with your specific bank before preparing this document.

CHOICES IN MEDICAL CARE: JIM AND DONALD

One of the nightmares of being in a non-married relationship is what may happen in the event of sudden medical illness. Donald and Jim had been together for years when Donald was seriously injured in a car accident on the way home from work. They lived in a state without a domestic partner law, and had never thought that they needed any sort of permission to make decisions for each other.

When Jim arrived at the hospital, he discovered that Donald was on a ventilator. There were some major decisions to be made regarding Donald's course of treatment, and Jim made a point of speaking to the surgeon in charge. He expected the doctor to discuss the alternatives and help him arrive at a decision for his partner's care. He found out his input was not considered valid, though, when Dr. Carlson asked, "Who are you?" Jim responded, "I'm Donald's partner." The doctor looked confused, asking if he was Donald's business partner or if they worked together in a law firm. Jim patiently explained that no, they were life partners, and had been for some time. The doctor shook his head and said, "I can only discuss Donald's medical situation with family members. Does he have any in the area that you can call?"

Jim couldn't believe what he was hearing, and tried to explain their living situation to the doctor. His pleas fell on deaf ears; the doctor would only talk about Donald's care with a wife, parent or other relative. Jim finally asked to go in and see Donald; surely they could sign some sort of form or document to clear this up. However, he wasn't allowed into the Intensive Care room because according to hospital policy, visitors were restricted to "relatives only." In this gravest of times, Jim was relegated to the status of stranger and had no power in the situation.

There are two ways around this problem. The first is to create and carry a document sometimes called a Living Will. This document states your desires for various medical procedures, in the event that you are unable to make such decisions for yourself. Depending on what state you live in, the document that you produce will have any one of a number of names. It can be called a Living Will, a Healthcare Directive, a Medical Directive, a Directive to Physicians or a Declaration Regarding Healthcare. This document clearly states your wishes for a variety of different scenarios regarding your own medical care, including whether you would want heroic measures to artificially extend your life. It also includes whether you want to be an organ donor. This document is considered legal proof of your preferences, and makes them very clear. The form for this document varies from state to state, and you need to use the form accepted in your state.

The second solution is to produce a durable power of attorney for healthcare. Depending on your state, this form can also be called a healthcare proxy. This document designates another person to make medical decisions for you if you become unable to make them yourself. For gay and lesbian couples, this document is crucial because it can be the only way a hospital will listen to your partner, rather than calling in some distant relative if you are injured in an accident. The durable POA should be filed with your particular health insurance carrier. If you're traveling, though, carry a copy of it with you at all times. It is an important document to have in addition to a living will because there may be situations which you're unable to anticipate while creating the living will; a durable POA covers all your bases by designating your partner to make decisions in your best interests.

HOSPITAL VISITATION

In addition to a Power of Attorney for healthcare, gay and lesbian couples should also fill out a hospital visitation authorization. This form, available online or through a lawyer, lets you designate specific individuals who are not related to you, either by blood or marriage, to be able to visit you in the hospital if you are unable to give direct authorization yourself. While it doesn't seem like such a form should even be necessary, it unfortunately is. Poorly-trained hospital staff, or even illegal hospital policies, may prevent your partner from seeing you in the event of an emergency, and that is the sort of situation that can be mitigated by preparing the proper paperwork ahead of time.

The form states that you authorize that if you are ever incapacitated by illness, it is your wish that a certain person or persons be given preference to visit you, whether or not there are other people related by blood or by law who want to visit you. The document remains in effect until you specifically change these instructions to your medical staff.

Imagine that you suddenly become very ill and end up unconscious in the intensive care unit, where visitors are tightly regulated. Your partner, or any children for whom you are not the legal parent, could be barred from even being able to see you. This type of policy could make a difficult situation even more heartbreaking for your loved ones. As horrible as it is to imagine, think about how your partner and children would feel if they were unable to say their last goodbyes to you. Now go fill out some paperwork!

Hospital visitation authorizations are also useful if you know in advance that you're going to be entering the hospital, as in the case of a planned surgery. You should not only file this form with your medical insurance provider, but also call the hospital and speak to someone directly about your wishes. Talk to the hospital administrator or the community outreach department. If they fail to address your concerns, contact the Gay and Lesbian Medical Association at http://glma.org for more help.

Again, while properly documented same-sex couples in CA (and VT and HI) should already have this right, it is an excellent idea to fill out this document just in case you find yourself in a hospital out-of-state where your relationship isn't recognized. Carry this document with you at all times.

MOUNDS OF PAPERWORK: HIRE A LAWYER OR DO-IT-YOURSELF?

Now that you have this daunting pile of paperwork ahead of you, there are two main choices for how to proceed with actually preparing and legalizing it. You can either consult a lawyer who is knowledgeable in estate planning and family protection of gay and lesbian couples or you can do it all yourself.

FINDING A LAWYER

While it may be tempting to get all of these documents in order by yourself, make sure you're being realistic about the prospect. It will take time, initiative, research and probably some online skills to be able to locate and fill out all the necessary forms. If you're not comfortable cold-calling various state agencies, are unable to sit on hold for long periods of time and do not enjoy speaking at lengths with strangers about your personal life, then using a lawyer may be a good option. They can do most of the research for you, and will limit the amount of direct interaction you'll need to have with government bureaucracy.

When looking for a lawyer, it's best to find someone who has dealt with non-traditional families before. Get referrals from other gay or lesbian couples, or consult your local gay and lesbian community center or gay newspaper for recommendations. If you live in an area without such resources, go online. Try searching for a gay and lesbian lawyers association in your state. If all else fails, find some lawyers in your area who advertise estate planning services. Call them up and ask if they've ever done documentation for a same-sex couple.

An excellent resource online is the National Center for Lesbian Rights, located in San Francisco, California. Their website is http://www.nclrights.org. This organization can provide information on gay-friendly lawyers in many areas of the country, as well as advice on other legal matters, for both gay and lesbian clients. The staff is very helpful, and they currently can offer suggestions via telephone and email.

Another good place to look online is Lambda Legal Defense and Education Fund. This is a national organization that helps gays and lesbians achieve civil rights. They offer all sorts of useful legal advice for a range of situations. Their helpdesk, located at http://www.lambdalegal.org, does not make legal referrals but they do maintain a list of attorneys who are sensitive to gay issues. This site is another great option to begin the process of finding a gay-friendly lawyer.

Once you think you've located an attorney who is willing and qualified, there are certain questions that you should ask by way of a screening process. Inquire if she has any experience with families like yours, and ask for specific references, if possible. Ask whether she has any personal doubts about equal rights for gays and lesbians – you do not want an attorney who is not really on your side. Find out if she is willing to look at sample documents produced by gay and lesbian organizations. Above all, trust your instincts – if you feel uneasy or notice that your lawyer is uncomfortable around you and your partner, keep looking.

If there are worries about the cost of using a lawyer, consider how important the documentation you'll be drawing up will be. These documents can have a major influence on the lives of you, your partner and any children you may have and need to be done one way or another. Make it a financial priority, if necessary. Costs will vary depending on your area of the country, and may also vary dramatically from attorney to attorney. Don't be afraid to comparison shop. Call a few different lawyers and ask for estimates. While the cost of most of these documents will vary, most lawyers will charge at least $500 just for preparing a will.

Some lawyers more experienced in estate planning for lesbian and gay couples may have a complete package deal. It may include pre-drawn-up forms that can be changed for your particular situation, for a set fee. This approach could end up saving money, especially if the documents you need to file are common in your state. However, if your situation is complicated or if you're dealing with complex trusts or other financial issues, expect to pay more in lawyer's fees.

When using a lawyer, expect an initial consultation for which you may or may not have to pay. There will then be a detailed meeting, which can last several hours, in which you lay out your desires and personal situations, and the lawyer will guide you through what documents will be necessary to protect you and your family. Depending on how complex your situation is, you may find lawyers who will do all this over the phone, though it's probably easier if you meet in person, especially if you want the lawyer to review financial statements or other documents. You can then expect the lawyer and/or members of her staff to prepare the paperwork. They may mail you copies to review before the final consultation. Once all papers are prepared to your satisfaction, expect at least one more meeting in the lawyer's office to go through all the documents and have everything signed and notarized. Most law firms will have a notary public on staff who can take care of that part of the process.

Make multiple copies of each item, and have each copy notarized separately. Yes, it will add to the fee, but notarized copies are often seen as more valid than simple photocopies. The originals should be stored in a safe deposit box or other safe location. Other copies should be filed at the appropriate institutions, including banks and hospitals as outlined above. Your lawyer may also be able to keep copies on file, in case future heirs need to locate them.

GO IT ALONE

If the expense of a lawyer is beyond your means, don't despair. You can locate and file most of this documentation completely on your own. It will, however, take sleuthing, research, perseverance and patience. While a general overview of the necessary processes is provided here, remember that the exact forms required may vary by state.

When considering drawing up legal documentation yourself, you have three major options. You can download sample wills and other forms from various websites, you can purchase a do-it-yourself Make Your Own will book or you can purchase software such as WillMaker, which guides you through the process of customizing your very own will.

Downloading sample wills from the Internet is an easy option because it can be as simple as doing an online search, locating a form, downloading it, printing it out and filling it out. The disadvantage of such a method is that any forms downloaded may or may not be legally valid in your state. Such standardized forms also may not take into account the specialized issues of gay and lesbian couples. They may only be valid for simple situations, and if your personal situation is more complicated, the generic forms may not apply.

For Medical directives and living wills, there is an excellent online resource that, fortunately, provides clear forms for every state in the country. All state forms can be downloaded from http://www.partnershipforcaring.org. Healthcare Power of Attorney forms can be downloaded from http://www.familycaregiversonline.com/legal-medical.html. These forms can also be obtained from large hospitals or from the medical association in your state. The American Medical Association's website (http://www.ama-assn.org) contains links to websites for medical associations in all fifty states.

If online forms are unappealing, or if you're not comfortable downloading forms over the Internet, there are several books for sale that instruct you on how to make your own will. Nolo Press (www.nolopress.org) publishes a number of particularly good do-it-yourself legal books, some of which include CD-ROMs with forms that you can fill in using a word processor. Such books will talk you through the process, providing specific advice and information for a range of situations. Make sure to get the latest edition of any book that you use, as laws change rapidly. Also be sure that any advice in the book is valid in your state.

Software provides a third way to make your own will relatively inexpensively. One popular example is Quicken WillMaker Plus (also by Nolo Press). This application includes wills, living trusts, healthcare directives, financial POA and various other documents for the executor of your will. There are many other software applications available as well, and most of them have a similar range of options.

The advantage of using legal software is that it can take you through a step-by-step process using documents and legal requirements that are specific to your particular state. You won't need to scrutinize every page to check for your own state, because it will be an option you can select when starting to use the software. You can fill in the blanks and print out forms, and the software will guide you through exactly what needs to be filled out. You also won't need to fill out the same thing more than once – the software will remember common entries such as your name and address and fill them in automatically for you.

Software is customizable for your situation, meaning you only need to fill out the forms (or parts of forms) that apply specifically to you. Software also allows you to make small changes to various parts of your legal documentation easily, without having to redo the entire process. On-screen help will provide links to explanations of legal terms and definitions, which will save you from having to look up unfamiliar words or purchase a legal dictionary.

If you take any of the do-it-yourself routes described here, once you've prepared your documents they will need to be notarized before they will be legally valid. You and your partner, along with valid identification, must go to a public notary. Notaries can be found in the yellow pages of most phone books. Places like copy and mailing centers often have a notary on staff, and many other places of business (such as your office) may have a notary.

In order to have your documents notarized, the notary public will need to verify your identification. You must then sign the document(s) in the presence of the notary. The notary will then sign and stamp the documents with her seal, making them legally valid. Expect to pay anywhere from two to ten dollars per page or document.

In addition, when using documents that you've prepared yourself, it's highly advisable to have a lawyer look them over before considering them finished. Preparing documents yourself and having them professionally checked is often much more affordable than having a lawyer do all the work, plus it provides enhanced legal protection in the case that you've omitted something or haven't taken into account a particular situation in your state of residence. Only a lawyer who's well-versed in estate planning in your own state will know the detailed ramifications, including tax implications, of the decisions you might make. It is well worth a brief consultation.

Unless your state or country has ratified laws on homosexual couples' rights, gay and lesbian couples will require plenty of documentation just to gain a few of the rights that are automatically granted to married heterosexual couples. However, until marriage is available equally to homosexual couples, it is important to do the best you can to protect your family. Simplify things by carrying notarized copies of documentation in your car, leaving them in your suitcase for traveling or sending a copy ahead when you're planning to travel and stay with a friend. An afternoon of paperwork may save you from serious heartache down the road. Of course, it doesn't seem fair, needing to do all this paperwork in the first place. However, with a bit of planning, some problems can be anticipated. Just think about the peace of mind you'll achieve when all your paperwork is in order and you won't have to worry about this stuff any more.

For more information on these processes, an excellent resource is *A Legal Guide for Lesbian & Gay Couples* (Nolo Press Self-Help Law Books), by Hayden Curry. This frequently updated guide helps couples anywhere in the country gain legal protection for their relationship, to the best of their ability in their particular states.

Another good resource with more information on the variety of documents discussed in this chapter is Lambda Legal's publication "Life Planning: Legal Documents and Protections for Lesbians and Gay Men." It is available online at http://www.lambdalegal.org/sections/library/lifeplanning.pdf . Another publication, from the National Center for Lesbian Rights, is "Lifelines: Documents to protect you and your family in times of trouble." It is available online at http://www.nclrights.org/publications/pubs/lifelines.pdf. This document contains appendices with samples of various legal forms.

CONCLUDING ADVICE

While starting a family will be one of the most important things in your life, protecting your family is a necessary first step in parenting. Gays and lesbians need to do more than heterosexual parents do, just to obtain the same or fewer rights. Unfair as it may seem, you still need to protect your children and partner. Write up a will or living trust, set up a Durable Power of Attorney for medical and financial cases and get all your paperwork legally documented. Hopefully none of these papers will ever be necessary, but if they are, you'll be glad to have them.

QUESTIONS FOR PARTNERS:

1. Have you and your partner registered as domestic partners, had a civil union or taken advantage of whatever level of legal recognition is available in your state, county or city?
2. Have you prepared a will or a living trust? Have you updated it to take into account recent births or adoptions of children?

3. Have you designated a third-party guardian, in the event that something were to happen to both you and your partner? Have you told your children who that guardian is?
4. Are most of your assets held jointly with your partner?
5. Have you filled out durable power of attorney forms for healthcare and finances? Have you had them notarized? Do you know where they are?
6. Have you discussed your wishes with your partner? Have you discussed your wishes with your relatives?

chapter three

ADOPTION AND FOSTERING

One of the most common ways for gay and lesbian couples to start a family is through adoption. There are many different options for adopting children, including domestic and international adoptions, and fostering. Which route to adoption you choose will be informed by mainly external factors: where in the United States you live (or what country you live in), the state of your finances, the age of child you desire and your willingness to be open about your lifestyle. See Appendix I for more information about adoption laws relevant to single parents or gay or lesbian couples in each state.

The most common type of adoption in the United States is domestic, meaning an American family is adopting a child born in the United States. Domestic adoptions come in one of two types; open adoption and closed adoption. They can be done either through a private or public adoption agency, or by using an adoption lawyer or facilitator. One of the first decisions an adoptive couple should make when entering this process is whether they prefer an open or closed adoption.

Until recently, closed adoptions were by far the most prevalent. Incredible amounts of secrecy surrounded adoption and, in fact, many children adopted in the 1950s and 1960s (and earlier) were never told they were adopted. Open adoptions became more common only in recent years. In a closed adoption, all records of the adoption are sealed and there is no contact between the birth mother and the adoptive family. In some cases, original documents relating to the adoption are actually destroyed.

In a closed adoption, therefore, it can be very difficult (if not impossible) for a person who was adopted to try to track down his biological parents, even once he or she reaches adulthood. More recently, in part because of an outcry from adults who were adopted as children, open adoptions have started to become more popular.

Open adoptions can range through varying degrees of "openness." In some open adoption situations, the birth mother and the adoptive family have each other's names and addresses. They can choose to have no contact at all, perhaps until the child reaches adulthood and may wish to initiate such contact. They may exchange yearly letters and photos, perhaps even presents and phone calls. In other cases, there is a much closer connection between the birth mother and the adoptive family–they may visit each other, and the birth mother (and other members of her family) may be fully accepted as an extended family for the child. If you wouldn't be comfortable having the potential for a relationship with the birth mother, then an open adoption probably isn't the best choice.

PRIVATE DOMESTIC ADOPTION

There are two main ways to go about adopting a child domestically. The first is to use a private lawyer, adoption facilitator or adoption agency; the second is to go through a public agency.

In the case of private adoption, one option is to find a lawyer who specializes in adoption law. This is often called an "independent" adoption.

Mary and Michelle, a lesbian couple in New York, had wanted a child for years. Both had infertility problems, though, and they ultimately decided to pursue a domestic adoption. They wanted to raise a newborn, so they retained a lawyer who had done about 200 private adoptions. He began the process of looking for a child on their behalf, placing advertisements in various clinics around the city. The women knew that they wanted an African-American baby, less than three months old, and in good health; at that point in their lives, they didn't feel that they could handle adopting an infant with special health needs. Because they were upfront about this with their lawyer, they were spared being offered children that they knew they couldn't accept.

Generally speaking, many private adoptions are for newborns. When a pregnant woman decides she wants to make an adoption plan for her child, she will often find and contact a lawyer. She may look in the yellow pages, check for ads at low-cost medical clinics or do a search on the Internet.

When Mary and Michelle registered with their private adoption attorney, they were given a lot of paperwork to fill out. "Our lawyer basically wanted to know exactly what kind of child we'd accept," Mary recalls. "But he also had to get to know us, personally. We told him everything from age and race, to our health histories. He had to know if we used any drugs, or had any major health problems." Michelle continues, "We also had to write a 'Dear birth mother' letter. We introduced ourselves as if the birthmother would be reading it to see if we'd be good parents for her baby. We described how much we love sports and music, and told them about our cats, the house we live in, our neighbors – everything we could think of that would make a good impression." These letters often include details such as religion, educational background of the potential parents, pictures of their homes and themselves, etc.

For gay and lesbian couples wishing to go through this process, the probability that a birth mother will choose them can be fairly low, depending on the area of the country. However, there are some circumstances in which a birth mother might actually prefer a gay or lesbian couple to raise her child. These include cases where the birth mother chooses a gay male couple perhaps because she believes that they will have a higher income, or because she doesn't want to be replaced as a mother figure in her child's life. Lesbian couples may be chosen by a birth mother who thinks that her child will thrive in an environment with two mothers rather than one, or by a woman who has had bad experiences with men and prefers that her child be raised by women. Mary and Michelle waited about ten months before they got the call they'd been waiting for – they had been chosen by a birthmother who was due in a little over a month. Michelle says "One of the reasons this birthmother chose us was that we were a lesbian couple – she didn't know any lesbians personally, but liked the idea of her child having two mothers. I guess being out in our profile actually helped us! She also said that our house looked cozy and friendly, and she liked the fact that we both have big extended families." Mary and Michelle soon adopted a newborn baby they named Angela, and exchange letters and photos with her birthmother once a year. "Maybe we'll meet her sometime, when Angela is older....but we'll leave it up to Angela how much of a relationship she wants," says Mary.

In some cases, birth mothers choosing a private adoption don't want to have any input at all into the selection process. Searching for parents for a child takes a huge emotional toll on pregnant women. They may leave the choice of the adoptive family completely up to the agency. In such cases, called "closed adoptions," the adoption agency will choose the best qualified set of parents on their waiting list of potential adoptive families. They'll often pick the family who has been waiting the longest. In cases where the birthmother has no express wishes, more equality is often created for gay and lesbian families; particularly in states or areas that are less accepting of homosexuality, a gay family may be picked by the agency, rather than the birthmother.

A private adoption is often the only way to adopt a healthy newborn (assuming that's what the parents want), but the cost can be prohibitive. While it is illegal to directly pay the birthmother for the adoption, oftentimes the adoptive family will be responsible for lawyer's fees, agency fees, hospital expenses and prenatal care for the mother. In some cases, the potential adoptive family will provide support for food and rent for the birthmother until the child is born. These costs can quickly exceed $20,000 or $30,000 and there's no pre-determined limit; the costs can keep soaring throughout the pregnancy.

In a private adoption, there is no requirement that you live in the same state as your adoption agency or the birthmother. This is important, because the rights of the birthmother and adoptive parents vary widely from state to state. In some states, such as New Jersey, the birthmother has only seventy-two hours after the child is born to sign a document relinquishing her parental rights; this document, once signed, formally frees the child for adoption. In other states, the birthmother has a much longer period, up to six months in some cases, during which she can change her mind before the adoption is finalized. An adoption is not finished until the birthmother has legally relinquished all parental rights and the appropriate waiting period has passed. If you don't want to take the chance of a birthmother deciding that she wants to retain custody, carefully consider whether private adoption is for you.

One of the biggest risks with a private adoption is that the birthmother may change her mind, either before the child is born or before the termination of parental rights is finalized. The birthmother may suddenly decide that she really doesn't want a gay couple raising her child, or that she wants to parent the child herself. If this happens, you may have no legal recourse to recoup any of the living or other expenses you've already paid.

See Appendix 2 for a list of domestic adoption agencies, sorted by state, that are reported to be friendly to gay and lesbian singles and couples who wish to adopt.

PUBLIC DOMESTIC ADOPTION

The second major type of domestic adoption is for prospective parents to go through a public adoption agency, such as the Department of Social Services. Although newborns are sometimes available via this route, most children available for adoption in this way are slightly older, ranging in age from a few months up to teenagers. The ages and races of children available for adoption through the public route vary widely from place to place around the country – some areas may have mainly older children, others may have many babies available. One of the big advantages of a public adoption is financial. Parents adopting through the Department of Social Services often pay minimal fees, and the children may even come with stipends to cover living and medical expenses for a number of years beyond the adoption.

Many agencies have foster-to-adopt programs, where a child can be placed with you as a foster child before her parents' rights are terminated and she is legally freed for adoption. Sometimes, the risk to the potential adoptive parents can be reduced because they can choose to consider only children who are legally free for adoption. This method eliminates the possibility of the birthparents changing their minds during the adoption process. However, it also limits the number of children available. Depending upon your state of residence in the US, adoption through a public agency may or may not even be available. On the other hand, in some more liberal areas, such as the San Francisco Bay Area, gay and lesbian couples are actively recruited by public adoption agencies.

WHAT ABOUT TRANSRACIAL ADOPTION?

While many families prefer to adopt a child of their own race in order to create the assumption that the child is biologically theirs, interracial or transracial adoption can be a very good choice for gay and lesbian families. James and Chad are a gay male couple living in Los Angeles; James is African-American, Chad is Caucasian. They decided that adopting an interracial baby would be the perfect way to expand their family, since both men felt that their cultures would be "represented" in their child. In addition, it actually sped up the adoption process; at the time they were looking to adopt, there were no white newborns available for adoption, but there were several interracial babies looking for a home.

While race isn't of concern to some adoptive parents, it should always be considered deliberately. Take some time to think about the reality of your life, the part of the country you live in and your personal feelings on the subject. Above all, be honest with yourself and your partner.

One thing to consider with transracial adoption is that the presumption of parenthood will be different than if you adopt a child of your own race. In families whose ethnicities all match, it's generally assumed that adults and children are biologically related. With a multiracial family, though, people's assumptions are challenged. This isn't a bad thing, but it's something to be aware of. When at the mall or grocery store, for example, you may be asked if you are babysitting. If just one parent is out with the child, people may ask or assume that the ethnicity of the other parent must match that of the child. Be prepared for intrusive questions, and also be aware that you'll need to protect your child from these questions as well. Plan out in advance what you can say to protect your children from cruelty or ignorance.

In the case of gay and lesbian couples with transracially-adopted children, some people in positions of power or authority may not conceptualize, understand or believe in your family. In one recent case that made the newspapers, a white male couple and their adopted African American daughter were stopped at a rest stop in a southern state and the police were called by a bystander, who assumed that the couple had abducted the child. The bystander didn't understand that the three were a family, and instead assumed a nefarious situation. The police later pulled over their car. Fortunately, the family was traveling with adoption papers and had photographs of the three of them together, and the child was old enough to refer to both of the men as her daddies. The police eventually recognized that they were a family and let them go on their way. If your family is multiracial, be prepared to define your family and prove your connections to each other.

A further consequence of transracial adoption is that the adoption becomes, in a sense, public property and public knowledge. In many parts of the country, for example, adoptions of children from China and other Asian countries are common enough that when a white couple is seen with an Asian child, it's assumed that the child must have been adopted. In adoptions where the ethnicity of the child matches the ethnicity of the parents, the adoption remains more private – it is something that can be told by the family, as desired, to friends, relatives or strangers, but is not immediately obvious at first glance to an outsider.

If your choice is international adoption, the adoptive parents commonly spend anywhere from a week to a month or more in their child's country of origin while finalizing the adoption process. You can learn the country on a more intimate level than what would be available in a standard tourist trip. In many parts of the world, there are various cultural groups that adoptive parents can use to keep their children in touch with their cultural heritage.

Transracial adoption is becoming more and more popular in the United States and other countries. One recent study estimated that about 10 to15 percent of adoptions in the US involved children and parents who were of different ethnic or cultural backgrounds. When Jerry, a single gay man, attended his first open house at a local adoption agency, he was told that in his area, 95 percent of the parents who wanted to adopt were white, while 95 percent of the children available for adoption were non-white! And, of course, most international adoptions are also interracial adoptions. After considering his options, Jerry went on to adopt an adorable five-year-old Hispanic boy, Juan, through the local department of social services. Jerry reports: "Juan is teaching me Spanish, and I'm helping him with his English. So far, he's a lot better in English than I am in Spanish! We enjoy exploring various ethnic foods and Hispanic parts of town, and I feel that bringing a child from a different culture into my life has really enriched my understanding of my part of the country."

DEMYSTIFYING INTERNATIONAL ADOPTION

Sarah, a single lesbian from New Mexico, had desperately wanted a child for years. She always thought that she'd wait until she found the perfect woman, but it appeared that she was destined to be single awhile longer. She'd dated, even been in a short-term relationship, but nothing had worked out. One constant in her life, though, was an urge to parent, and it was growing ever stronger. She had traveled to Russia during her college years and loved the people, the language and the gorgeous scenery. Her great-grandparents also hailed from Moscow. For her, adopting a child from Russia was an obvious choice, and one she began to pursue seriously.

International adoption is an increasingly popular choice for many singles and couples. These sorts of adoptions are typically done through an international adoption agency, rather than a state-run department or a private attorney. There are many different international agencies to choose from, depending mostly on where you live and what country you want to adopt from. Your own location, though, isn't that important; if you live in Arizona, for example, you could easily work with an agency based in New York.

The international adoption process is fairly complicated. You will first locate an international adoption agency. You will fill out some paperwork and will be accepted (or rejected) by the agency; there is usually a deposit required at this point. The agency will then show you videos, photos and medical charts for children who are available for adoption. Around this time, you will also begin some extensive paperwork required to adopt from any country; you'll need to solicit and obtain letters of recommendation, certifications of employment, a medical checkup, financial verification, fingerprinting, proof of no criminal record, a current passport and a host of other documents. Expect all of this to take several months to complete. In the meantime, you can select a child and begin a separate set of paperwork for the actual adoption. In many cases your agency will prepare a dossier of paperwork and ship it off to the country you've chosen to adopt from.

Eventually, the foreign country will approve (or reject) your desire to adopt, and you'll make a trip to see your child. Some countries now require two separate trips, while some allow you to stay in-country for several weeks and finish the adoption in a single overseas trip. Other countries only give you a referral for a child right before your travel date is determined. Once there, you'll meet your child and should have the opportunity to decline the adoption if the child doesn't meet your expectations (or has medical problems that were not apparent before). If you choose to go ahead with the adoption, you'll go to court, obtain a judgment certifying that the child is now yours, and will fill out yet more paperwork to secure a new birth certificate, travel visa and passport for your child. The child will also get a thorough medical exam in-country before he is allowed to leave. Eventually, all the paperwork will be completed, and you and your child will be on an airplane headed for home and your new life together.

There are many major decisions to be made, but the first crucial thing to decide when considering international adoption is the country you'd like to adopt from. Sarah knew that she wanted to adopt a child that shared her ethnic heritage, hence her decision to adopt from Russia. Race may also play a role in your selection of a country to adopt from; if you will only accept a Caucasian baby, for example, you may not consider agencies that only work with Guatemala and India. You should instead focus on agencies that work with Russia, the Ukraine and other European countries.

Sarah didn't have a gender preference. In Russia, she had a choice of genders; at the time she was adopting (1997) there were both girls and boys available. While most countries will offer children of both genders for adoption, be aware that some (like China) are much more likely to have baby girls up for adoption, while others (like Vietnam) often have more boys available than girls. In general, adoptive parents seem to preferentially choose to adopt girls rather than boys, so in some countries the wait for a girl may be longer than the wait for a boy.

Many countries will give preferential treatment to parents of the same ethnic background as the child they wish to adopt; for example, if you're of Indian descent and want to adopt a child from India, you may get a referral faster than someone of another background. To adopt in Japan, only married couples are allowed and one must be of Japanese descent. Most gay couples will want to look to countries with less severe restrictions.

HOW YOUNG WILL MY BABY BE?

Almost all countries have regulations and waiting periods that will make it impossible for you to take home a baby less than six months old. The reasons for this are complex, but most other countries want to give their own citizens (or the child's birthparents) time to adopt a child before surrendering it for international adoption. Six months is a typical waiting period. Discuss with the agency the youngest child you can adopt, and ask which countries currently have the youngest children available and ready for adoption.

Sibling groups can sometimes be adopted at the same time, which saves on travel expenses and other fees. If you're sure you want a large family, it may make sense to look into adopting two siblings from the same orphanage. A sibling adoption may often go faster than a single; most often these children have been waiting for some time to be adopted, and will have already gone through the required holding periods. Some countries also allow the adoption of two unrelated children at the same time, though many agencies discourage what is known as "artificial twinning" when two unrelated children of approximately the same age are adopted together.

WHAT IF MY CHILD IS SICK?

Making a decision as to your willingness to take a child with potential health complications will be important in your decision. Some children placed for adoption in other countries will have some sort of health problem. The problem may be no more serious than head lice or an upper respiratory infection, but it could also include birth defects like a cleft palate or serious medical issues. Of course, children available for adoption domestically can also come with their own medical issues, but they are easier to diagnose and understand from nearby rather than relying on long-distance diagnoses that are often fraught with translation problems. In international adoption, most agencies will supply videos, photos and other information about the child, and you'll want to bring or mail these videos to a doctor who specializes in children from foreign orphanages. He'll be able to examine the video and give you an idea of how healthy your child actually is.

With Sarah's adoption, she was surprised to find that her potential daughter had about twenty listed problems and disorders – everything from schizophrenia to Down's syndrome! "I sent the videos to a doctor who'd dealt with a lot of Russian babies, and she told me that they (the orphanages) often do this – list tons of medical problems that the baby may or may not have. Apparently, they have these "full disclosure" policies so that if something ends up wrong with the baby, I can't sue them later. I figured the baby looked healthy, the doctor thought she looked healthy, and there was no way she could have had ALL of these problems anyway!"

Adopting children with special needs comes with its own set of problems and joys. You'll usually need to prove that you have adequate medical insurance that will cover care and treatment for the child. On the plus side, these adoptions often go faster and are less expensive than adopting a healthy newborn. These children may have been waiting for months or years, and the paperwork will usually go through faster. Adopting a child with medical issues, such as a cleft palate, that are easily addressed in the United States but might be beyond the capabilities of the child's birth country, is one way that an international adoption can make a huge difference in the life of a child.

CAN I EVEN AFFORD TO ADOPT FROM ANOTHER COUNTRY?

The actual adoption expenses may be less than $10,000, but there are many other fees to take into account. An agency will surely charge a fee for their services, probably ranging from $2000-$5000, as will many of the agencies in-country. Sarah tried to recall all of her expenses. "Bear in mind that this was seven years ago, but here goes. The adoption itself was around $7000. The agency charged me about $8000 on top of that. Travel expenses for my aunt and me were about $4000. All the gifts we brought cost close to $500. And don't even get me started on the apostiling!"

Sarah is referring to the fact that all documents, from health and bank statements to home studies, have to be notarized and apostiled (a state-level notarization that insures that your notary public is properly registered) before they can be sent to the country you're adopting from. Both of these services come with fees, which can add up when you consider the number of documents you'll need to have officially verified. International travel costs can also be considerable when you take into account that you may have to make more than one trip and you're responsible for your hotel, travel and other expenses in-country.

International adoption can cost $35,000 or more, and the prices can vary somewhat from agency to agency, so it's a good idea to compare prices before committing to one particular agency. When Sarah was working with her adoption agency, she mentioned that she had lived with a family in Russia before; because she had kept up contact with them, she was actually able to stay with her host family for part of her time in-country. This saved her from paying hotel fees for her entire visit, which took about $500 out of the cost of the adoption. Every bit helps!

DO WE TELL THE AGENCY THAT WE'RE GAY?

Perhaps one of the most difficult parts of adopting as a gay or lesbian couple will be finding an agency who will work with you. In the case of international adoptions, if your application is rejected, it will usually not be because the agency in the United States is homophobic. Rather, almost every other country has rules restricting adoptions to heterosexual couples or singles (and single women may adopt in far more countries than single men). Be forewarned that almost no countries are willing to work with homosexual couples.

Before even approaching an agency, you should decide if you want to present yourselves as a gay couple, or whether you will choose one partner to act alone. Some agencies have a "don't ask don't tell" policy and if you don't mention outright that you are a gay couple, they may work with you; others may reject you outright if they later discover that you're a gay couple, so it's best to learn an agency's policy before committing. One way to do this is to make an anonymous phone call to inquire about the agency's policies; you can also network with other gay and lesbian adoptive families to find which agencies they used.

If the agency is known to be gay-friendly, then you should be as open about your relationship as you're comfortable being. In this friendly scenario they should treat both partners as equal parents of the child-to-be, and they'll advise you as to which countries allow homosexuals to adopt. It's important to understand ahead of time that, as a gay couple, you will be expressly forbidden to adopt in just about every other country. If you want to adopt internationally, you'll need to accept these limitations. Ultimately, many people feel, the child is what matters, so if you choose to pursue an international adoption expect to swallow your pride at certain points along the way.

While most countries prohibit gay couples from adopting, most do allow single individuals to adopt. Currently, these include India, Kazakhstan, Russia and Ukraine. Some countries, like Japan, heavily discourage single people from adopting; other countries may have different age limits and other requirements for would-be single adopters.

Although we are not advocating not telling the truth, we wish to present all options. If you're in a gay or lesbian relationship and want to pursue adoption, one choice may be to pass yourself off as a single person with a "roommate." This approach may be morally distasteful to couples who don't want to feel they have to be dishonest about their relationships. Legally speaking, in most states a gay couple does actually consist of "roommates" rather than two people married to each other.

There is no legal obligation to present yourselves as a married couple if you're not. An exception will be in states within the United States that allow domestic partnerships; these can be legally-binding arrangements, depending on the state. In this case, locate a gay-friendly adoption agency and ask them how to proceed.

If you're in a gay or lesbian relationship and want to adopt from a country that only allows married couples, you may find it tempting to consider a "quickie marriage" to gain eligibility. Kelly and Greg, a gay male couple from Portland, had been together for several years before deciding to adopt. Although they tried, they were unable to adopt as a gay couple and became frustrated. "I'd had my heart set on adopting a baby from India," Kelly says, "but India doesn't allow adoptions by single men, let alone gays."

Kelly and Greg had several close lesbian friends, and Kelly married one of them so that he and his "wife" could qualify for the adoption. If you choose this type of arrangement be aware that most countries require a married couple to have been married for a certain length of time (usually at least three years).

If you decide to present yourself as a single person, be ready for some preparatory work. Inform the people writing recommendation letters for you to portray you as a single person. When the social worker comes for the home study, you must present two separate sleeping rooms for you and your "roommate." In some cases, one of the partners might move out for the duration of the adoption process, so that no one from the agency can later "accuse" the two partners of being a couple.

Any such subterfuge may place great strain on your relationship. If one partner is undecided about adoption, these requirements may be substantive. On the other hand, if you've been in a committed relationship for years you and your partner may decide that the child is more important than anything else.

In the interviews with the social worker (there will be several, both before and after the child arrives), think carefully about how you will discuss your plans to take care of the child. If you decide to present yourself as a single parent talk about "me" and "I" rather than "we" and "us."

Some countries require an affidavit of heterosexuality. Part of the adoption paperwork may demand that you sign a document certifying that you are not homosexual. Currently, such countries include China and sometimes Guatemala. The danger of proceeding in this situation is that the adoption could be revoked if the foreign country eventually finds out that you are, in fact, gay. While the odds of such a reversal happening are slim, some gay couples may decide to abandon the idea of adopting from these countries.

ARE WE TOO OLD TO ADOPT?

Most foreign countries have age requirements for the parents, though they can vary quite a bit. Many countries require the parents to be at least thirty. Generally, adoptive parents also can't be more than thirty-five or forty years older than the child they're adopting. Married couples often are required not to be more than a certain number of years apart in age. www.adoption.org is a great resource for quickly researching the adoption laws of different countries.

CAN WE BOTH TRAVEL TO THE FOREIGN COUNTRY?

When the adoption has been finalized and you're making plans to pick up your child, a major issue for gay couples who are adopting as singles will be whether your partner comes on the trip. The agency with which you're working may specifically advise you not to travel together, as some countries have rejected adoptions if, for instance, a "single woman" walks into court holding hands with a female partner. It is particularly unlikely that two men would be allowed to travel together – some gay men doing international adoptions have brought their sister, or even their mother, along to help provide some child-rearing expertise. Sarah, one of the prospective adoptive parents of whom we've spoken, was traveling to

Russia with her aunt. She still had to convince the adoption agency that her aunt wanted to come along to help out, and also to see some of the country: "The agency kept insinuating that she was really my girlfriend. They tried about six times to get me to go alone, but we finally convinced them."

Remember, as we've said before, the adoption will be a life-changing event for all parties involved. Both partners in a couple will probably want to pick up their child. If you're willing to be discreet, some agencies will allow you both to travel; the non-adopting partner usually takes the role of a "support person" or "best friend" who's traveling to help with the new child. However, if the agency tells you early in your working together that you that this won't be possible, you may need to consider adopting in a different country or investigate working with another agency.

Bear in mind that many countries, particularly Russia, now require prospective adoptive parents to make two trips. If one partner cannot miss work twice for international travel, then it may make sense for the other partner to be the parent of record for the adoption. These sorts of issues need to be considered well in advance.

FOSTERING

Some families may decide to provide foster care to one or more children in need of a temporary home.

Some gay families may choose fostering over adopting because it allows them to help both a needy child and the community. Many United States agencies are willing to let gay parents serve as foster parents. Perhaps one partner may have been in foster care as a child and feels a strong urge to "return the favor" by serving as a foster parent himself. Foster parenting provides a needed home for children, though often on a short-term basis; it is a route well worth considering.

FOSTERING IS THE SAME AS ADOPTING, RIGHT? NOT EXACTLY...

Foster parenting differs from adoption in that children placed for adoption have been legally freed when their birth parents' parental rights are terminated (for a variety of reasons). Children in foster care are not legally free for adoption. The goal in most cases, when children are removed from their original homes and placed in foster care, is for the eventual reunification of the children with their biological families. Thus, foster care is seen as a temporary solution, while the birth parent or parents undergo such measures as drug treatment, parenting classes or finding employment.

SO HOW DO I GET STARTED?

Becoming a foster parent is a process that will take some time and perseverance. The first step is usually to visit a local foster parent, talk to them and get some idea of what to expect from the experience. Following that, the prospective parents should contact their state's department of children and families to request information on foster care agencies. These offices will have applications for becoming foster parents, which can be quite extensive – they'll include medical and physical tests, financial reports, references and usually a letter from the parent on why they want to foster. If your family is approved for foster care, you'll undergo extensive training to help your family cope with your new charge (or charges).

As with adoption, a prospective family should decide what age and race of child they'd be willing to welcome into their home. They'll also need to decide if they can handle a child with special needs. A major factor is that, unlike a newborn coming from an orphanage or hospital, most children in foster care are older and may have been the victims of abuse or neglect. They're likely to come with some sort of physical or emotional problem, and foster parents need to be prepared for anything.

One pathway through which some couples adopt is called "Foster-to-adopt" or "Fost-adopt." This method involves taking a child who has not yet been legally freed for adoption (i.e., termination of parental rights has not yet taken place), but the court system and Department of Social Services all agree that this is the route which is being taken. In this situation, a child can live with you on a temporary basis with the possibility of making it permanent, once parental rights are terminated, if the child is a good match for your family.

When any family is trying to get approved as foster parents, part of the process will be to have a home study in which the house (and people living in it) are certified for fostering. This home study is usually less intense than that of an adoption, but the same rules for gay families will apply. If you're attempting to foster as an out gay couple, make sure that you find out ahead of time whether your particular region is amenable to having homosexual foster parents. Be prepared for the possibility of rejection based solely on your sexual orientation. If you've applied and been certified as a foster parent but have yet to have any children placed with you, don't be afraid to inquire directly with a case manager or foster care supervisor. If you and your partner think that you're being passed over because you're a gay household, you may unfortunately have little or no legal recourse. However, sometimes a personal approach can make all the difference. If you can change one person's mind, you may go on to great success as a foster parent.

Since foster parenting is often done on a county or city-wide level, it's possible to circumvent regulations at the state level which may be hostile to gay and lesbian families. John is a single gay man, living in Florida, who wanted to start a family through adoption. The state of Florida has an outright ban on gay and lesbian people adopting children, and unfortunately John wasn't able to move to another state; his parents were ill, and he wanted to remain close to them. John consulted with a lawyer and found that Florida has allowed gay couples to act as foster parents in certain regions, and he is currently fostering two babies. Inform yourself of your own state's laws.

As a potential foster parent, you can choose the age range of children that you're interested in fostering. One fact to consider when contemplating fostering a school-age child or teenager is that he or she may have some preconceived notions about gays and lesbians. Especially with a teenager, you may encounter some outright hostility. Be upfront about your sexual orientation at all stages of the process, and make sure your case manager informs the child before he shows up at your door; this sort of "complete disclosure" may avoid unpleasantness later. On the other hand, your family may be ideal for a young gay or lesbian teenager! Being placed in a supportive, nurturing family is the best thing that could happen for them.

One of the most difficult parts of fostering is the fact that you are, essentially, a temporary parent. There's always the chance that you'll be giving the child back to child services at some point, and your family will need to be able to deal with this emotional upheaval successfully. There's a balancing act involved here: providing a loving family while not growing completely attached. Make sure you and your partner are up to this challenge before endeavoring to become foster parents.

CONCLUDING ADVICE

The decision to adopt is one that has to come from within. Once you arrive at this decision, though, you'll constantly need to interact with agencies, courts, lawyers, social workers and all the other people who will help make your particular adoption a reality. Have patience with the paperwork; there will be a lot of it! One day, though, you'll achieve what makes it all worthwhile, bringing home a beautiful child of your own.

QUESTIONS FOR PROSPECTIVE ADOPTIVE PARENTS:

1. Will I be satisfied and fulfilled by adopting, as opposed to giving birth to a child? Am I okay with the fact that my child will not be biologically related to me?
2. If you have tried infertility treatments, are you finished with them? Many agencies require that all attempts to become pregnant stop before the adoption process begins.
3. How do we feel about interracial adoption? Explore any preconceived notions that you and your partner have about adopting a child of a different race. Be completely honest about your comfort level, and make sure that you and your partner are on the same page.
4. How do parents and other relatives feel about adoption?
5. Would we consider adopting an older child? What age range? Under a year? School-age?
6. Would we consider adopting a child with special needs?
7. How do we feel about open adoption vs. closed adoption? How much contact with the birthparents would we be comfortable with?
8. How would we deal with an adoption disruption?
9. Can we afford an international adoption or a private domestic adoption?
10. Am I comfortable with hiding my sexuality from certain agencies or others involved in the adoption process?

chapter four

SURROGACY

In the case of surrogacy, a woman gives birth to a child who is intended for someone else from conception. Thus there is a surrogate womb. Most of the time, surrogacy includes the genetic material (sperm or egg) from at least one of the intended parents, although in some cases both an egg donor and a sperm donor are utilized.

Surrogacy is commonly used by both gay male couples and heterosexual couples with fertility problems. There are two main types of surrogacy: traditional and gestational. The difference involves the egg source – in traditional surrogacy, the surrogate is fertilized using sperm from the intended father, and carries to term a child who is genetically related to both her and (one of) the intended father(s). In gestational surrogacy, eggs from an egg donor (or mother with infertility problems) are fertilized with sperm from the father (or donor sperm), and then implanted in a surrogate who will carry to term a child to whom she is not biologically related.

Choosing between traditional and gestational surrogacy in the case of heterosexual or lesbian couples involves a major decision. In the traditional case, the intended mother will not be biologically related to the child, while in the gestational case she will be. For a gay male couple, however, the difference is not as large – in either case, the sperm of one of the intended fathers will be used, with either an egg from the surrogate herself (in the traditional case) or from an egg donor (in the gestational case). Of course, choosing which man will be the biological father can become a huge issue for gay male couples, just as choosing which mother will be the egg donor can become an issue for lesbian couples.

Another difference between the two types of surrogacy is the level of fertility procedures required – traditional surrogacy often requires only basic medical procedures, while gestational surrogacy requires a much higher level of procedures and therefore costs. This is because in gestational surrogacy, similar to IVF (in-vitro fertilization, see Chapter Five), the egg donor must have eggs extracted, requiring fertility drugs to stimulate the production of multiple eggs and to synchronize her cycle with the gestational surrogate's. Then the surrogate has the eggs implanted, and must be on a variety of fertility drugs to help increase the chances of implantation. In addition to the increased costs, gestational surrogacy also comes with all the risks of IVF, including a higher risk of miscarriage and a longer recuperation time between cycles.

From the point of view of the intended parents, there is the possible increased risk of a disruption in the process due to the biological relationship between a traditional surrogate and the child she carries. While such disruptions are very rare, they do happen and in a custody dispute the courts might be more likely to rule in a surrogate's favor if she is biologically related to the child she carried than if she isn't. In the case of gestational surrogacy, the only biological claim on the child will be from one of the intended fathers, thus providing a bit more legal protection.

CONSIDER A SURROGATE EVEN IF YOU DON'T HAVE A PARTNER

Gil, a single gay man, very much wanted to be both a parent and a father. "I've been wanting to be a father to a child since I was a kid!" he said. He didn't want to adopt, because he wanted to have a child that was "his" – for him, biology was a very important factor. "When I was young, people always told me how much I looked like my father. I was so proud to resemble this great man, one that I looked up to every day. I want that sort of familiarity, that connection, with my own child." Single gay men who wish to become parents may be especially drawn to surrogacy, though there may not be much of a cost savings compared to adoption.

A major emotional decision to make, in the case of a couple, will be the issue of whose sperm to use. In the case of a single man, there will be no one to consult or haggle with about the many decisions involved. For single men, surrogacy may actually be easier from a legal perspective than adoption. Surrogacy provides a clear alternative, albeit with many pros and cons.

VARIATIONS ON SURROGACY

In addition to gay male couples, some lesbian couples suffering from infertility also choose surrogacy. It is an excellent way to incorporate one's genes into a child that one then plans to raise, even though neither individual will physically carry the child to term. With gay male couples or singles, a variety of options are possible in addition to the typical "traditional" and "gestational" routes. The usual procedure is for one man to donate sperm, which will be used in fertilizing the egg of an anonymous donor. This embryo is then implanted into a surrogate, using regular IVF procedures. Nine months later, with luck, the couple will have their own biological child.

Variations on this procedure are also possible. In some cases, where a gay couple doesn't wish to know who the biological parent is, they may ask for their sperm to be mixed before being used to fertilize an egg. Some fertility specialists think that this actually cuts down on the chances of conception because the sperm from the two men "compete" with each other. Most specialists think it is preferable to pick one man to be the sperm donor.

In other cases, sperm from one of the men can be used to fertilize an egg from a woman related to the other member of a couple, such as a sister or other close female relative. By going this route, the child has a biological connection to both men. If such a connection is important to both members of the couple, then it can be an excellent avenue to explore. However, it relies on both the willingness and availability of female family members.

Miguel and Robert, one gay couple, used a family member as a surrogate. Miguel's sister, Maria, and her husband, already had two children, and Maria had had easy pregnancies with both. When Miguel and Robert approached Maria about being a surrogate, she was a bit hesitant at first – the idea of being a surrogate had never occurred to her, though she knew how much Miguel and Robert loved children and how they were devoted uncles to her two girls. After discussing the idea with her husband, Maria decided to go ahead with the procedure. Robert provided sperm, and Maria became pregnant after only two tries. She had an easy pregnancy again, and Robert and Miguel were there at the delivery and got to hold their new daughter Rebecca right after she was born. Miguel says, "Robert and I were lucky to have a close relative who was willing to be a surrogate for us – this way, Rebecca is really part of both of us. And Rebecca has an especially close relationship with her two cousins, as well – we see them all the time, and she knows that Auntie Maria carried Rebecca in her tummy, because her daddies couldn't get pregnant themselves!"

PROS AND CONS OF SURROGACY

To Gil, it was be important to pass on the family name, as well as genes, to the next generation. Gil says, "Surrogacy is clearly an extremely personal decision of a highly emotional nature, and only you and your partner, if you have one, can make these choices together.

In surrogacy, the child is planned from the very beginning. The eventual parents can be involved in the pregnancy from the very earliest days. It allows a degree of control and reassurance for the parents – they know that the surrogate is getting good prenatal care, isn't smoking or using drugs and is otherwise taking care of herself during the pregnancy. If all parties agree, the intended parents can even attend medical appointments with the surrogate, hear the heartbeat and see the baby on ultrasound. They may also be allowed to be present during the birth. This degree of access is sometimes available in an open adoption situation, but in many cases is not.

The decision to place a child for adoption is often emotionally charged. With a surrogate, the woman decided to go into the procedure; the surrogate may not consider the child as hers, whereas a woman giving her child up for adoption is always considered the birthmother. Also, in the case of adoption, the birthmother usually has the option to change her mind about giving up her child. With surrogacy, there is little doubt that the contractual parent will receive his child once the baby is born.

One disadvantage of surrogacy is that it is an extremely medicalized process with many interdependencies. There are medical exams and procedures for just about every party involved, and all aspects of the concerned party's health will be examined and subject to scrutiny. The least intrusive route possible, using a traditional surrogate and doing at-home inseminations with fresh sperm, is still somewhat invasive and may make some surrogates uncomfortable. Remember, though, that a gay man's part of the process will actually be fairly limited. Once the sperm sample is taken, assuming that there aren't any fertility problems on the man's side, the man shouldn't need any more medical contact. The rest of the medical procedures (egg harvesting to embryo implantation, pregnancy and birth) will all involve the woman.

If you're a particularly private person, or can't tolerate multiple doctor's visits and probing questions about your health, adoption may be a better choice (though of course, adoption comes with its own intrusions in the form of court petitions, the home study, etc.).

WHAT ARE THE LEGAL PITFALLS?

Surrogacy usually involves a legal contract wherein the surrogate relinquishes any and all parental rights toward the child. Surrogacy is not the same as adoption, and the surrogate mother is not usually considered a "birthmother." It is a type of legal transaction.

When considering surrogacy be aware that this is one area of reproductive technology in which the law has not yet caught up to society. Surrogacy laws are highly variable from state to state (and region to region) in the United States. Because of this uncertainty, it is very important to consult with a local lawyer, preferably one who has experience with surrogacy contracts, before proceeding. A summary of laws in each state can be found in Appendix I; more details on laws in various states are available at www.surrogacy.com or www.hrc.org.

In some states, surrogacy is illegal. In other states, it is legal, but the surrogate cannot be compensated financially for her role in the birth. In many states, surrogates cannot be paid directly for bearing a child to term. If you live in one of these states, other arrangements for compensation will need to be made or you'll need to find a family member or close friend who will be a "compassionate surrogate" out of the goodness of her own heart. In Miguel and Robert's case, Miguel's sister Maria refused to take any money from the grateful couple. Robert reports: "We made sure to offer to babysit Maria's two girls as often as we could, especially during Maria's third trimester when she was very tired. We had them over at our place just about every weekend. It gave Maria a break, and definitely helped us get ready for parenthood!"

A workaround to living in a state that doesn't allow surrogacy is finding a surrogate in another state. You may actually need to have the procedures performed in this other state. You may find, however, that some agencies will refuse outright to work with couples or singles in states where surrogacy is illegal or of an uncertain legal status. In terms of fairly compensating the surrogate, in states where that is allowed, it is legal and permissible to pay them for travel expenses, medical fees, emotional distress and everything else relating to the conception and pregnancy. Some states also allow payment for living expenses while the surrogate is pregnant.

Of course, there are horror stories about surrogacy just as there are about adoption – a few cases over the years have made the news, where a surrogate refused to surrender the child she bore for someone else upon the child's birth. It is important to investigate the laws of your state and if you live in a state where surrogacy is unregulated or disallowed, be prepared to make alternate arrangements.

WHAT ABOUT THE COST?

Between finding an egg donor, locating a surrogate, fertility procedures, legal fees and pregnancy expenses, having a baby via a surrogate can cost between $25,000 and $50,000 depending on your area of the country. The cost can increase if many IVF attempts are required; remember that payment is due even if pregnancy is not achieved on a particular attempt. There is no guarantee that the surrogate will become pregnant, and there is always a risk of miscarriage or other problems during the pregnancy. Attempting surrogacy without substantial savings is a questionable decision.

Something to be aware of is that, even if the surrogate has health insurance to cover pregnancy, many insurance plans specially exclude coverage for pregnancy by a surrogate. Check into the surrogate's health insurance policy, so that there are no unexpected bills or claims. Depending on the state, the surrogate may or may not be allowed paid leave after giving birth – California, for example, is one state that allows surrogates the same paid family leave time that women who give birth to their own babies receive.

ARE WE MORE LIKELY TO HAVE TWINS?

In surrogacy, as with IVF for a lesbian couple, the risk of multiple births increases with the number of embryos that are implanted in a particular cycle. However, the situation surrounding surrogacy differs slightly because medical insurance often does not cover the expenses associated with the procedure; if there are pregnancy complications due to multiple fetuses (ranging from bed rest to premature birth to time spent in the neonatal intensive care unit), all of these costs must be borne by the intended parents. These fees can easily reach into the hundreds of thousands of dollars. If you cannot commit financially to these sorts of unforeseen expenses, surrogacy may not be the best option for achieving parenthood.

In Gil's case, talking with the doctor reassured him. "I wasn't particularly worried about having multiples, but, as a single gay man, I wasn't sure I wanted to end up with five children! Mostly, it was financial – I don't think I could afford to raise that many kids on a journalist's salary. The fertility team told me about ways to reduce the chance of multiples: mainly, we could transfer fewer embryos at a time."

HOW DO I LOCATE A SURROGATE?

Finding a surrogate can be a challenging process. Matthew and Damian, a gay male couple living in Massachusetts, decided to use a lawyer for the search. "We had a hard time finding a surrogate, so it seemed that the best way to go was just to find a lawyer," Matt says. "We met with a few lawyers before settling on one who had worked with surrogates and parents before." They recommend looking for a lawyer who will work entirely on your behalf, though. "One of the lawyers we met had another surrogacy client at the same time, and we were always sort of worried about having to compete with this other couple for a child. We knew that the one we picked was totally on our side."

Another good choice is to contact an agency that specializes in surrogacy (see Appendix 2 for some gay-friendly surrogacy agencies). An agency may have broader services, including contacts in different locations (which can be especially useful if you live in a small or conservative town, or want to take advantage of favorable laws in a different state). Agencies take on the brunt of the footwork involved with medical exams for the surrogate, matching of surrogate to parents and legal paperwork. They will also do both medical and financial screening of all involved parties. In Matthew and Damian's case, this wasn't an option. "There just weren't any agencies in our area, or if there were, we couldn't find them."

A third option is to work with a fertility center that specializes in surrogacy. The main advantage here is that you can often avoid a common agency problem of "middle man markups." Some agencies charge an extra fee for the services of finding and matching prospective parents with egg donors and surrogates. Working directly with a medical center can keep you focused and may also save money.

Using some sort of service to help you locate an egg donor and surrogate has many benefits over going it alone. They will do the background research on your potential donor and surrogate. They can certify that her healthcare is up to date and that she doesn't have any known fertility problems. They can do thorough background checks to make sure that the women involved truly want to contribute a child to a deserving, caring parent and are not trying to make a quick buck.

Be sure to find an agency that is enthusiastic, or at least willing, to help gay couples. If you sense any sort of discrimination, find a new agency.

If using a lawyer or an agency isn't for you, or if you can't find these resources in your area, another option is to be your own 'independent contractor." In this approach, you would have to locate both the surrogate and the egg donor on your own. Depending on where you are in the United States, this may be your only option – especially if you live in a state where surrogacy is actually illegal.

There are many issues to be aware of when locating and fomenting a relationship with your surrogate. You will need to take responsibility for managing a relationship with the surrogate. The extent of this relationship needs to be spelled out precisely. The arrangements you will need to make include specifics for prenatal visits, agreements for when and how often you can call her to check up and acknowledgement of whether or not she can meet your family and you can meet hers.

Working without an agency will also require that you create your own legal contracts. You may want to consult with or hire a lawyer for this part of the process. The contract should cover every possibility. What happens if the surrogate wants to abort a pregnancy? What if the surrogate decides she wants more of her fee up-front (before the baby is delivered)? Prepare yourselves for these sorts of situations by clearly spelling everything out in a contract. See Appendix 4 for a sample surrogacy contract.

Also, don't underestimate the emotional stress of acting as your own agency. You will need to deal with the surrogate's emotional ups and downs, as well as your own. Everyone needs to be treated fairly; as the woman progresses in her pregnancy, though, tempers may flare up over the smallest of issues. Without a fully legal contract, there could be difficulties, and a clear head is required to deal with anything that might come up. An agency would normally take care of these sorts of emotional issues, so if you go it alone, be prepared to navigate these waters.

WHAT SHOULD WE LOOK FOR IN A SURROGATE?

Choosing the woman to carry your child is a decision to make with great care. The ideal candidate for surrogacy is a woman who has already had one or more healthy children. Some women are much more prone to pregnancy complications than others and having had at least one healthy full-term child will increase her chances of having another. She will also be familiar with what it means to be pregnant and is less likely to back out. Miguel's sister Maria had already had two healthy children with easy pregnancies and wanted to help her brother, who she felt would make a good parent. This made her a suitable candidate.

For Gil, it was very important that his surrogate be healthy. "I'd heard so much about fetal alcohol syndrome, and babies born with breathing problems, so I considered only women who were willing to stay fit and active, eat healthily and refrain from drinking or smoking." An agency will be able to screen out candidates who are unlikely to follow these basic rules; if you choose to find your own surrogate, be sure to put the requirements in writing.

OPEN SURROGACY

As with adoption, there are two main varieties of surrogacy: open and closed. With "open surrogacy," the surrogate often is contractually allowed to have a relationship with the intended parents after delivery. This can mean anything from occasional cards and letters with pictures of the child to full involvement in the child's life. The nature of the agreement will specify the extent to which the surrogate will maintain contact with the child.

Open surrogacy can provide a warm, caring circle of parents for a child. A single man or gay male couple may welcome a potential female role model for their child at some point in the future. While this isn't the case for all gay male couples, some who end up having a girl want to have the involvement of a caring female parental figure. If they don't have many close female friends, the surrogate could be just such a choice. Also, if the surrogate uses her own eggs, any genetic health problems that show up later can be explained or better dealt with if the surrogate remains involved in the child's life. Cases where a family member or close friend acts as a surrogate, such as Miguel's sister Maria, are almost always open surrogacy situations.

One additional advantage of open surrogacy is that if you decide you want another child in the future, you could use the same surrogate again! Especially in cases of traditional surrogacy, where the surrogate uses her own eggs, this may be a particularly appealing solution. One method that some gay male couples who want more than one child have used is for the men to take turns providing sperm to a traditional surrogate (or using the same egg donor); this way the children have a biological relationship to each other as well.

CLOSED SURROGACY

Many couples may not wish to have any third parties involved in the upbringing of their child. If the couple really does not want any sort of contact with the surrogate, they need to find an agency or lawyer that works specifically with closed surrogacy agreements.

In a "closed surrogacy" situation, surrogates are recruited specifically because they do not wish to have any contact with the child after birth. In some cases, the contract may actually require that the surrogate not try to contact the parents after delivery. Variations on the contract might include an option for the parents or child to contact the surrogate at a later date.

Matthew and Damian went this route. "We're pretty private people," Matt says, "and we just didn't want the surrogate, wonderful woman that she was, involved in our lives beyond the birth." The men drew up a contract. "She agreed, in writing, not to contact us or try to find out anything more about us and not to have any role in the baby's life." Once the parents have made a decision as to which type of surrogacy they wish to use, they need to ensure that their agency or lawyer offers this type of service. Make sure that all legal agreements are in effect and correctly worded well before the child is born.

FINDING AN EGG DONOR

Some gay couples using a surrogate will also need to locate an egg donor, if the surrogate is not going to be using her own eggs. A full-service agency, will have already done this part of the process for you; they may offer you a list of possible egg donors to choose from, much as a lesbian couple would look through the database at a sperm bank before deciding on a candidate for an insemination.

There are, of course, key differences between egg donors and sperm donors. While sperm can be cryogenically frozen for months or years without losing its potency, unfertilized eggs currently cannot be safely frozen for later reuse. Fertilized embryos can, however, be frozen. What this means for a couple using an egg donor is that the donor herself must be available at the exact time of the procedure. She cannot simply donate eggs at some prearranged time in order to have them frozen for future use. Also, another implication is that the egg donor and surrogate must physically be in the same part of the country at the same time in order for doctors to harvest eggs, take a sperm sample, create an embryo and implant the fertilized embryos into the gestational surrogate.

GETTING HELP

Agencies will be able to coordinate all the parties, along with medical professionals, to ensure that the whole process goes smoothly. However, doing it yourself is certainly possible and may save money, although it will involve significantly more time and effort on the part of the parents.

Josh and Stephen, a gay couple deciding on surrogacy, wanted to locate a surrogate on their own, but realized that they needed help finding an egg donor.

"One of Josh's friends from college was totally into being a surrogate, but she didn't want to use her own eggs; she had some genetic problem she didn't want to pass on, and felt weird about knowing that we would be using her eggs." Stephen did some research and found that there were entire agencies devoted to egg donation. These agencies serve two purposes: to provide a place for women to donate eggs, and to provide a resource for couples to look for an egg donor. Using an agency is probably the best way to go, unless a couple happens to know a woman who wants to donate her eggs. While some people do advertise in local papers for an egg donor, a more rigorous screening process is highly recommended.

When looking for an egg donor, the same basic criteria apply as when looking for a sperm donor. Consider whether the woman's race, ethnic origin, religion, height, academic skills or athletic prowess are important to you. Read her application thoroughly; perform a background check to be sure that her assertions are facts (or make sure that your agency does one for you). Pay careful attention to the woman's medical screening and history, and ensure that there are no red flags.

Age may also be important when choosing an egg donor. Women's egg quality starts to decline around age thirty-five, meaning that in the case of an egg donor, younger is usually better. When a gay couple is paying per pregnancy attempt, they probably want to maximize their chances of quick success.

Be aware that in most states, it is illegal to pay for a woman's eggs (or other genetic material). It is permissible, though, to pay for everything relating to egg donation: travel expenses, hospital care, medical procedures, lost wages from work and other items. Most egg donation centers charge $10,000 - $20,000 or more for medical expenses related to egg donation, but in many cases that fee also includes implanting the egg in a woman such as in IVF. If you are planning to use a different woman as a gestational surrogate, make sure to discuss this arrangement with your agency ahead of time. Procedures that can raise the cost include freezing extra embryos and extra medical testing that may be required.

THE PROCESS

Generally speaking, when doing a surrogate insemination, the first thing that needs to happen is that the cycle of the egg donor and the surrogate will be analyzed and synchronized so that eggs from the donor will be ripe at a time when the uterus of the surrogate is ready for implantation. This involves the use of various fertility drugs to suppress and then stimulate fertility in both women. The egg donor is given these drugs to hyper-stimulate her ovaries, so that as many eggs as possible are produced. The cycle of the egg donor will be monitored on a daily basis and when her eggs are large enough, they will be harvested using a simple procedure under local anesthetic.

At this point, the male member of the team (usually one of the intended parents) comes in and donates a sperm sample. The eggs are fertilized in a lab using the donated sperm, and are carefully cultured so that as many as possible fertilize and become embryos. Once the embryos are at an appropriate size, an agreed-upon number will be transferred to the uterus of the gestational surrogate. The egg donor and the father-to-be are done with their responsibilities for this round, and all parties will have to wait and see if one or more embryos implant in the surrogate. If they do, the pregnancy will be carefully monitored in the early stages, but once it is well established the surrogate will be released to general prenatal care.

If the embryos fail to implant and if surplus embryos were produced and frozen during this cycle, then the surrogate can prepare (with the help of fertility drugs) for another cycle. This process can continue until the woman gets pregnant, or you run out of frozen embryos. If you get to that point, the egg donor will need to be recalled for another cycle, and the process begins again. Since you get charged for each cycle, whether or not it is successful, using a surrogate can get very expensive very quickly.

ONCE THE BABY'S BORN...

Following the nine months of a successful pregnancy, the last task in surrogate parenthood is how the child is passed to his/her intended parents at birth. Depending on which state the delivery takes place in, actual procedures may vary. In general, the lawyer for the intended parents petitions the court to get an order directing the medical records department at the hospital to put the names of the legal parents on the infant's birth certificate. In many places, the surrogate's name never appears on the birth certificate although she actually gave birth to the child. This sort of situation is a result of using an antiquated document (like a birth certificate) to indicate legal parenthood for a child today. Unfortunately, until there is a better system, such conundrums will continue to exist.

The reality is that, in some cases, the legal end of the process will not be nearly this simple. The hospital may refuse to put two men's names on a birth certificate, court order or not. Or you may run into trouble trying to get a birth certificate with the mother's name left blank, in the case of a single father. If this happens, you and your lawyer will need to take it up with the Secretary of State's office (Department of Vital Records). Depending on the laws in your particular state, a gay male couple using the sperm of one man plus an egg donor may only be able to place the name of the biological father on the birth certificate; they will then need to go through a second-parent or domestic-partner adoption process to assert the parental rights of the non-biological parent.

Once the surrogate gives birth, her role in the legal process may end, depending on whether the intended parents have chosen an open or closed relationship with her. Depending on the nature of the contract, the woman may hand over the child as soon as birth is complete. Sometimes the intended parents may be in the delivery room, or they may see their child soon afterwards. In some cases, the surrogate breast-feeds immediately following the birth, but in other cases the intended parents may not want her to bond with the child, or the surrogate may not wish to have such contact with a child who is not legally hers. These issues should be resolved well ahead of the birth, but all parties will want to be somewhat flexible. In Robert and Miguel's case, the whole family was present when their daughter Rebecca was born – Maria, her husband, their two daughters, and of course Robert and Miguel. Robert says "The happiest moment of my life was when I held my new daughter for the first time and felt all the love surrounding us."

FAMOUS SURROGACY EXAMPLES

One of the most famous surrogacy cases concerns "Baby M," the case in which a woman named Mary Beth Whitehead was contracted in 1985 to be a surrogate for an infertile couple, William and Elizabeth Stern. Whitehead agreed that she would relinquish all parental rights after the child was born (and signed a contract to this effect). However, once the child was born, Whitehead decided to keep the child and return the fees she had agreed to accept from the Sterns. After a lengthy court trial, Whitehead's parental rights were terminated and custody was given to the biological father (whose wife adopted the baby immediately thereafter). A year later, though, this verdict was overturned and Whitehead's parental rights were restored. Partly because of this court case, New Jersey (and many other states) have invalidated surrogacy contracts unless the surrogate is given the right to change her mind, thereby asserting her parental rights, after the birth of the child.

Another seminal surrogacy legal case was Johnson vs. Calvert, in 1993. This California case ruled that a gestational surrogate in fact had no legal parental rights to the child she gave birth to, paving the way for California's favorable surrogacy laws today. This court ruling stated that in cases where there were two potential mothers (or parents) of a child, one who gives birth and one who is genetically related, the test should be that the legal parent is the one who intended to bring about the birth of the child and intended to raise it as his or her own. This court decision was later extended to apply to births in which neither of the intended parents is biologically related to the child, such as where a heterosexual couple used a donated egg and sperm as well as a gestational surrogate. The intended parents can therefore obtain a judgment before the child is born and appear on the original birth certificate as the child's legal parents. In places like California where domestic partnership laws allow for two men or two women to be legal parents of any children who enter the relationship, a similar case should hold true.

There is a legal distinction, however, between a woman acting as a traditional surrogate (i.e. using sperm from the intended father and her own eggs) and a woman acting as a gestational surrogate. In the case of a single man or a gay male couple who are using a surrogate, the surrogate has a stronger legal position if she changes her mind and tries to claim maternal rights if she has used her own egg rather than a donor egg. Therefore, from a legal point of view, it is safer to use an egg donor and a gestational surrogate, so that the intended father(s) and sperm donor have a greater legal right to the child than does the surrogate.

CONCLUDING ADVICE:

One of the most difficult parts of using a surrogate is that you'll have to find a healthy woman who is willing to donate her womb to making your wish for a child come true. It is important to go through the appropriate legal channels and locate a surrogate and egg donor with whom you're completely comfortable with. Then you will be able to enjoy the pregnancy and birth of your child!

QUESTIONS FOR PROSPECTIVE PARENTS:

1. Is surrogacy legal in my state? If not, is it legal in my state to work with a surrogate in another state? Can we compensate her?
2. Do we have any close friends or relatives who would be willing to act as a surrogate or egg donor? Or do we prefer a closed, anonymous arrangement?

3. Are we prepared to have a woman, probably a stranger, carry our child?
4. Are we financially prepared for the costs of surrogacy?
5. Can I deal with the emotional ups and downs of insemination cycles, knowing that it could take many attempts?
6. Are there lawyers or agencies to work with in our area?
7. If in a couple, which man would donate sperm (first)?
8. What qualities would we want in an egg donor or in a surrogate?

chapter five

DONOR INSEMINATION

For lesbian couples, one of the predominant ways to achieve parenthood is through donor insemination, sometimes known as artificial insemination or alternative insemination. There are many options for donor insemination; they can range from the very low-tech, to cutting-edge reproductive technologies. When considering donor insemination, it's important to think about the particular laws of the state in which you reside, in addition to the physical health of the partner(s) involved. Despite the sheer volume of decisions required, donor insemination has far fewer legal entanglements than other methods.

WHAT IS DONOR INSEMINATION?

Donor insemination is the method wherein a woman achieves pregnancy through the use of sperm from either a known or an unknown donor, without heterosexual intercourse. Through this method a child can potentially be conceived as close to "naturally" as possible. This method can, in some cases, minimize medical interference and cost.

WHO GETS PREGNANT?

If you and your partner are a lesbian couple who have decided to become pregnant through donor insemination, your next big decision is which partner will become pregnant and carry the (first) child. In the case of Joan and Samantha, who had been together for five years before deciding to have a baby, Samantha made it very clear that though she was supportive of the decision she did not want to carry the child. For Joan, on the other hand, pregnancy was a lifelong dream. "I don't know if the biological clock is fact or fiction, but I can tell you that my body feels that it is time to have a baby. I don't know how to explain it, other than to say that I've never been more sure about anything in my life."

In other situations, if one partner is infertile or has a health problem, then the choice is clear. However, if both women are healthy and eager to get pregnant, the decision could be more difficult.

There are many factors to take into consideration – one of the most important is age. If either partner is in their mid-thirties or older, that partner should be the first one to get pregnant since, as we have discussed, a woman's fertility begins to decline from this point on. If both women are younger than thirty-five or the same age, other considerations might include health insurance, since not all plans include infertility coverage, as well as job security and flexibility. Partners should discuss their options and decide which partner would handle pregnancy better and who would make a better support partner. Both roles are equally important. The role of support partner is critical during pregnancy, and especially important during the birth.

Some couples who both want to undertake pregnancy go a different route, and have both women undergo insemination at the same time. While this method promotes equality, it introduces a whole new set of possible complications, such as having two newborns and two women who've recently given birth. Both the birthmother and the newborn will need supportive care, including running errands and dealing with other household responsibilities and in some cases this may be best achieved by one partner choosing not to get pregnant. Inseminating both partners at the same time can also cause complications if one woman gets pregnant quickly and easily, but the other has more trouble conceiving. This situation can lead to resentment. Try to anticipate issues which might come up, like this one, ahead of time, and talk with your partner about how you would deal with them.

USING A KNOWN SPERM DONOR

At this point, both sperm and egg are required to produce a child. While there is medical research being conducted in the field of reproductive technology, today's lesbian couples still need a source of sperm. Once you have decided on insemination the next major thing to resolve is the selection of the sperm donor. There are two main options: choosing a known donor or using an anonymous one.

There are several advantages to using a known donor. If you wish your future child to have a particular religious or ethnic background, you can look for these attributes in a male friend, associate or relative of the non-carrying partner.

On a lighter note, it's possible to look for someone who resembles one or both of the partners. Joan has straight black hair, while Samantha's hair is lighter and curlier. As a compromise, they decided to look for a sperm donor with wavy brown hair, so that the baby would have a chance of looking like either mother. "Hair color certainly wasn't the most important thing for us," Samantha recalls, "but we did try to find a donor whose looks resembled ours."

Also, a known donor who is actually related to the non-carrying partner will give the baby biological ties to both mothers. This advantage may be a big one, depending on the mothers' wishes. Joan and Samantha originally wanted to use sperm from Samantha's uncle – he was a close friend of the couple and even had wavy brown hair. Joan was excited about having a child who was biologically related to both of them.

A similar advantage can be found in a known donor's health profile; his medical history should be readily available. The potential donor obviously knows his blood type and food allergies, but one of the first steps will be acquiring his complete family medical history. If the donor is a relative or close friend, there should also be few surprises in terms of the baby's appearance, talents and aptitudes – although with genetics, there's never any guarantee!

There are many other reasons to choose a donor that both the partners know. They have time to interview and discuss the situation with the man and can feel comfortable knowing that a third party may (or may not) participate in the child's upbringing. For some couples, a "third parent" is an ideal situation, because a child raised by lesbians can then have an easily-accessible male role model. Some lesbian couples or single women choose to co-parent fully with a male donor or a male couple. When this arrangement works well, it can be beneficial for the child, who will have a male role model.

However, this arrangement can also be one of the greatest downsides to using a known donor if you and your partner have decided not to have him involved in raising the child. Unless the donor fills out legal paperwork specifically giving up all parental responsibilities, he may try to impose his rights or even sue for partial custody. The donor's desires and legal status must absolutely be established prior to engaging in any donation. Beware: even the most carefully drawn-up donor agreements have been successfully challenged in court, so make sure to work with a donor who's not only known, but also trusted. See Appendix 4 for a sample known-donor agreement, but make sure to consult with a lawyer before proceeding.

In some states, legal agreements created before the birth of a child won't hold up in court, so even the most carefully-constructed legal contract could be thrown out when the baby is born and the donor suddenly decides to claim his "parental rights." Courts have even awarded partial custody to donors. The best way to approach this situation is to draw up the strongesr possible legal agreements both at the start of the sperm donation process and after the birth of the child. If anything in the donor's words or intent arouses suspicion or worry, pick a different donor. Make sure to consult with a local lawyer who is well-versed in the legalities of donor insemination in your area, so you are protected to the greatest extent possible.

An important side note: when using a known donor who lives out of town or is away on business frequently, one option is to have him go to a sperm bank and freeze sperm samples there. Once that's done, sperm will be available for use whenever it's needed. The disadvantage of this method is that many sperm banks impose a quarantine of a few months, to make sure the donor has passed all medical exams. Also, the woman sacrifices the effectiveness of fresh sperm over frozen. However, in some cases it may be the only option.

If you don't know anyone who might want to be a donor, one option is to try connecting with a single or coupled man online. Websites such as www.gayfamilyoptions.org provide a way for lesbians to find possible donors and gay men to find possible surrogates. Such sites also allow people to connect who want more opportunities to co-parent. Another way to find a donor is looking at, or placing an advertisement in, local gay and lesbian publications.

BEING ANONYMOUS IS ANOTHER OPTION

If you and your partner don't want or can't find a known donor, the next recourse is to choose an anonymous sperm donor, and this method is achieved most effectively by going to a sperm bank. Sperm banks are available in many states. Realize, though, that not all states allow this, and they do not all have sperm banks (and if they do, they may not allow lesbian couples to partake of their services). Do not despair, however; many sperm banks will mail-order to anywhere in the country. See Appendix 2 for a list of sperm banks reported to be lesbian-friendly.

An advantage to an anonymous donor is that there might be a greater selection, if particular attributes (hair color, eye color, religious background, etc.) are desired. Particularly if a donor of a certain ethnic group is desired, using a large sperm bank may provide more options than are available in the local community.

When using anonymous sperm, the bank will have a profile for each donor. It should contain a detailed medical history, as well as an evaluation filled out by the donor himself. He's usually asked to write some short essays so you can get a feel for his personality. The donor will list his likes, dislikes, hobbies, proficiencies in sports or music and other personal traits that will give women a good indication of his interests and characteristics. Some sperm banks provide more information, such as baby pictures, detailed information on facial features and even audio files recorded by the donor himself. Of course, expect to pay more for all this information.

An important note is that some sperm banks have a program where some anonymous donors will make themselves available to the child after s/he reaches the age of eighteen. This concept is usually known as "identity release." In the identity release program, a child can contact the agency independently after age eighteen to secure this information, with or without your permission, if their donor allows it. Note, though, that the donor usually cannot contact the child; contact must originate with the child and is only possible after age eighteen. However, investigate the sperm bank you choose and its particular rules. At least one sperm bank we've looked into allows the donor to contact the child directly at very young ages, so read the fine print!

Another option for women who want the ability to use fresh sperm, but don't know of any potential donors (or don't want to use a known donor) is to find a person who will act as a go-between. Perhaps the friend of a friend knows a perfect donor and someone can act as an intermediary between the couple who wants to become pregnant and the man who wishes to donate. This way, both parties remain completely unknown to each other, but the ability to use fresh sperm is preserved. There is also a degree of intimacy impossible with using a purely anonymous donor (at least in this case, the friend can vouch for the donor). Of course, as in any arrangement of the sort, proper legal measures are advised before insemination actually takes place.

Many people who make the decision to use anonymous sperm do so because of the clear legal situation: the sperm donor has no parental rights. However, the actual legal status can depend on where the insemination takes place. It may seem strange, but doing an insemination in a doctor's office can have a different legal impact than doing it yourself at home! This caveat can apply to known-donor sperm as well as unknown-donor sperm. Make sure to investigate all the legal options in your state before beginning to inseminate – see Appendix I for a summary of donor insemination laws by state.

WHICH IS BETTER COST-WISE?

Some mothers don't have a preference for using a known or unknown donor, but have budget constraints. Joan works as a checkout clerk at a grocery store, while

Samantha has a steady but low-paying job in library sciences. "We both work full-time," Joan says, "but we have school loans to pay off, Sam has some credit card debt from years ago, so we don't have much in savings." In their case, using a known donor would be much more affordable than going to a sperm bank. Although, remember that a donor can be as expensive (or not) as the donor requires. Many donors simply donate sperm, though for a contract to be legally binding in most states, they need to charge at least a nominal fee. Sperm banks, on the other hand, are not free and there are usually many fees associated with using banked sperm.

Known-donor sperm can also be less expensive because, depending on the woman's health, it may require fewer inseminations. Fresh sperm is more effective simply because the freezing process kills a certain percentage of the swimmers, and donor sperm obtained through a bank is almost always frozen for health reasons.

Using a known donor may have other "hidden" costs. Lawyers may be required to draw up legal agreements. You will probably also want the donor to have a complete health screening, and that may not be covered by your, your partner's or the donor's health insurance. If you plan to store some of the donor's sperm with a local sperm bank for future use, those services have to be paid for and such items can get pricey, especially if you're planning long-term storage. If the donor doesn't live in the local area, travel expenses also can mount up quickly.

ARE SPERM BANKS EXPENSIVE?

Yes, but even when using a sperm bank, there are ways to save money. Most banks use overnight mail to transport frozen sperm in either dry ice or tanks of liquid nitrogen. Using a local sperm bank provides a distinct advantage since you can pick it up yourself and take it to either your home or a doctor's office. The cost savings here can be considerable.

Money can also be saved in the selection of the actual donor. Some sperm banks provide extensive information on their donors, including audio tapes and baby pictures; this information comes with a higher price. These banks may have other donors with less information available, for a lower price. When first looking at lists of donors, generally the sperm banks provide a summary of each for free; to get a full history of any donor, additional fees are required, so it makes sense only to request full reports on a donor when you're quite serious about that particular donor.

In addition, identity release donors tend to be more expensive than non-identity release donors. There is extra time and paperwork required in keeping track of these donors for eighteen or more years, and the woman ends up bearing some of this cost. There may also be a program registration fee upon the birth of a child, so make sure to ask these questions before selecting a donor.

Sperm availability generally influences price. Fresh sperm is usually available upon demand, but it requires the donor to be available when the woman is ovulating. Using a non-local donor can be difficult, since fresh sperm has a very short shelf life and must be used almost immediately. Frozen sperm can be obtained ahead of time so that, with a little planning, the sperm is available whenever it's needed. However, sperm banks do not have a limitless supply and it may be difficult to get large numbers of vials from the same donor. Be prepared to be flexible and switch donors if necessary.

PREPARING YOUR BODY FOR PREGNANCY

Although the process of choosing a sperm donor (and getting any necessary legal agreements in place) can seem interminable when you want to get pregnant right away, take things one step at a time. There's plenty to do to prepare for pregnancy while you're getting the details of your sperm source worked out.

See your doctor for a full physical, especially if you haven't had one recently. Make sure there aren't any nagging medical problems that would be easier to take care of before pregnancy – there are many medications that aren't safe to take while pregnant, so if you're currently taking any prescription (or over-the-counter) drugs, make sure to discuss this with your doctor. Also, you will want to see your gynecologist for a checkup as well, although many will do an annual exam/pap smear at your first prenatal appointment if you're due for one.

In the months before pregnancy is actually achieved set up some wholesome habits that can carry you through a healthy pregnancy and beyond. If you smoke, now is the time to stop! Examine your diet and general fitness level—make sure you're eating plenty of fruits and vegetables, whole grains and limiting the junk food. If you don't exercise much, now is a good time to add a gentle exercise, like swimming or walking, to your daily or weekly routine – these are both low-impact ways to keep your body moving and both are sustainable during pregnancy.

Even if you're worried about your weight, pre-pregnancy crash diets are not recommended. These can actually be bad for your metabolism and for an upcoming pregnancy, since quickly losing large amounts of weight can release toxins that were stored in fat cells. Instead, focus on eating healthily and getting exercise, and work toward improving your overall fitness level. Excess weight can sometimes cause difficulties with ovulation, which can in turn prevent you from becoming pregnant; if you're considerably overweight, shedding a few pounds may make the difference between conception and frustration. However, if your ovulation is regular and you don't have other weight-related problems, your weight alone shouldn't have much (if any) effect on your ability to get pregnant and have a healthy child.

Other healthy habits should be started early—some people cut back significantly on caffeine before trying to get pregnant, and some begin cutting down on their alcohol consumption (since both caffeine and alcohol can be detrimental to a growing fetus). It's also a good idea to start taking a prenatal vitamin or folic acid supplement. Folic acid can prevent neural tube defects as long as it's present in sufficient quantities in the early weeks of pregnancy, so it makes sense to get in the habit of taking it now.

GETTING COZY WITH YOUR BODY'S CYCLES

Start charting your menstrual cycles. Especially if you're planning to try an at-home insemination, you'll need to be intimately familiar with the rhythm of your body. This information can also be very useful even if you plan to conceive in a more medical setting. Since your menstrual cycle can vary slightly from month to month, it's best to have at least six months of cycles charted before you plan to try to conceive; this process will provide a good idea of the average length of your cycle.

There are many different aspects of your cycle that should be charted. The simplest approach is simply to keep track of when your menstrual period starts and ends each month—you can mark the start and stop dates on a calendar. If you're willing, however, there are a number of additional factors that can also be useful to keep track of. These include basal body temperature, cervical fluid and cervical position.

Taking basal body temperature is a relatively easy way to determine where you are in your menstrual cycle, and it can indicate whether or not you're ovulating regularly. This is very useful information when trying to get pregnant. Your basal body temperature is taken after you've been sleeping for at least four to six hours, so for most people it's taken first thing in the morning.

Joan says, "We ended up buying a special 'Basal Thermometer'—it wasn't too expensive, and the drugstore down the street sold them. Since you're supposed to take your temperature right after you wake up, I just kept it on my nightstand. I also got a clipboard with the charts and kept that on the nightstand too." Use the thermometer before sitting up, having anything to drink or using the bathroom.

The basal body temperature measurement is most accurate when it's taken at approximately the same time every morning, so this method of determining your fertility may not be appropriate if you work shifts or have varying sleeping habits. Once you've taken your temperature, it's best to record it on a special chart that you can download from various fertility websites. (For example, you can download one in PDF format from here: http://www.babycenter.com/files/bbt_acro3.pdf)

Make a dot on the chart to indicate your temperature each day. You'll notice that during your period and the first part of your cycle, your temperature will generally be fairly low. You can expect it to rise as you approach ovulation, and then drop significantly once ovulation has taken place. If you were actually pregnant, you would expect a rise at ovulation, and then instead of a post-ovulation drop, your temperature would rise even higher. Thus, taking your temperature can actually help determine if you're pregnant before a pregnancy test could even work!

If you don't see a regular pattern in your temperatures, or you simply want more information, there are other fertility signs that you can chart in addition to temperature. One of these is cervical fluid—in the days leading up to ovulation, your cervical fluid (the mucus in your vagina) will change in character from its usual watery state to a much thicker, more slippery form. Right before ovulation, it's often called "egg-white clear mucus"—it should have a clear, stretchy character. Plotting the changes in your cervical fluid on your temperature chart can give you another piece of information to suggest that ovulation is approaching.

Other methods of monitoring fertility include plotting the changes in cervical position. You can either just use your fingers to keep track of its position or try to use a mirror to actually look at its changes—a partner can be useful for this second one. In addition, there are kits that allow you to examine your saliva for changes that can indicate impending ovulation. There are even commercial monitors that use test strips and temperature readings to help indicate your "fertile window," and can be an easy alternative to the do-it-yourself techniques described here.

There's no need to go overboard with all of these techniques; for most people, just charting their temperature will give them a good idea of their cycle. If you're curious or just want more information, however, feel free to explore these alternatives. Once you are actually doing inseminations, you can use "ovulation predictor kits" (a simple urine test) to indicate that ovulation will take place within the next day or two. Even if you are doing inseminations in a doctor's office, the doctor may have you use a commercial ovulation predictor kit to help determine the best time for insemination.

For more information on these techniques, there are two excellent books currently available. One is *Taking Charge of Your Fertility*, by Toni Weschler (Perennial Currents, 2001). This book goes through detailed instructions on how to chart your cycles using the techniques described above, along with actual pictures of cervical fluid at various stages in your cycle and careful analysis of various possible temperature charts. The author even offers software that helps analyze and track your cycles, available from http://www.tcoyf.com. Another good resource is *The Essential Guide to Lesbian Conception, Pregnancy and Birth* by Kim Toevs and

Stephanie Brill (Alyson Books, 2002), which has information applicable to lesbian couples or single women wishing to get pregnant.

THE NITTY-GRITTY OF MAKING A BABY

Getting pregnant through donor insemination can either be an incredibly easy do-it-yourself at-home process or it can be an expensive, invasive medical procedure. Starting at the low-tech end, in order of increasing complexity, the methods include at-home insemination with fresh sperm, at-home insemination with frozen sperm, doctor's office insemination with frozen sperm, doctor's office medicated cycles using fertility drugs, medicated cycles in a doctor's office using injectible drugs and in vitro fertilization procedures.

I.C.I.

The simplest of these is intra-cervical insemination, done at home with the help of a partner. To inseminate at home, the woman must have been charting her cycle for at least a few months, so that she knows which days she's most fertile.

When using fresh sperm, there are a few primary considerations. If you're using a known donor, you should make sure that he's going to be in town during your most fertile days. He needs to be available on short notice! Insemination can occur at your home or the donor's, wherever everyone is most comfortable. Make sure to obtain the specimen in a clean, dry container.

Insemination using fresh sperm needs to occur within several hours of obtaining the sperm, since it can't survive outside the body for long. It should be kept at body temperature for any necessary travel time, and should then be drawn up into a small sterile needle-less syringe. The smaller the syringe, the better - you'll be surprised at how little fluid there actually is. Syringes are usually available in pharmacies and are often sold as children's medicine droppers. Make sure to get the plunger, not the squeeze type. Use a clean dry syringe, and try not to get any air bubbles in it when you draw up the semen.

A LITTLE HELP FROM A FRIEND

Insemination is hard (though not impossible) to do on yourself, and is much easier when assisted by a friend or partner. The woman should lie comfortably on her back, preferably with her hips slightly elevated. It's easiest to just use a pillow or two under the hips. The partner should take the prepared syringe and insert it into her partner's vagina, slowly pressing down on the plunger. The woman should remain lying down, with her hips elevated, for at least half an hour. Some people think that having an orgasm after insemination can help the process along, because, the theory goes, contractions cause the cervix to dip into the vaginal canal, speeding up the sperm's swim upstream. Even if it's not medically necessary, it can make the process more fun and inclusive for both partners.

Using frozen sperm changes the process slightly. If you rent a liquid nitrogen tank, the frozen sperm can be obtained from the source (sperm bank or doctor's office) up to a few days before you plan to inseminate. When using such a tank, be sure to wear gloves and be careful when removing the cane (the rod that the vials are placed in) from the tank. If you plan to use the sperm the same day you acquire it, it's possible to save money by packing the sperm in a cooler filled with dry ice.

With either method, thaw the sperm about half an hour before you plan to use it. Generally, the sperm can just be taken out of the tank in its vial and placed on a countertop to thaw. Don't use the microwave or oven, since excess heat may kill the very substance you're after. The sperm bank will have specific instructions on thawing and handling the frozen vials. They may also supply the syringe. Be very careful when handling the vial, since the amount used for one insemination is quite small. Once it's completely thawed, proceed as you would using fresh sperm. Before using, be sure to match the donor number with the donor you've selected.

IF AT FIRST YOU DON'T SUCCEED, TRY, TRY AGAIN

One insemination, while the least expensive method, may not suffice. Many couples inseminate two or even three times per cycle to increase the odds of conception. Typically, when inseminating at home, inseminating once a day for two or three days around your time of expected ovulation is a good idea. Remember that once your temperature goes up, you've already ovulated so there's no point in inseminating after that. While frozen sperm only survives inside a woman for about twenty-four hours, fresh sperm is expected to live for forty-eight to seventy-two hours. Therefore, inseminating with fresh sperm provides a wider window of opportunity for conception to occur. Also, an interesting note about fresh vs. frozen sperm is that, since frozen sperm doesn't survive as long, inseminations are usually timed to be as close to ovulation as possible. This approach favors male sperm—sperm that produces male babies—because these sperm seem to swim faster than female sperm, but do not live as long. Using fresh sperm gives the female sperm (which swim slower, but live longer) a more equal chance. Studies have confirmed that babies conceived through artificial insemination using frozen sperm have a slightly higher chance of being boys than babies conceived through conventional means.

Some people buy a speculum to use for at-home inseminations so that the inseminating partner can see the cervix and aim the syringe more carefully. While this may increase the accuracy of the insemination, it can also cause problems, because withdrawing the speculum can take a portion of the semen with it. Also, it can make the procedure much more uncomfortable for the woman trying to get pregnant.

WHEN HOME INSEMINATIONS DON'T WORK

At-home insemination simply doesn't work for all couples. If you're under thirty-five and have been trying unsuccessfully to become pregnant for a year or if you're over thirty-five and have been trying for about six months, then a trip to the fertility clinic is probably warranted. The reproductive endocrinologist will do a thorough exam and medical history before advising you on your options. They will probably want to watch and detail at least one un-medicated cycle, performing vaginal ultrasounds to observe the follicle growth and ovulation. They may also do blood tests at key points in the cycle to check hormone levels.

The doctor may also check your progesterone level. Very low progesterone can interfere with conception, and supplemental progesterone is an easy first step. This test proved pivotal for Joan and Samantha. "We didn't get pregnant on our own, so we went in for a few insemination cycles at the fertility clinic. When that didn't work, they finally tested my progesterone and found it to be almost nil. Once they started me on supplements, I got pregnant within three months." Joan warns that taking the supplements isn't exactly fun. "The ones they gave me were suppositories, which were just a great big mess. But you know, you do what you gotta do!"

Another important test when using a known sperm donor, if it hasn't already been done, is to have a doctor's office test the sperm for viability – if this is the problem, it is easily remedied by picking another donor. Using frozen sperm from a sperm bank will sidestep this issue, since the sperm bank will have already tested the sperm to make sure it has good motility and a high enough count. Joan and Samantha ran into this issue, as well – they tried to use Samantha's uncle, but after getting his sperm tested they found that his very low sperm count would make conception difficult. "It was a hard decision," says Samantha, "but eventually we decided that it made more sense to go with an anonymous donor that we knew was fertile."

AIDING THE PROCESS WITH MEDICATION

If basic hormone levels and sperm viability aren't the problem, the next step is to ask the doctor about fertility drugs. First-line drugs usually include Clomid, which stimulates ovulation and increases the length of the luteal phase. Clomid is generally taken on days 3-8 of the cycle and once ovulation occurs an insemination will be performed in the doctor's office. When taking fertility drugs, careful monitoring is required to make sure that the ovaries do not hyperstimulate and produce an unsafe number of eggs, so expect all inseminations to take place in the doctor's office. Also expect frequent vaginal ultrasounds to monitor follicle growth and help predict when ovulation will take place. These ultrasounds are more invasive than an external one, but are tolerable; doctors use a well-lubricated wand-shaped ultrasound probe.

Sometimes, a shot of HCG (Human Choriogonadotropin) is used to trigger ovulation when one or more follicles are deemed large enough to ovulate. If this shot is necessary, be forewarned that, from this point on, insemination will be very closely monitored by the doctor. HCG narrows even further the window during which ovulation will take place.

Joan recalls, "They had me come into the office nearly every day for ultrasounds, then just before ovulation, I had to go into their office *again* for the HCG shot. I missed tons of work while we were trying to get pregnant, from all the driving to doctors' offices." But Joan's employer was understanding, and she was able to take unpaid leave for the extra missed time.

If drugs like Clomid (which is taken orally) and progesterone (which can be oral or in the form of vaginal suppositories) don't do the trick, the next line of attack usually consists of injected fertility drugs like Pergonal. These drugs can be much more expensive than Clomid, so your costs can escalate dramatically. And, of course, many health insurance plans don't cover expensive fertility treatments, so watch your budget if your doctor recommends moving to injections! Usually there are a limited number of cycles over which Clomid is safe and effective, so if you haven't conceived by that point, stepping up to more potent drugs will be the plan of choice.

Inseminations done in a doctor's office are generally intra-uterine (IUI) inseminations. Inseminations at home are called ICI (intra-cervical), because the sperm goes into the vagina as close to the cervix as possible, but not actually in the uterus. When doing an IUI, the doctor uses a speculum (the same used for an annual pap smear) to open the cervix and inserts the sperm directly into the uterus through a small catheter. This gives the sperm a good head start on its journey, though the actual insemination may be uncomfortable for some women.

It's actually possible to do IUIs at home, though it's much more difficult than doing ICIs. If one partner has a medical background or is trained by a nurse or midwife, then at-home IUIs become more of a viable option. The biggest risk in doing these at home is infection – a doctor's office is simply a more sterile environment for inserting anything through the cervix. In some places, midwives will actually make house calls to do IUIs in the comfort of your own home. This option can provide the best of both worlds, but is not available everywhere.

If IUIs still fail to achieve pregnancy, another diagnostic procedure that can be done is called an HSG (Hysterosalpingogram). This procedure checks to see if either fallopian tube is blocked. It is an in-office procedure where dye is shot into the fallopian tubes and X-rays are taken to make sure that the dye can traverse the tube's entire length. There are even anecdotal reports that the cycle or two after an HSG can offer an enhanced chance of conception – the theory is that perhaps the HSG actually "flushes out" the tubes. There is little (if any) medical knowledge to support this theory, though.

IN VITRO AND OTHER METHODS

Sometimes, even after ICIs and IUIs, a woman may still not have become pregnant. In these cases, even more medical intervention may be required. If finances or insurance make it possible, the next step may be in vitro fertilization (IVF). In this process, a woman's eggs are actually removed from her body, fertilized in a laboratory setting, and then the fertilized embryos are returned to her uterus where (hopefully) they will implant and thrive.

This process is not simple. First, the woman is given hormones to stimulate egg production. Just before ovulation would occur, a procedure is performed in a doctor's office under local anesthesia and the eggs are extracted vaginally. Ultrasound is used to guide the placement of a needle through the vaginal wall. The eggs are removed, and then placed in a laboratory where they are watched until it's time for fertilization with donor sperm. Sperm is placed in the dish with the eggs, and the eggs then develop into pre-embryos. Once they're big enough (in about two days), they are passed through the vagina and into the uterus using a special catheter in a procedure similar to IUI. The egg retrieval process sounds scary, but actually feels similar to a pap smear.

The nice thing about the IVF process is that for a lesbian couple, there's the option of using the partner's eggs if both women are healthy. Eggs can be extracted, fertilized and implanted in the other partner for a truly joint birth experience. The two women's cycles will need to be synchronized using various fertility drugs, though, which increases the cost.

IVF is not cheap and is not covered by most health insurance. Currently, IVF can cost $10,000-$20,000 per cycle and there are many factors which can increase or decrease the price.

If straightforward IVF doesn't work, there are even more complicated (and more costly) techniques. Doctors can, for example, inject sperm directly into the eggs once they've been extracted. This method increases the chances of fertilization, but it costs more since more medical intervention is required. For many, IVF is the only way in which two women will be able to conceive. If finances allow it, IVF may be the method that will be successful. If not, though, or if IVF just doesn't work for you, perhaps it is time to consider other options: adoption, fostering, donor eggs, or impregnating the other partner.

One danger with fertility drugs or IVF is the risk of multiple births. While many women desperate to get pregnant often disregard this danger, it can be quite real. In the general population, the twin rate is one set per eighty births. With Clomid, the chance of having a multiple birth increases by 10 percent. With IVF and with multiple embryo transfer, up to 25 percent of pregnancies are twins or higher order multiples. While twins are certainly a blessing, quadruplets, quintuplets or more can present difficulties. Some of the babies will probably be smaller than others, and some may suffer health consequences—and the mother's health is at risk too.

Careful monitoring is always required when using one of these conception techniques, as is selecting an ethical fertility doctor who will carefully help you decide how many embryos to implant per cycle. Before considering IVF, then, it is essential to consider how important it is for the woman to conceive, when there are many other options available for raising a child.

CONCLUDING ADVICE:

Locating sperm might be thought of as a daunting task, but it's really pretty straightforward. If you know a male friend who wants to be the donor and you choose him to father the projected pregnancy, have him tested. If there is no one you're comfortable asking, contact a sperm bank and start working on your medical exam and other paperwork. The resources in this chapter will help you get started once you're committed to inseminating. Find the method that is right for you and, if you choose, work with a medical professional to achieve pregnancy.

QUESTIONS FOR CHOOSING INSEMINATION:

1. Is one of us in good physical health, with regular menstrual cycles? If so, is she willing to try and become pregnant?
2. If part of a couple, and both women want to try to become pregnant, have we discussed who gets to go first? Will we alternate?

3. Has the potentially pregnant partner been tracking her cycles for at least three to six months?
4. Do we want a known or an anonymous donor?
5. Do we know of a healthy male friend or relative who's willing to donate sperm? What sort of parenting agreement would we have with him?
6. If using a known donor, have we found a lawyer to draw up a contract waiving the parental rights of the donor to the extent allowed in our state? Do we need to have a doctor's involvement to allow the donor to waive parental rights if we choose this option?
7. If we use an anonymous donor, what characteristics do we want? Do we want a donor whom our child could contact at age eighteen?
8. How long do we want to try to get pregnant? Will we start with at-home attempts and move to a fertility doctor if necessary? What degree of medical intervention are we comfortable with?
9. Does my health insurance cover infertility treatments? To what extent? What will we have to pay for ourselves?
10. How do we feel about the risk of multiples when using fertility treatments? Would we consider selective reduction or implant fewer embryos or only inseminate on cycles with two or fewer ripe follicles?
11. Is there a limit on time or money that might cause us to switch to trying to get the other partner pregnant, or switch to considering adoption?

chapter six

MOMMY AND DADDY ROLES

For many gay and lesbian couples, having a child is their first immersion in the heterosexual world of child-rearing. For couples who tend to socialize mainly with other gay and lesbian people, this new world can be a bit intimidating.

Paul and Dennis are a gay couple with one income. Dennis works as a lawyer, while Paul is a stay-at-home dad. Part of Paul's daily routine with their two small children is a trip to the playground, and he often feels the eyes of the playground mothers upon him. "I can just tell that the 'other mothers' are looking at me as if I'm some sort of child molester, just because I'm male and hanging out on a playground! I usually have to keep talking about our family to one of my daughters, just to make sure the other moms know it's okay for me to be there. It shouldn't have to be this way, but better that I demonstrate my role as a parent than someone calls the cops about the strange guy that's always at the playground."

In families with two mommies or no mommies, how can parents best deal with the stereotype of the mother as the nurturer and the father as the provider? Many of these issues will be resolved as your child grows and your roles as parents evolve over time, but some should be prepared for and discussed before you become parents.

An integral relationship of male and female parents is not the only way to go. Many lesbians choose what can be called a "Donor Daddy" – a gay male who donates sperm, but only visits a few times a year. His role may be that of father, or it may simply be that of close family friend. This sort of arrangement can work out extremely well for cases where the women need to be the primary parents, but the sperm donor wants to play a minimal role in the child's life. Such a "known donor," of course, doesn't need to be gay—he can be any male chosen by the lesbian couple, even a relative of the non-carrying partner.

PRECONCEIVED ROLES OF "MOTHER" AND "FATHER"

The concept of a child being raised exclusively by one mother and father is a relatively new one. In the Sioux tradition, for example, babies are routinely breastfed by every nursing mother in the tribe. An old African proverb (brought to light in recent years in a book by Hillary Rodham Clinton) claims, "it takes a village to raise a child." In many African and other cultures around the world, extended families are more common than a single mother and father raising a child on their own. Aunts, uncles, grandparents, cousins and friends can play just as important roles.

A variety of responsible adults can enhance a child's growing-up experience in several ways. Children can learn much from the wisdom and experience of their grandparents. In addition, aunts, uncles, cousins and close family friends can provide much-needed insight and can give advice that may not be obvious to those who are with the child continuously.

The idea that a family consists of only one mother and father is, in our opinion, only one of several possible parenting models. Children need to be surrounded by loving, caring adults who can protect, make early decisions for and teach children how to make good, responsible decisions for themselves. Paul feels; "Caretaking is completely gender-neutral. Aside from actually giving birth, there's nothing that two men can't do in raising children."

However, most people still expect to see children being reared by a (usually married) male and female. Of course, the "traditional family" is hardly ubiquitous in modern American culture. The prevalence of divorces, remarriages and other changes in family structure has resulted in new demographics. Many children in the United States today are not being reared solely by their biological mother and father.

However, expectations and preconceived ideas about gay parents place an extra burden placed upon them. Not only do they have to rear their children to the best of their abilities, but they often have to defend themselves against bigoted or uninformed people. Despite a different family structure in gay families, gay parents have strong desires to nurture their children and protect them from hate speech or any perception of inequality.

FAMILY NOMENCLATURE

For gay families, composed of two women or two men, there may be a desire for one or more parents to take on the traditional name of "Mommy" or "Daddy." Perhaps you or your partner have fond recollections of calling your own parents by these names. For many people, it seems like the right thing to do. Plus, these names confer a level of societal approval and recognition—every parent on a playground will identify with a child calling for "Daddy," but won't understand the relationship as quickly if the child calls for "Walter" or a made-up name like "Bibby." By definition, since a gay family will have two parents of the same gender, a naming conflict quickly becomes apparent and can actually be one of the more substantial conflicts that gay and lesbian couples have before starting a family.

One solution is simply to call both mothers "Mommy" or both fathers "Daddy." Critics argue that the child will be confused, calling two parents by the same name. However, children aren't likely to confuse two completely separate caretakers simply because they have the same name.

Dennis and Paul debated this issue extensively before adopting their first child. "Denny thought we shouldn't have Nick call us both 'Daddy,' because he'd get confused... but come on! Kids have friends in school with the same name all the time, and they manage to keep them separate." They decided to use Daddy for both parents, and they say that it has worked out beautifully. "As the boys get older, they're starting to call Denny 'Dad' and me 'Daddy,' but in the beginning, we were both Dada."

Some families use the partners' names to distinguish them, such as "Mama Kate" and "Mama Jane." Families with step-parents, where one parent comes into a parenting relationship later on in a child's life, may find it most natural to have the first parent called "Dad" and the second called "David."

Another option is to use variations on traditional or nontraditional nicknames. One mother can be "Mommy" and the other "Mama" or "Mom." You can even make up a name or find a non-traditional one for one or both parents. A good option, if one partner has a different ethnic background, is to use a word for mother or father in their native language. Some Jewish families, for example, may choose to call one mother "Ima" (Hebrew for mother) and the other "Mama." However you choose to identify yourselves to your children, rest assured that one day, all parental nomenclature will eventually deteriorate into a simple "Hey, can I have the car keys?"

All naming issues aside, despite the lack of mother and father stereotypes, both parents will have distinct roles in their children's upbringing. It's likely that one parent may work more hours outside the home, while the other may spend more time with the children; this sort of arrangement will create different relationships for the child with each adult. One parent may have more free time to attend school functions and to chaperone play dates, while the other parent may be more of a "weekend warrior" in leading activities.

However gay parents choose to label themselves, their children's relationships with them will be similar in many ways to relationships with two opposite-gendered parents. What matters when raising a child is that the child's physical and emotional needs are met.

Another issue that gay families sometimes struggle with is which last name to give the children. Some families give each child the last name of the parent who gave birth to them or adopted the child. Some families do the opposite – when Joan got pregnant, she and Samantha decided that the child would have Samantha's last name to emphasize that the child was a part of both of them. The important thing is that your choice is legal in the state you reside in. Some states don't allow a "single" woman to give a child any last name but her own, while other states allow you to use whatever surname you choose. Other couples may decide to give their children a hyphenated last name and then have to decide which name will go first. Hyphenating can result in some awkward combinations, though, and hyphenated last names sometimes confuse computer systems. Other options include using one partner's last name as a middle name or choosing a new family last name that all family members will take. Your choice of last name will influence how society defines you as a family, so it's worth some thought about how you want your family to be perceived.

FULFILLING "ROLES"

Lesbians who've just had a baby need to be conscious of the roles they choose. It's important to understand that you don't have to fall back on the time-honored stereotypes of father and mother roles. Perhaps the most important role decision to undertake will be: who will be the primary caregiver? The woman who gets pregnant is not the fallback de-facto parent. The birthmother may return to work and choose to pump breast milk for her partner to feed the baby during the day. On the other hand, the birthmother may choose to quit work to stay at home with the child, or perhaps she didn't work before the baby was born.

In most families, at least one partner has to work. While some will be able to work from home, most have to commute to an office or other business locale. However, both are apt to want equal time with the baby, and both deserve the opportunity if they choose to try to share the role of primary caregiver.

Biology does, of course, lay some of the groundwork for stereotypical roles. In a lesbian couple, usually one partner becomes pregnant while the other does not. The non-carrying woman, though, does not necessarily play the same role that a male husband would play. Pregnant or not, female partners have different issues and needs than male partners would, even if their roles are fairly similar.

The non-pregnant woman's role in the pregnancy of her partner can be as active as both decide. Thus she may attend all prenatal appointments, asking questions about her partner's and the baby's health. She may be completely involved in the pregnancy, from doing the insemination to watching the baby move on the ultrasound. She can feel the baby kick as it grows and may be an active partner during labor and delivery.

Nevertheless, though both partners participate, the woman carrying the child has her own set of responsibilities. She needs to stay active and healthy during the pregnancy, taking care of herself in order to take care of the baby. She also has the additional duty of looking out for her partner. Female partners are not always automatically welcomed at prenatal visits and the pregnant woman needs to assert her partner's rights whenever it may be necessary. The best way to make it clear to the doctor that both of you are equally involved in this pregnancy is by introducing the partner to any new doctors and making sure to include the partner in all appointments and decisions.

The pregnant woman should make sure to ask her partner if she has any more questions at the end of each appointment, as well. To make matters easier, when looking for an obstetrician, request one that is willing to accommodate a female partner, or be ready to switch if you encounter a doctor who either ignores or is outright hostile to your female partner. Take the same approach when seeking a birthing class instructor. Be proactive and the entire pregnancy will go that much more smoothly for both women.

Male couples should also make preparations for an impending newborn. When using a surrogate, depending on their relationship with the birth mother, they may be able to participate in the pregnancy and birth. If she does not want them to be involved, they're still likely to experience that "nesting urge" and will want to start preparing their home for the baby. These preparations usually include designing the baby's room, building or buying baby furniture or creating financial plans while waiting for the arrival. They may work on birth announcements, arrange to take family leave time from work, purchase a child's car seat and take care of the hundreds of other details that come with becoming a parent.

Once the baby is born, the issue of roles takes on new meaning despite pre-birth discussions. In a lesbian relationship, it is important to remember that the woman who gives birth should not automatically assume that she now is the primary parent. Both women need to be aware and conscious of the fact that they both will have maternal instincts that can, at times, be consuming and both need to be given the opportunity to be nurturing, protective mothers.

IT'S YOUR TURN TO FEED THE BABY!

If a birthmother and her partner choose to breastfeed, the non-birthing mother may often feel left out. She may withdraw and, as a result, work more outside the home and take on more of a father-like role. However, breast pumps make it possible for the partner to feed as well as the birthmother and, if all parties are willing, both partners to be involved in every aspect of their new baby's growth. The key factor is communication; this issue is one that should be discussed before the baby is born and may need to be re-discussed afterward. Generally speaking, newborns can easily adjust to either breast or bottle, and there's no reason for either partner to take a back seat.

If the parents wish to avoid using bottles, a device called a "supplemental nursing system" allows formula, or expressed breast milk, to be fed to a baby as she sucks at the non-lactating partner's nipple. These devices are often used by adoptive mothers or those who can't produce their own breast milk, and can easily be used by the non-birthing partner in a lesbian relationship. They can also be used by one or both fathers in a gay couple.

This idea of roles, of course, is equally true for gay men raising a child. Dennis and Paul ended up taking on fairly traditional roles: Dennis works outside the house, Paul stays home with the kids. But they made an effort to keep Dennis involved in the day-to-day trials and joys. "I call him on his cell whenever one of the kids does something new, sometimes I'll have him paged. I also e-mail several times a day to let him know what's going on."

Paul remembers one time when keeping in touch may have gone too far. "I was sending my partner text messages with some graphic details of our son's potty-training, and one of the partners in his law firm happened to read the screen on his cell phone. That took some explaining!" But Dennis really appreciates all the effort Paul goes to to involve him even when he is working. "When I come home from work, I know just what questions to ask the kids and I know what they've been up to. It feels like I was right there with them all day."

Paul and Dennis prove that while one partner may work outside the home full-time and the other may take care of the baby full-time, there's still no need for one to be *The Parent*. The partner working outside the home can be an equal parent.

Many studies have been done of gay and lesbian couples raising children. In most cases, they indicate that these couples have a more even division of labor between the two parents then in heterosexual couples–usually both parents are equally involved and responsible for things like child care and household tasks. Studies reflect that even in cases where one parent stays at home and one works outside the home, those in gay and lesbian relationships reported that the parent working outside the home was more equally involved with taking care of the baby when he was home than his heterosexual counterpart.

While the lack of pre-defined roles can take some negotiating, this can allow both partners to decide between themselves for which tasks each is better suited. One partner might do the laundry, diaper changes and car maintenance, while another might do the cooking, bathe the kids and take out the trash, or these responsibilities could be divided. Rather than dividing up tasks along traditional gender roles, each parent can choose what they prefer to do or at least decide which parent hates the task less!

CO-PARENTING ARRANGEMENTS

Families are one of society's most fundamental units. Even within the gay community, there are many ways to make a family. "Aunt," "uncle" and other names come into play while creating words to describe a child's loved ones. While the most common scenarios for gay households with children will be to have two "mommies" or two "daddies," there are other possibilities that can work extremely well.

One arrangement is for a lesbian couple to co-parent with a gay couple. Sperm is provided for the lesbians to achieve pregnancy and, at the same time, the men can participate in the pregnancy. This may be a very cost-efficient method and not just for the sake of becoming pregnant. There are potentially four people who can now share in the lifelong financial responsibilities of raising a child, including sending the child to college and providing for other major expenses as well as the nurturing responsibilities.

To meet a gay single or couple of the opposite gender for the purpose of creating and rearing a child, start with the simplest approach: ask around. When Darlene and Janet were ready to get pregnant, they talked to some of their friends in the lesbian community and through one met a wonderful gay man, Charlie. After they spent a couple of months getting to know each other, he agreed to serve as their sperm donor. Once Darlene got pregnant, the friendship between the three blossomed and the women decided that they wanted Charlie to play more of a role in their baby's life.

What they weren't sure about, though, was exactly how much they wanted Charlie to be involved. "Suddenly deciding that we might want a man to help raise our child was a really soul-searching decision," Janet says. "But from talking to and getting to know Charlie, we knew that he'd make a great part-time Dad."

For women considering sharing child-raising responsibilities with a male couple there are many decisions: Are the women expecting the men simply to serve as sperm donors and nothing more? Are they hoping that the men will be Daddies to the extent that they are Mommies? Are they expecting only financial help? Or do they want all four people to play active roles in the child's life? All these issues need to be discussed and clarified.

It is becoming more and more common for lesbian and gay couples to fully share parenting responsibilities, beginning with the pregnancy. The men may want to come to the inseminations, ultrasounds and other pre-pregnancy procedures. Once conception occurs, they may want to come to prenatal appointments and the ultrasound examination usually conducted between sixteen and twenty weeks. All parties may want to take part in baby showers, buying baby furniture and clothes and other preparations.

Then again, the male couple may not expect much in the way of involvement. They may simply have made the decision to help father a child. They may want nothing more to do with the child and may not want to have any financial responsibility.

Darlene and Janet decided to take a middle ground with Charlie. "He wanted to help out with the parenting and wanted to be in the baby's life, but he didn't want to be there every single day. He's a young single guy and he didn't want to commit to raising a kid yet." The women worked out an arrangement in which Charlie could come over whenever he wanted, go on vacation with them if he wanted to and his title would be "Uncle Charlie."

One of the most rewarding aspects of a co-parenting arrangement is that everyone may have a role in the actual birth. The men may want to be in the room for the birth and perhaps even to take some role as a birthing partner. Though this level of involvement is uncommon when the birthmother already has a partner, the lesbian couple still needs to be aware and respectful of the men's wishes.

It is important to make sure that the hospital is aware of the entire family's role in the child's life. In the event that the sperm donor wants to take part in the birth, it's advisable to contact the hospital administrator well ahead of time to make arrangements. They probably won't be expecting so many people to take part, and birthing rooms are not very spacious. Also, depending on the state (or country), the parents may face varying degrees of discrimination, and discussing the birth in advance will help the entire process go more smoothly.

These sorts of issues should be spelled out (both verbally and in writing) before conception ever takes place. While it may seem like the birth is far off, emotions run high as such an important event in everyone's lives comes closer, and it will be better for all involved if these sorts of details are agreed upon well in advance.

Remember flexibility is key to successful parenting, so both gay women and men should be open to evolving decision in relation to bringing up their child.

WHOSE HOUSE DO WE LIVE IN?

While some gay and lesbian couples who cooperate in parenting may choose to live together in one home, a more common arrangement is for the two families to live in separate houses but nearby, often in the same neighborhood, to make it easy for the child to go back and forth between homes. The families may choose to alternate weeks with the child or one family may have "custody" every weekend while the other rears the child during the week. Special times, such as holidays and school vacations, will need to be agreed upon.

This sort of relationship can work to the child's and parents' benefit. Both couples are involved in child-raising, and the child has twice the number of loving parents. However, it may not always be smooth sailing. On big and sometimes small matters, the child will have to get consent from four adults. And if two consent but the other two do not, who wins? Disputes may arise over doctor's visits, inoculations, school field trips—suddenly, there are a lot of parent figures who may demand to be considered in every important decision. Parties should discuss and understand that these (and many more) decisions will be forthcoming.

Before entering any sort of arrangement about raising a child, take the appropriate legal measures to protect rights. Hire a lawyer to draft documents that will specify who has parenting responsibility or who does not. Remember also that many parenting agreements are not legally binding until the child is actually born. If one or more parents dramatically change their expectations at the sight of that adorable newborn, be forewarned that even carefully drawn-up documents which illustrate intent can be nonbinding and a court battle could be in your future.

Another issue to consider is the birth certificate and the concept of legal parentage. Usually a child can only have two legal parents, although a few jurisdictions have approved third parent adoptions in some situations.

For instance, two couples may choose to parent together. If the birth mother and sperm donor both choose to be recognized as legal parents of the child, neither of their partners will be able to do a second-parent adoption to also gain legal parental status. In this case, the easiest and most straightforward way to proceed will just be to list one female and one male on the child's birth certificate and then protect the non-biological parents with guardianship agreements. The problem with this difference in legal status, though, is that not only will different parents have differing abilities and choices about things like schools and medical care, but there may be resentment between the legal and non-legal parents.

TWO PARENTS OR ONE?

Another arrangement may be for a single lesbian to co-parent with a single gay man who has served as the sperm donor. Sometimes a single lesbian decides it's time to start a family with or without a partner and she may turn to a gay male friend for assistance by his contributing sperm. While in most cases the two may go their separate ways after conception occurs, in some cases the two may decide to co-parent the child together. There are special challenges and pitfalls to be aware of with this sort of relationship; the lesbian and gay male will need to be very clear about their family structure, especially when it comes time to register the child for school or fill out other important paperwork.

However, if/when the parents eventually want to partner with other people, the adults and child need to be clear about how the living situation might change. The child will also need to know and understand his parent's sexuality and his or her feelings need to be considered when his parental foundation is subject to change by the addition of an extra partner.

Communal parenting is yet another co-parenting arrangement that can work successfully. Some communities might choose to raise children in one large "family by choice," either living in a large communal living situation or in separate but nearby residences. One of the downsides to such an arrangement is that children may be confused about who has final authority and discipline could be difficult if no single person is considered to be in charge.

Other ways to raise families communally, but with a bit more privacy, are land developments where all families who buy into the plot agree to be part of a central community. This trend is called "co-housing." The families may have a meal together each day, and may all chip in toward grocery and activity purchases. Many co-housing communities also include gardening projects where everyone can take both responsibility for, and pride in, the fruits of their labors.

In addition to gays and lesbians parenting together, another co-parenting style that has been popular in many countries is intergenerational parenting. Some couples may choose to live with their parents or with other siblings or relatives. Currently, when both parents are likely to work outside the home, having a close tie to Grandpa or Auntie can be a huge help financially by helping save on rent or mortgage payments and also by surrounding children with loving, understanding and tolerant adults, where the extended family may provide that caring and attention.

FAMILIES OF LOVE

When one's family of origin is not willing or able to be involved, some gays and lesbians create "families of choice" to help raise children. This could involve moving in with a close friend, or a lesbian couple moving in with a gay male couple (non-sperm donors). The idea behind this type of communal parenting arrangement is that, while Moms (or Dads) make and enforce the rules, there are other caring adults who become part of the child's life.

Childless friends can also take a part in raising children. Many gay and heterosexual couples choose not to procreate or adopt. While one's priorities and interests definitely change when a baby is introduced, friendships with childless adults should become no less meaningful. On the contrary, adult conversation may be a much-needed blessing. Don't lose touch with childless friends, busy as your new life may be. Remember never to judge those couples who decide that family life simply isn't for them. Cherish their difference while, at the same time, growing into your own family.

Encourage and allow childless friends to be as involved with the new baby as they want to be. While some offers of help may never materialize, other single or coupled friends may offer attention, cooking, cleaning and babysitting. These relationships can provide caring throughout the life of your child. Remember, a child can never have too many "aunties" or "uncles."

CONCLUSION:

Don't be afraid to create your own names for yourself, your partner and other meaningful adults in your children's lives. Just because you do more of the cooking and cleaning, the kids don't necessarily have to call you Mama. Adjust traditional roles to your and your children's needs. Raise them to be aware that the stereotypes that society often expects from us are not necessarily good models for changing roles in real life. Loving parents come in many sizes, shapes and both genders.

QUESTIONS ABOUT PARENTING ROLES:

1. Will you and your partner be equal parents or will one partner take on more of a parenting role?
2. What do / will your kids call you and your partner?
3. If the name "Mommy" or "Daddy" has special meaning to you, is your partner willing to be called by another name? Can you come up with names that denote equal parental status?
4. What last names will you give your children? How do you feel about hyphenated names, changing your last name or picking just one last name for all the children?
5. Will you have a stay-at-home parent and a working parent? How do you both feel about those roles?
6. If you will be the birthmother, are you willing to pump breast milk so that your partner can also feed the baby? Do you object to her taking on some of the "mother" roles?
7. If you're interested in co-parenting, do you think you could be happy living with a member of the opposite sex?
8. If you are planning to co-parent with another single or couple, do you have legal arrangements in place to protect the child's best interests if you decide to stop the co-parenting arrangement?

chapter seven

MAKING SAME SEX PARENTING LEGAL

Heterosexual couples can enter into (and exit from) marriage; their relationships are universally legitimized and if they have children the two parents are automatically recognized.

Unfortunately, these same assumptions are not extended to gay couples starting a family. While friends and family will probably recognize your children as being truly your own, the legal system may not be so understanding. A partner who bears no legal relationship to her child will not be able to register the child for school, place the child on her health insurance, make medical decisions for the child in an emergency or perform myriad other tasks that require legal recognition of the relationship.

WHY LEGAL RECOGNITION IS NEEDED

Both parents and child benefit from a legally recognized parent-child relationship. Helen and Joyce have one daughter, Miranda. The baby was born to Helen in a state that allowed domestic partner adoption (California) and Joyce legally adopted Miranda. Their daughter now has the proper legal status to inherit from both her mothers should anything happen to either one of them. Miranda would be eligible to get Social Security survivor's benefits (something denied to same-sex partners) or worker's compensation benefits, should these benefits ever become necessary. A major bonus to the adoption was that Joyce became eligible for parental leave to care for the child under the Family and Medical Leave

Act; if Miranda becomes ill or requires more of Joyce's time, Joyce can take the time to be with her family without fear of losing her job.

The child also benefits from having two legal parents if those parents separate; she will be eligible for both financial support and ongoing visitation with both parents, thereby ensuring that at least some parental relationship will be maintained with both parents. Numerous studies have shown that parental contact is extremely important for the child's emotional well-being, even if the family no longer functions as a unit. Similarly, if the legal parent dies, a second parent without the properly recognized legal status may be unable to keep custody of his own child – in a worst case scenario, the child could become a ward of the state or be sent to live with distant, unknown relatives. Even if the legal parent has named the second parent as the designated guardian in his will, there is no guarantee that the court system will honor this request if the second parent does not have any legal status.

In many states, gay couples can achieve the necessary parental status. It won't come easily or cheaply, but it is doable—and highly important. Helen and Joyce, for example, went through a fairly smooth process for Joyce to achieve the full status of parent: from start to finish, the adoption took less than six months. In some states, as you will see, the process is more complex.

CHOICES FOR PROTECTING SAME-SEX FAMILIES

Depending on where you live and the circumstances under which you become parents there may be a variety of options for achieving recognition of both parents as legal parents. If you are adopting a child domestically, either through a public or private agency, a joint adoption may be possible. This means that both partners will become legal parents from the very beginning. If one partner has given birth to the child, then the other partner may achieve equal parental status through a second-parent, domestic partner or step-parent adoption. In some places you may petition the court to obtain a judgment of parentage before the child is born.

The second-parent/step-parent/domestic partner adoption procedure is one that allows the legally-recognized parent to share parental rights with her partner, without relinquishing any parental authority of her own. Different states have different types of adoptions available – second-parent adoptions are most widely available, but require most of the same hurdles as a standard domestic adoption of an unrelated child, including an in-depth home study and background check.

Some states allow true marriage or full-featured civil partnerships between homosexual partners. In these cases, a child born to one member of a legally-joined couple automatically gains parental rights for both members of the couple; at least both partners will be allowed to place their names on the birth certificate from the day it is granted. However, in some places like California, it is still recommended to do a universally recognized procedure like a step-parent adoption to insure that the parental rights of both partners are recognized everywhere. There are a number of different ways to safeguard your family.

JOINT ADOPTION

If you and your partner are adopting a child who is unrelated to both of you, find out if a joint adoption is possible in the area in which you live. Where available, joint adoption provides one of the simplest ways for both parents to achieve legal status. Joint adoption is only available for domestic adoptions.

California, Massachusetts, New Jersey, Vermont and Washington, DC, allow joint adoptions by gay and lesbian couples. In some cases, it may be easier for a single gay person to adopt than a gay couple. Florida is the only state that specifically forbids adoptions by any gay person, single or otherwise, although similar bans have recently been considered in a number of other states. As of this writing, these states include South Carolina, Georgia, South Dakota, Texas, Arkansas, Idaho, Indiana and Oklahoma. Ohio presents another option by specifying that single lesbians and gay men are not barred from adopting. Oregon has no statewide ban or acceptance of single or gay couples adopting but in many counties, gay adoptions are routine. See Appendix I for more information.

Consult a lawyer in the state in which you live before you look at adoption. Laws change all the time, so keep up to date.

If your state allows joint adoption, the legal paperwork is easier than you might imagine. After you go through the normal adoption process there will be a hearing at which both parents are made legal parents at the same time. There is no need for one parent to adopt first and the other to catch up with a "makeup adoption," as both parents become legal parents simultaneously.

Adoption law is generally governed by the state in which the birth mother gives birth, rather than the state of residence of either the birthmother or the intended adoptive parents. Thus, when working with an agency or a private adoption, you might, if you are able, consider relocating to a state where adoption laws favor gay and lesbian couples. Of course, this option is usually only possible in the case of an open adoption, where the birthmother and the adoptive parents have at least some contact before the birth of the child.

Depending on your state of residence, then, it may be possible to have the birthmother relocate shortly before the birth to give birth in the state of your choice. For instance, a lesbian couple in New York might choose to have a local birthmother give birth nearby in New Jersey, since the child would then be subject to the short relinquishment period and favorable laws of that state. A gay couple in California, who have been matched with a pregnant birthmother in Texas, might choose to have her come to California to give birth there, so that both members of the couple will be able to adopt the child from the beginning. Of course, this route can expose both sides of the arrangement to both financial and emotional risk if the adoption does not go as planned, so it should be done in careful consultation with your lawyer or agency.

SECOND-PARENT ADOPTION

In cases where one member of a gay or lesbian couple has parental rights and the other does not, the usual way to give parental rights to the other member of the couple is through second-parent adoption. This procedure differs from a standard "stranger adoption," because the initial legal parent does not give up any of his or her rights; instead, a second-parent is added with full parental status.

Second-parent adoption often is utilized when a gay or lesbian couple gives birth to a child or adopts a child in a state which does not allow joint adoption. It may also be a desirable choice in places that do not automatically bestow parental rights on both members of a same-sex couple when one member gives birth to a child. In the case of a lesbian couple where one partner gives birth, once the child is born the couple must do a second-parent adoption to add the other partner to the child's birth certificate and to bestow legal parental status on her.

Second-parent adoption can also be used in cases where one partner has full custody of children from a previous relationship, whether heterosexual or same-sex. In this case, any parental rights of the previous parent, whether the ex-husband or former partner, must be terminated before a second-parent adoption can take place. If this termination of rights occurs, the new second mother or father may be added as a legal parent, if permitted in the state of your residency. Second-parent adoption can also be used in cases in which a single man or woman had a child, either through artificial insemination or adoption and later wants to add a new partner as a legal parent. In some cases, these situations can be governed by the simpler "step-parent" or "domestic partner" adoption process, to be discussed later.

Second-parent adoptions are currently allowed by about half the states in the United States (see Appendix I for a list). Not coincidentally, these are mostly states which have been shown to have neutral adoption laws and which have not explicitly passed bans on adoption by gay men and lesbians. The status of second-parent adoptions may vary from county to county, or even judge to judge, within a particular state. Thus, in less hospitable states, it can be very important to enlist the advice of an experienced lawyer in your local area who knows the laws and who can give up-to-date advice on which areas and judges are the best bet to approve your adoption.

The general process of second-parent adoption is similar to a regular "stranger" adoption. This process can therefore seem intrusive to families where the child and second-parent are already a de facto family, but is unfortunately required by the legal system in most places.

A second-parent adoption almost always starts by finding an experienced lawyer in your area who preferably has done second-parent adoptions successfully before. The lawyer will usually have an initial intake questionnaire, and in many places may charge a flat fee for the whole adoption. The cost will probably be several thousand dollars, depending on where you live. Don't be afraid to shop around, as prices may vary, but in general this is a situation where it makes sense to go with experience over cost.

Once you have filled out the initial paperwork for your lawyer, you will need to locate and provide a variety of documentation for both partners and the child. These papers will include things like a birth certificate, domestic partnership registration certificate where available (and required), any divorce decrees from previous relationships and other legal documents. In some places, the adopting partner will need to undergo a background check and may be fingerprinted. Depending on the state and county you reside in, documents may need to be originals or certified copies, or you may be able to use photocopies.

TRIAL BY FIRE: THE HOME STUDY

Once you have gathered all the necessary documentation, the case will be referred to a county social worker who will perform a home study. Having an experienced lawyer may make a difference, because she or he may be able to refer you to a gay-friendly social worker. This will make the whole process go much more smoothly. If you encounter any problems during the home study, you also have the option to use a private social worker, though this option will cost more.

Will and Lance are a gay male couple who started to make arrangements for a second-parent adoption. Will's child was from a previous marriage, and his ex-wife had passed away several years before. Will met Lance through a bisexual dating service and their relationship had blossomed. They decided to pursue the second-parent adoption to firmly establish Lance's role as one of Will's child's parents and to help secure their son's future. When it came time for the home study, their lawyer recommended a social worker who had worked successfully with gay couples in the past.

While preparing for the home study, Lance was nervous but took an active role. The home study included two visits to their home by the social worker, and Lance's fears were alleviated by the social worker's friendly attitude. She interviewed Will, Lance and Jared, Will's son, separately, then sat down with all three family members for a joint discussion. By the end of the process, she was convinced that allowing Lance to adopt the child was in each family member's best interest.

The wait for the home study can often be a long one, depending on the social worker's caseload. Once the home study is completed, the social worker will write up a report hopefully recommending that the adoption take place. In most cases of a second-parent adoption the family is already functioning as such, which makes the report much less formidable. Read it through thoroughly (the social worker should send you a copy), to make sure that there aren't any errors such as birth dates etc. which could cause problems later on.

Once the home study is completed, your lawyer can schedule a court date for the adoption hearing. This hearing may be done in open or closed court and will include both partners and the child being adopted. In some cases, the court will allow other children, if they are part of your family, to attend as well, in addition to other interested parties such as friends and relatives. In other cases, the court may be closed and only allow the petitioning parties to attend.

The court hearing will likely be brief—your lawyer will present the facts of the case, the judge will ask both partners a few questions and obtain their consent, under oath, to the adoption. If the child being adopted is old enough, she may be asked for her consent as well. Once the hearing is completed, the judge will sign an order of adoption which your lawyer will help you file with the court. Get several certified copies of this court judgment, which you can then use to petition for a new, amended birth certificate with the names of both legal parents on it. The birth certificate process may take months, so until you receive an amended birth certificate (and even after that) the court order of adoption will be your legal "proof" that both of you are legal parents. Many parents choose to keep the whole adoption process secret from their children if very young; they may not want the children to see their family as any less of a "real" family before the legal process is completed. However, it is important to realize that in most cases the children will be interviewed about the adoption by the social worker, so you'll need to have a basic discussion with them about the legal process.

When Lance and Will went to court for the formal hearing their son was shocked when the judge wrapped up the proceedings by saying to him, "Welcome to the family!" He later asked Will if the judge had made a mistake. "Wasn't I already in the family, Dad?" he asked. With children preadolescent and older, a preliminary discussion of what the adoption process is about will help the child understand the court hearing better. Later, as the child gets more mature, he or she may be ready for a more in-depth discussion.

STEP-PARENT ADOPTION

In some states, a simpler procedure is available that uses the step-parent adoption legal guidelines, for families in which the child already lives with both intended parents. In California, for instance, the step-parent adoption proceedings have been amended by the legislature to include domestic partner adoptions. The process is available to any registered domestic partners, and allows one legal parent to share parental rights with her registered domestic partner. The advantage of using the step-parent (or domestic partner) adoption process is that it's much quicker and easier than a second-parent adoption. It's set up to deal with a family that already lives together and functions as a family, but wishes to have their relationship legalized.

Helen and Joyce went this route. After Helen gave birth, Joyce submitted the paperwork to begin a domestic partner adoption, which follows the step-parent adoption guidelines in California. "We looked into several other options," Joyce recalls, "and even talked to a lawyer about it, but step-parent adoption was the easiest process, the least expensive and it offers the most protection."

Another advantage of a domestic partner adoption is that since the paperwork follows the step-parent adoption pathway through the court system, the procedure usually is smooth and efficient. In fact, in some places you can do a step-parent adoption yourself, without using a lawyer. Since step-parent adoptions often use pre-prepared forms available for download from the county or state court's website, there is none of the complicated legal language necessary in a legal proceeding with less precedent. So even if you decide to use a lawyer, it's likely to be several thousand dollars less expensive than doing a second-parent adoption.

Helen and Joyce say that cost was a major factor for them in choosing a step-parent adoption. "It was just a few hundred dollars. There were a couple of filing fees, a court fee, and that was it." Joyce says that her lawyer also advised going this route. "Since there was no one contesting the adoption," Joyce says, "this was clearly the best way to go. Apparently you can't do the adoption yourself if there's any problem – like if there was a father somewhere whose parental rights needed to be terminated. But in our case, it was really pretty easy."

The partner responsible for the paperwork should be good at following directions and following up on filing forms correctly. Dealing with the court system requires both care and perseverance. Helen recalls, "There was an awful lot of paperwork. And we had to go to the courthouse a few times to drop off documents, but that's a pretty small inconvenience. Especially since it saved us thousands of dollars in legal fees."

The general process for a step-parent or domestic partner adoption is quite similar to a second-parent adoption, but it's often faster and easier. Whether you are doing the process yourself or using a lawyer, you'll start by filling out some background forms which you can download from the state or county court system's website or pick up in person. If you are doing the adoption yourself, you will need to file the forms with the court, which means taking them to the appropriate office and handing them in. Expect a small filing fee.

Then you will have to gather a list of appropriate documents, including birth certificates and other documents for all involved parties (the current legal parent, the adopting parent and the child being adopted). These documents will be sent to a social worker, who will also send you a background questionnaire and schedule a home study. The home study in a step-parent adoption case is usually quite different from that in a second-parent adoption case. The step-parent adoption assumes that the child is already living with both partners and merely needs the parental relationship formalized. Thus, the home study can be abbreviated, in some cases only a single interview in the social worker's office and no actual home visit. The social worker still will want to talk to each adult separately, just to confirm that all is as you say it is, and will probably observe the family briefly as a unit. He or she may also want to talk briefly to any children who are old enough to understand the process.

As in the case of the second-parent adoption, the social worker will send out a home study report for your review, in which he or she (hopefully) recommends that the adoption go forward. At this point, a court date will be scheduled for a hearing in which the judge interviews each parent briefly, makes sure they consent to the adoption, and then signs an order of adoption which establishes legal parenthood for both partners. This court order can then be used to obtain an amended birth certificate.

UTILIZING THE UNIFORM PARENTAGE ACT (UPA)

All the adoption options mentioned previously can only take place once the child is actually born. Some people really prefer the extra security of knowing that their unborn children legally belong to both partners. An option that accomplishes this result, available in some places, is to petition under the "Uniform Parentage Act."

This process is generally intended for use in the case of an unmarried heterosexual couple when the father wants to protect his parental rights to the unborn child without marrying the mother (which would come with a de facto assumption of parenthood of any child born during the marriage). It is also sometimes used in surrogacy arrangements, to decree the intended parents of a child before it is born.

In some counties in various states around the USA (mostly ones with gay-friendly laws), the UPA has been used to decree two women the legal parents of a child with whom one of them is pregnant, before the child is born. The advantage of this process is that it can all be done before the birth of the child – many couples find it a relief to be legal parents right from the birth, and not have to deal with a tedious adoption process with a newborn. In addition, a UPA petition bypasses the need for an intrusive home study or other court interference in their lives.

Since the UPA does not provide a generally-accepted and-performed procedure like a step-parent adoption, you will need a lawyer with experience with this act as it is applied in your particular county. Ideally, the lawyer will know how to word the petition to your best advantage. A UPA petition requires filing unique briefs with the court and so it is sometimes more expensive than a second-parent adoption. However, the whole process can be faster than a second-parent adoption because it does not require a home study or any intervention by social service agencies.

The UPA procedure starts like other adoption processes. It is best to find a lawyer with experience. You will likely fill out a questionnaire, and may need to provide documentation such as birth certificates, though the amount of documentation is much less than for an adoption. Of course you will have no such documentation for the unborn child.

It is best to start the UPA process once the pregnancy is well established and the risk of miscarriage is past, but not too close to the due date. Remember, the main advantage of this process is completing it before the birth! The fifth month of pregnancy is usually a good time to begin the paperwork. Your lawyer will file various briefs with the court and will need to wait for the appropriate responses. Eventually, a court hearing will be scheduled.

In many places, a UPA hearing differs from an adoption hearing, because it occurs in open court, along with a number of other cases, rather than in a closed hearing or in the judge's chambers. Depending on the jurisdiction, it may be performed in family court rather than in juvenile court (where adoptions are performed). On the day of your court hearing, if it is in open court, expect to be ushered in to a big court room where no other children or other spectators are allowed – make arrangements to have someone care for any other children during the hearing.

Once your case is called, you and your partner may be placed at different tables for the two opposing sides of a case, a scene that may be familiar from legal television shows. Since the UPA is not disputed, the judge will ask each of you a few questions verifying your understanding and consent to the process. A UPA hearing is usually much more formal than the warmer, friendlier adoption hearing. Once the brief interview before the judge is over, the judge will review and sign the court order. You may receive it at the close of the hearing, or you may need to wait for the judge to review it and return it to your lawyer, who will let you know when it has been filed with the court. Then you can go and pick up a certified copy for future use.

Once you have a court judgment declaring both you and your partner legal parents of your unborn child, bring that document with you to the hospital and use it to have both you and your partner listed on the birth certificate. However, when you attempt to do this, you may encounter unfamiliarity with such a concept or even outright hostility. One possible way to avoid problems is to talk to the birth records office or the hospital administrator before the birth, explain the situation, and ask if there is anything you can do to smooth the process. If the birth records person refuses to list both of you on the birth certificate, expect a process that can take months and months to resolve before you get a corrected birth certificate. In the meantime, however, at least you have the UPA petition itself to prove that both of you are legal parents and eventually you will get a corrected birth certificate.

GUARDIANSHIP

In states or counties which do not permit sharing legal parental status for both members of a same-sex couple, you can protect your family as much as possible through a series of legal documents. The most important of these, from a family protection status, is a guardianship agreement. Remember that these documents do not provide the same legal protection as an actual adoption – they are certainly better than nothing, and can be used to prove intent to the legal system if the need ever arises, but they do not create a universally recognized parental relationship between the non-legal parent and the child. For this and other reasons, many gay and lesbian couples have chosen to move to more gay-friendly states so that they can obtain the highest degree of protection and therefore peace of mind, for their families.

The nomination of guardian for a minor is a legal form that can be filled out, in places where adoption is not available, to assign the care and responsibility for a minor child to another adult. This is necessary when the legal parent or parents become unable to care for the child due to serious disability, or when the parent has died. The designated guardian gains physical custody of the child as well as control of the child's financial assets.

Such a document is not legally binding, however. Most courts will consider a guardianship agreement and give deference to the wishes of a person who has been parenting a child in cases where there is no other legally recognized second parent. However, such an agreement can be challenged by relatives of the child and depending on the jurisdiction they may be given preference over a former same-sex partner.

The format of a nomination for guardianship of a minor varies significantly from state to state. If you live in an area of the country where same-sex adoption is not a possibility, you should find a lawyer familiar with the laws in the county in which you live who can draw up a guardianship agreement that will be valid in your area of residence.

LEGAL RAMIFICATIONS

It is important to have legal recognition for both parents in a gay or lesbian family. Yet the biggest legal challenges to parental recognition have actually come from lesbian and gay couples who are in the process of separating. In states where lesbian and gay families can choose from more than one option for legal recognition, it is critical to know the status of various legal challenges to procedures like second-parent adoption and UPA petitions.

Recently in California, two separate legal cases have challenged the legal standing of both second-parent adoptions and UPA petitions. In the second-parent adoption case, a lesbian couple did a second-parent adoption to make both partners legal parents of their child. When the couple separated a few years later, however, the biological mother launched a legal challenge to the parental rights of her former partner. She argued that the second-parent adoption was invalid under California law. The case is still pending in appeals courts, but has the unfortunate possible consequence of invalidating not only the second-parent adoption in question, but potentially all second-parent adoptions performed in California over the last fifteen years! A similar case has challenged future and perhaps past UPA petitions.

In light of these court decisions, one of the safest legal bets to ensure your child's future is a step-parent/domestic partner adoption. These adoptions use the same proceedings and laws for both heterosexual and same-sex couples, making it extremely unlikely that a single court case could threaten to undo their provisions. For that to happen, the thousands of heterosexual step-parent adoptions that take place each year would also have to be challenged and that would be extremely unlikely.

Step-parent adoptions are valid in all states of the USA. Will and Lance, happily living in California, suddenly had the opportunity to move to Texas when Will's employer offered him a transfer with a nice salary increase. Because Lance had adopted Will's son via a second-parent adoption process that is not legally valid in Texas, he was worried that their child would no longer be considered his. They decided to contact a gay-friendly lawyer in Texas and have not yet decided whether or not they want to move to a state that may not honor their child's adoption.

Even if you live in California and have the advantage of the 2005 domestic partnership law, it may be best legally to do a step-parent adoption to provide full legal protection for parents and child. California's law states that both partners in a registered domestic partnership are to be treated in the same way as a married heterosexual couple. Thus, they should be considered full legal parents of any child that enters the relationship. This means that if one of a pair of registered lesbian domestic partners gives birth, the child is considered legally parented by both women from day one. Theoretically, the birth certificate should reflect this. In reality, however, it may take some time to gain true legal recognition and in the meantime a step-parent adoption will provide the most legal safety. In the case of a gay couple using a surrogate, however, the couple must still obtain a court judgment of parentage before both partners can be listed as legal parents on their child's birth certificate. A heterosexual couple using a surrogate must obtain a similar court judgment of parentage.

In an illustrative case in Vermont, a child was born to a couple in a civil union. The couple later broke up and the birth mother moved to Virginia (a non-gay-friendly state), where the birth mother challenged the presumption of parenthood of the non-biological mother due to the Vermont civil union. Since the civil union was unrecognized in the state of Virginia, the biological mother might gain full custody of the child. Judgments of parentage or adoption are much safer from a legal standpoint and should provide the best protection available to families.

TAX IMPLICATIONS

One final important point to consider is that the federal tax code provides generous tax deductions for adoptions. These tax breaks may or may not be valid for second-parent or step-parent adoptions, and are not valid for UPA petitions. The criteria for tax deduction eligibility state that they are not valid for the adoption of a "spouse's child," meaning that for a married heterosexual couple doing a step-parent adoption, the tax credit would not usually apply.

However, gay and lesbian couples cannot legally marry (at least not as recognized at the federal level). Therefore second-parent and step-parent adoptions by gay and lesbian couples may qualify for the tax credit. See a lawyer or qualified tax professional to help sort out these complicated issues.

CONCLUDING ADVICE FOR PROSPECTIVE PARENTS:

Make sure that your family's rights are protected. There are a variety of means for you and your partner to adopt each other's legally-acquired children: joint adoption, step-parent adoption, second-parent adoption and a Uniform Parentage Act judgment are in some places all viable choices. Your state of residence will greatly impact which of these proceedings. Consult a lawyer in your home state. Even though your family will have love and commitment, go through the extra steps to make it legal. Should a challenge ever arise, you'll want these protections in place.

QUESTIONS ON SAME-SEX FAMILY LEGAL PROTECTIONS:

1. Are both you and your partner legal parents of your children?
2. If not, what adoption procedures are available in your state or country? Have you met with a lawyer to see what your options are?
3. If you've been putting off that adoption, have you thought about what would happen to your children if the legal parent were to die? What would happen if you and your partner separate?
4. If more than one option to obtain legal parentage is available in your area, have you weighed the pros and cons of each method to pick the one that works best for your family?
5. Do your children have any other legal parents whose rights would need to be terminated before your partner could adopt them?
6. If no adoption processes are available in your area, do you at least have a guardianship agreement to protect your family to the best extent you are able?

chapter eight

TRANSGENDER PARENTS

"Transgender" is a term used to refer to someone who does not adhere to all the societal norms attached to their biological gender; it says nothing of a person's sexual orientation. A "transsexual" is someone who feels that their psychological gender does not match their physical gender. Transsexuals usually dress and live as their preferred sex, and may undergo surgery to complete the transformation. "Transvestites" are people who simply enjoy wearing the clothes of the opposite gender.

Gender and sexual orientation are two different aspects of a person. Thus, a person who is born male and chooses to transition to female (called a male-to-female, or MTF, transsexual) could be attracted to either men or to women. This attraction could change with the gender transition, or it could remain the same. Thus, if originally Mark were a male attracted to women, he could undergo hormone therapy and surgery and eventually transition to become Marcia. Marcia could maintain her original attraction to women and be seen as a lesbian, or she could be attracted to men and be seen as a straight woman. Sexual orientation and gender are complex, fluid aspects of a personality. Some people believe that they can change over time, while others believe that it is only their expression that changes over time (i.e. Mark might have been attracted to men all along, but it was only once he transitioned to becoming female that Marcia felt free to act on this attraction).

Transgender people feel the same urges to parent as other members of society. Transgender individuals may experience discrimination while trying to adopt, and may face unique fertility issues if trying to conceive or help their partner conceive. In the end, though, your gender and how you arrived at it have as little to do with your suitability for parenting as your sexual orientation.

TRANSITIONING AFTER HAVING KIDS

One of the most important aspects of transitioning with kids is to be as open (in an age-appropriate manner) as possible during the process. Kids can be extremely accepting, and are often much more open and flexible about gender roles than adults are. Don't be surprised if your children, especially younger ones, take your transition in stride without much, if any, concern or confusion.

Depending on your individual circumstances, the possibility of your family composition changing post-transition may be a much larger issue for your children to deal with than the fact that one of their parents is changing gender. For example, take the case of Mark and Sharon. They had a typical heterosexual relationship, but Mark eventually realized that he needed to live life as a woman to be true to himself. While he did consider dating men while undergoing the transition, he realized that he loved his wife too much to give her up without a fight.

Sharon was understanding, but didn't think she wanted to continue living with Mark once he became Marcia. She still loved him, but just wasn't sure what she thought about suddenly appearing to be a lesbian, since she'd be living with a female partner.

The eventual family composition, of course, depends on the ultimate sexual orientation and flexibility of both parents – in some cases, a relationship can survive the gender change of one of the partners. After Mark became Marcia, Sharon realized that her love for her former husband hadn't changed. "The person under the clothes was still the same person that I married," she says. "I don't know what'll happen legally with our marriage, but we're sticking together. The kids deserve it, and so do we."

In another parallel case, consider a lesbian couple where one of the partners decides to transition to male. To the outside world, any pre-existing children will go from having two mothers to having a mother and a "father" – interestingly, becoming more in tune with the heterosexual majority, especially if both parents remain together as a couple.

SOMETIMES KIDS UNDERSTAND MORE THAN ADULTS

One of the hardest situations to deal with can be when a spouse does not understand a transitioning spouse. George and his wife, Mandy, have two children. The couple had been married for fifteen years, and over that time George slowly came to the conclusion that his true gender identity was as a woman. After years of counseling, George was ready to tell Mandy the truth. Mandy, unfortunately, was not as understanding as George had hoped. At first she thought George was telling her that he was really gay, but George explained that he was still attracted to women and to Mandy, just that he wanted to live life as a woman.

George began going out dressed as a woman and eventually spent a year living full-time as a woman before undergoing sexual reassignment surgery. During this time, as George became Georgia, her relationship with Mandy began to unravel further. Unable to deal with Georgia's new identity, Mandy asked Georgia for a divorce, and Mandy assumed that she would retain full custody of their two children. Georgia, however, had always been an involved parent, and refused to give up seeing her children. Eventually the custody dispute ended up in court. Mandy's lawyers argued that the children, now pre-teens, would be damaged by having a "gender-confused" parent. Georgia's side argued that she was still the same parent she'd always been, just that she was now a mother instead of a father to them. The court eventually sided with Georgia, and awarded shared custody to the two parents.

The decision could easily have gone the other way, however. In the recent past, and still today in some states, the transgender status of a parent has resulted in an automatic loss of custody. Fortunately for transgender parents, however, courts and psychological experts are beginning to realize that just like sexual orientation, gender identity or a change in gender has nothing to do with the ability to parent.

While adults may have trouble dealing with a transgender spouse, children can prove remarkably adaptable. Once Georgia's legal battles were over and she had shared custody of her children, she heard her younger daughter talking to some friends one day. The daughter was explaining that "Mama used to be my daddy, but now she's my mother. I still have a Mom, too, in my other house." Georgia was amazed by her daughter's matter-of-fact acceptance of a situation that most adults found confusing and even disturbing.

BECOMING A PARENT POST-TRANSITION

While some individuals may transition later in life, once they have already had children, others may transition earlier. They may be in a relationship while they transition, or may find a partner during or after the transition process. Once one or perhaps both members of a couple have undergone the transition from one gender to another, many will reconsider their initial desires for a family. Perhaps they wanted to start a family earlier, but never felt that the time was right, or perhaps they were concerned about the final costs of transition surgery. Many couples also feel that they don't want children until they are "really themselves." However they ultimately arrive at the decision to start a family, many transgender families find themselves in the position of wanting children, but not sure how to go about it.

Transgender individuals or couples may want to adopt a child. However, there may be some problems once the agency begins its background check. They will discover that the transitioned person has switched genders when they examine social security numbers and given names. Medical records will show surgeries, hormone treatments and other office visits that will need to be explained. While there is no law forbidding transsexual individuals from adopting, it will help to have an understanding social worker and an adoption agency willing to work with you.

There may be the same problems with international adoption as those facing a gay couple. Be forthright with the adoption agency and they can tell you which (if any) countries will attempt to exclude you from adopting their children. You may also be able to find an understanding doctor who is willing to fill out medical forms describing your "hormone imbalance" and the required medications and surgeries to correct it, without coming out and saying that it was for a sex change.

As with gay and lesbian couples attempting to adopt, the best strategy may be one of "don't ask, don't tell." Unlike gay and lesbian couples, however, the potential heterosexual appearance of a couple in which one person has transitioned may make things more difficult. For domestic adoptions, for example, birthmothers may not choose your family; if they wanted a heterosexual couple they might pick one, passing your family over, and if they wanted a gay or lesbian couple they might pick one, again passing over your family. Like any type of adoption, however, perseverance is the key, and with time and patience you will be able to find a child to join your family.

Some couples in which one or both partners are transgender choose to use their personal experience to help out a child who would particularly benefit from it. For example, transgender parents could be a good choice to adopt a child who is born intersex, or with ambiguous genitalia. Such children are usually assigned a particular sex at birth, and often given surgeries at a very young age to "normalize" their appearances. However, intersex adults have begun to speak out against this practice, suggesting instead that such children be left as they are until they are old enough, post-puberty, to choose the sex that they feel best fits them. Transgender parents may also be a particularly good fit to foster or adopt a teenager who is transgender – such children often have difficulties in their families of origin or in typical foster families, but a transgender family might be a perfect place to support them as they find out who they really are.

FERTILITY, PREGNANCY AND SRS

For couples in which at least one member is fertile as a female, pregnancy is another option for having children. Before undergoing the hormone therapy and any type of sexual reassignment surgery (SRS), it may be worth considering whether you might want to have children. For a MTF transsexual, this may be as easy as freezing some sperm before undergoing hormone treatments that might impair fertility, or surgery that might permanently remove it.

For a FTM (female-to-male) transsexual, these issues are more complicated. Hormone therapy and surgery will eventually remove your ability to become pregnant. Freezing unfertilized eggs is still an experimental idea; while freezing embryos is a possibility, you would have to have eggs extracted, fertilized with sperm from a partner or donor, and then frozen until some point in the future when you had them either implanted in yourself or a gestational surrogate.

Another option is to leave your options open. If you think you might want to get pregnant at some point in the future, you can preserve your anatomical ability to bear children. This will, of course, have implications about how well you are "read" as a member of your true gender. The issues are complicated by the hormones that you might be taking. If pregnancy is something that you are contemplating, either now or in the future, it is extremely important that you discuss your desires with your medical specialist before starting a course of hormone treatment. It is important not to expose a baby to any risk from hormones you may have taken in the past or currently may be taking.

THE PREGNANT DAD?

Even in the case of women who have begun taking hormones to masculinize their appearance, or who are considering transition surgery to become male, pregnancy is still a possibility, depending on where they are in the process.

One famous example of such a couple is Patrick (formerly Pat) Califia-Rice, a well-known lesbian author, and his partner Matt. Both Patrick and Matt are female-to-male transsexuals. Matt had been undergoing hormone therapy and surgery in his transition from female to male for a number of years, but had stopped taking testosterone because of the side effects. When the couple decided to have a child, they consulted a series of doctors. The doctors determined that even though Matt looked male, biologically he was still fertile as a female.

For other people who are in a similar situation, consulting with good, sympathetic doctors is mandatory before attempting pregnancy. Whether or not fertility is still a possibility will depend on the particular hormones that have been used, how long they have been taken and how recently they have last been taken. Surgery can, of course, change fertility as well. If an FTM has had top surgery to remove breasts, then pregnancy may still be possible (as in the case of Matt), but breastfeeding won't be an option. An MTF who has had bottom surgery probably won't be fertile, but freezing some sperm before undergoing this final operation is always a possibility for those who might want the option of biological children in the future.

In the case of Matt and Patrick, once the doctors had determined that their plans for pregnancy would be no risk to the future baby, they decided to proceed. While both of them appeared male, they needed a sperm source. After a search, the couple found a few biologically-male friends to serve as sperm donors, and mixed their sperm so that they wouldn't know whose genetic material would end up being passed on. Matt became pregnant, and the couple is now raising a healthy son.

To people who don't know their history, Patrick and Matt appear to be a gay male couple raising a child. Those close to them generally accept their unusual parenting journey. However, they have encountered the most resistance from straight-identified FTM transsexuals who see themselves, post-transition, as "real" men. Patrick and Matt knew, however, regardless of their genders, that they belonged together and wanted to raise a family. Their public exposure has reportedly encouraged other transgender couples to consider parenthood as a possibility.

PREGNANCY AND MALE IDENTITY

Getting pregnant as an FTM is an extreme act. When someone who identifies as male, or someone who identifies as "butch," becomes pregnant, it can bring its share of attention and problems. Once you become pregnant, it's very difficult to be read as male. The bulging belly and enlarged breasts are a dead giveaway, and are nearly impossible to disguise toward the end of a pregnancy. Factors as simple as maternity clothes may become a problem; it can be hard to find tailored or masculine-looking maternity gear, although careful shopping and judicious use of larger men's sizes can turn up some good choices.

When the child is born, a butch woman and her partner will need to reconsider and adjust their roles as parents. Some butch women may have trouble accepting the fact that they can breastfeed, especially when it comes to nursing in public places. They may feel that such an act is "too feminine" for them, and would rather bottle-feed; some would actually prefer that their more "femme" partners do most of the feeding, changing and other minutia relating to caring for a newborn. Formula-feeding is a perfectly acceptable way to nourish a newborn, but pumping breast milk at home is also a good option – it's healthy for the baby, and is much cheaper than formula. Wearing breast pads can eliminate most leakage, a major giveaway of a lactating woman.

Remember that pregnancy is a temporary state with certain long-lasting aspects. While the large belly only lasts for nine months, increased breast size can last as long as the mother is breastfeeding, and may sometimes be permanent. Still, there is no reason why a butch woman or FTM cannot resume her previous role in the world after the baby is born.

CONCLUDING ADVICE:

Many transgender individuals have raised families successfully and more will continue to do so. Whether or not you can get pregnant or contribute sperm will depend on what type of surgery and/or hormones you've had. Your ability to raise a child, though, depends exclusively on you and your partner. Have you both come to terms with your sexuality and the roles you intend to play? Can both of you deal with a newborn, male or female, and all that's involved with caring for a baby? If you choose to adopt, how much are you willing to share with the adoption agency? Consider all these issues but, most importantly, listen to your heart. If you're ready to parent, your past-present-future sexuality is not a barrier.

QUESTIONS FOR TRANSGENDERED PROSPECTIVE PARENTS:

1. Do you think that you can't become a transsexual if you already have children?
2. Are you worried about what your children will think if you mention that you're considering Sexual Reassignment Surgery?
3. Do you think you'll lose your spouse if you come out as a transsexual? Would you want to stay with your spouse?
4. If you are considering SRS before you have children, have you thought about freezing some sperm or eggs so that you would be able to have children that are biologically yours at a later date?

5. Have you taken hormones for SRS? Have you spoken with your obstetrician about the effects such hormones might have, if any, on the unborn child if you were to become pregnant?
6. Have you considered adoption? Have you thought about adopting or fostering an intersex or transgender child?
7. Have you thought about the effect pregnancy might have on your butch or male identity? Would you be comfortable being a pregnant or breastfeeding "dad"?

chapter nine

A HEALTHY PREGNANCY

There are so many emotions that accompany a pregnancy: worry, health cares, stress... as well as love, caring, excitement and wonder. While joy far outweighs most worries about diet, fitness and giving birth, it's important to have a healthy pregnancy. Labor will be easier, recovery faster and those nine months will be more pleasant and enjoyable.

Regardless of how you became pregnant, once you are with child, all pregnancies (whether you're heterosexual or lesbian) are equalized. However, there are some differences of experience and habit that lesbian couples should be aware of. This chapter will focus mostly on single women or lesbian couples who are pregnant. However, gay men using a surrogate to become parents are strongly advised to read through this section, as it will heighten awareness of your surrogate's experience.

CARING FOR MOTHER, CARING FOR BABY

After pregnancy has been achieved, you need to choose your prenatal care provider. In the case of Emily and Jasmine, a lesbian couple from California, the couple was embarking upon Emily's second pregnancy. They really liked the obstetrician who had taken care of and delivered their first baby. "We felt totally comfortable with her," Emily said. "She was completely gay-friendly, very professional and listened to all of our small worries and complaints. She never once disregarded something we were concerned about and she treated my partner as kindly as she treated me." Their doctor had a policy of always accepting "return customers," so they didn't have to worry about being placed on a waiting list or being denied by their obstetrician.

For many women, especially those having a first baby, choosing a practitioner takes considerable time and effort. If you achieved pregnancy through the services of a fertility clinic, expect them to follow your pregnancy until the tenth or twelfth week. However, after this time the fertility clinic may refer you back into the pool of "normal patients." Managed healthcare facilities often work this way, as do other medical groups that have separate facilities for infertility patients and mainstream ones.

This switch can be a difficult transition at first, depending on your circumstances and how long you've been trying to get pregnant; you may have grown close to the fertility team and become accustomed to weekly or daily visits. You also may have gotten used to constant attention and monitoring. During a typical pregnancy, though, regular prenatal visits will only be scheduled once a month or so. Even if the facility has provisions for pregnant patients, you'll need to get used to both this reduced schedule of office visits and probably new staff members.

OBSTETRICIAN VS. MIDWIFE: THE FIRST BIG DECISION

The main providers of prenatal care are a traditional obstetrician or a midwife. If you don't already have an obstetrician, your choice may be influenced by nearby hospitals that are covered by your insurance. If there is a hospital close to your home, your best choice may be to locate an obstetrician or midwife who has privileges at that hospital.

If you're considering using a birthing center or doing a home birth, your options increase, but be forewarned that you may be responsible for more of the costs. If you've decided to use a birthing center, for example, you may want to consider a midwife who practices at that location. Alternatively, if you choose a home birth, you'll need to find a midwife specifically certified for home birthing. (See Chapter Nine for more detailed information on alternate birthing locations.)

A traditional obstetrician and a midwife may have differences in philosophy. Midwives are often trained to consider pregnancy as a normal extension of a woman's health, while mainstream obstetricians tend to view pregnancy as a condition to be managed. However, if you have medical complications with either the pregnancy or birth processes having a medical specialist may be of paramount importance. In practice, your prenatal visits whether they are handled by an obstetrician or a midwife, involve ultrasounds, blood tests and regular monitoring.

Some midwives are able to provide the bulk of your prenatal care at your home, or in a clinic or birthing center; obstetricians will work from a doctor's office or hospital. If you'd be more comfortable with home care, are having a routine pregnancy and are expecting an uncomplicated birth, then a midwife may be a good choice. Midwives tend to be lower-tech in their practice of medicine than obstetricians; expect fewer ultrasounds and more physical hands-on examination to determine the size and position of the baby. Midwives often use a "fetoscope" to listen for the fetal heart rate, rather than the transducer or Doppler ultrasound more commonly found in a doctor's office. Some midwives may be less likely to insist on routine prenatal testing than an obstetrician; however, it is always possible to request a specific test.

If you're the type of person who wants every security and as many assurances as possible concerning your baby's health, an obstetrician may be a better choice. High-risk pregnancies and birthing complications should not be cared by a midwife and need to be handled by an obstetrician.

Another factor to consider when choosing an obstetrician or midwife is how aggressive their typical standard of care is and how their methods fit into your wishes for the pregnancy. If you've had a previous C-section and wish to try to have a natural birth, does this doctor support VBAC (Vaginal Birth After C-section)? If so, what are her rates of successful VBAC attempts and how do they compare to other doctors at hospitals in the area? Other factors to consider are what percentage of patients with this doctor have episiotomies, whether she or he routinely induces patients at forty weeks or forty-two weeks, philosophy on elective C-sections and any other matter you feel is important. If you are certain that you will want an elective C-section, for example, and your current obstetrician won't allow it, consider choosing a new doctor.

Pain relief is another subject to look into when selecting an obstetrician or midwife. If you and your partner are committed to giving birth naturally and without any sort of pain relief, find out if possible what percentage of your doctor's patients have epidurals or other forms of pain relief. Emily and Jasmine were committed to having a drug-free pregnancy, and their OB group was supportive. "Of course, they asked us a few times at the hospital if we wanted pain relief, but we just kept saying no. They eventually realized that yes, we were going to have the baby without drugs. You'd think we were the first people there to turn down the anesthesiologist!"

If you choose a medical group and not a sole practitioner, while you will have one primary obstetrician for your prenatal care, there usually is no guarantee that your doctor will actually be there for the birth, particularly if you have managed health care. Even if you have your own private physician, many doctors practice in teams, because no one doctor can be on call 24/7. It is important, therefore, to get to know your doctor's colleagues.

ASSERT YOUR RIGHTS

Make sure your potential obstetrician or midwife treats you and your partner as an equal couple. The best way to discover her willingness to work with a gay couple is to introduce your partner at your first appointment and see how well the doctor involves her in the visit. The pregnant partner will have to do her part as well, making sure her partner is involved in the conversation, but you'll most likely be able to judge your practitioner's comfort level just from a single visit. If you pick up any negative cues or find the physician avoiding eye contact with one of you, finding a different doctor may be your best option.

There are other situations in which a non-pregnant person(s) may need to be involved with prenatal care. Common scenarios include a gay male couple using a surrogate, a gay male couple who is co-parenting with a lesbian couple or a couple doing an open adoption with a pregnant birthmother. If it's all right with the pregnant woman, you can help her find a practitioner who understands and is supportive of your family situation.

Decide ahead of time how to present your relationships—being open and honest with the doctor is probably the best choice. The practitioner may ask the non-pregnant partner to leave for part of the appointment so that she can have a private conversation with her patient. Don't feel offended; this is normal, so there's no need to worry about what's going on. Above all, remember that the pregnant woman wants control over her own body. While you can make encouraging and helpful suggestions and help her take the best care possible of her unborn child, these decisions are ultimately hers.

STEP IT UP! THE PREGNANT WORKOUT

Take care of your body while you're pregnant. Exercise, to the extent that you are physically able, is important. Exercise stimulates the bowel, which helps digestion and may help prevent constipation. It also has many more benefits. Most women who exercise during pregnancy have an easier delivery, shorter labor time and quicker recovery.

If you're not currently exercising regularly, start slowly by walking at a relaxed pace, and gradually increase your speed. Swimming is also fantastic exercise for pregnant women, since it doesn't strain joints and the feeling of weightlessness may be a pleasant change. Avoid contact sports, because they may cause injury to the fetus; skiing should be avoided for the same reason, since a forward fall could have bad consequences.

While exercising, aim to keep your heart rate below one hundred and forty beats per minute, since your baby's heart rate is tied to your own. Heart-rate monitors can help you keep track and will let you know when it's time to slow down. If you feel out of breath, take a break. For some women, one hundred and forty beats per minute may be too high, so always rely on the so-called "talking test" – if you can't talk or are out of breath while exercising, you're working out too strenuously.

Always stay hydrated while exercising; the standard fluid intake suggestion is one cup per fifteen minutes of exercise. As the pregnancy nears its end, ease off your exercise. Consult your health practitioner for specific advice. Also, your body will let you know what it can and can't handle. Particularly in the last few months, avoid jumping- and bouncing-related sports such as aerobics, since they can strain the floor of the pelvis. High-impact sports should also be avoided, because pregnant women produce relaxin, a hormone that softens the ligaments. While it allows your bones to spread so that the baby can grow, it will also increase your chance of injury from high-impact exercise.

Toward the fourth or fifth month, watch your balance – a pregnant woman's center of gravity will change as the baby grows, so balancing may be more difficult. Also around this time, be sure not to do any exercise lying flat on your back. Depression of the vena cava results from lying on your back, and this can reduce blood flow and oxygen to the baby. The major rule for exercising while pregnant: listen to your body. If you start feeling dizzy, start having contractions or notice any sort of fluid leakage, stop exercising. Sit with your feet up, drink two cups of water, and see if you start feeling more normal. If not, contact your physician.

Even if the time and expense of joining a fitness club is out of reach, incorporate more exercise into your daily routine. Emily, one of the pregnant women with whom we talked, found that she could get more exercise by making some very simple changes to her daily routine. "I started parking at the far end of the parking lot when we were going to the grocery store or mall. It was actually sort of a relief, not having to wait around for that perfect parking spot! We also started taking the stairs instead of the elevator."

Try a pregnancy fitness videotape or DVD; some provide a very good workout for pregnant women. Two particularly good ones are the *Denise Austin Pregnancy Plus Workout* and the *Kathy Smith Pregnancy Workout.* Get your partner involved; trying to kick and step in rhythm can make for some great laughs and good shared time.

PROPER NUTRITION DURING PREGNANCY

Healthy eating while pregnant is basically the same as healthy eating when you're not pregnant, with a few important exceptions, of course. First and foremost, all pregnant women should take prenatal vitamins, preferably starting a few months before attempting to conceive. One of the most important component of prenatal vitamins is folic acid, which can prevent serious birth defects if taken in sufficient levels in the first few weeks of pregnancy.

Pregnant women need a slight increase in calories, but not enough to demand ice cream at any hour of the day or night. Early in the pregnancy, women may need only an additional two hundred calories a day; after the first trimester, the additional requirement may increase to an extra three to five hundred calories a day.

This is, of course, not to say that pregnant women will not have food cravings. They will. While some really do crave pickles and ice cream, others crave protein. Anemia is common during pregnancy and one of the body's ways of letting you know it's anemic is to crave red meat. If you're a vegetarian, go with beans and other iron-containing foods.

Once Emily was a few months along in her pregnancy, she found that she actually craved foods that were good for her! "My partner and I kept reading about how important folic acid is, so we did some research on the Internet. Even though I'm taking prenatal vitamins, we decided to add in extra things like spinach and fortified cereals to get a little more folic acid in. Slowly, I'm learning to actually *like* spinach."

Many pregnant women also experience constipation. This condition generally results from the body's increased hormone production during pregnancy, which can sometimes slow down bowel movements. To avoid constipation, eat foods with plenty of fiber. These include beans, broccoli, bran cereals and whole grains. Other anti-constipation recommendations include eating stone fruits (apricots, prunes, peaches) and drinking lots of water.

All pregnant women need more protein. Non-pregnant women should take in fifty grams a day according to the US RDA, but once you're carrying a child you'll need about sixty grams a day. Note, however, that the World Health Organization actually recommends closer to seventy-five grams a day of protein while pregnant. Some schools of thought believe that eighty to one hundred grams of protein per day can actually help prevent pre-eclampsia, a serious pregnancy complication involving high blood pressure.

The bad news? Many pregnant women just can't stomach the idea of a slab of red meat. Some alternatives include fish, which is an excellent source of protein, and is low-fat as well. However, be especially careful about mercury levels and other toxic chemicals (such as PCB's) found in some fish. Do not eat catfish, bluefish, striped bass, tuna, shark, mackerel, tilefish and swordfish. Even canned tuna, especially albacore tuna, can have unacceptably high levels of mercury, so avoid it while pregnant.

Recently, farmed salmon (the most common kind available in the United States) has been found to contain high levels of contaminants due to the environments in which the fish are raised. Wild salmon is considered a safer choice while pregnant. Low-fat fish are considered a good choice: white fish, such as cod, haddock and pollack, are safe to eat within reason. Also, make sure to avoid raw fish (such as sushi and sashimi) and shellfish, because they can be contaminated with raw sewage.

While some pregnant women may crave an Italian hoagie with bologna, salami and mortadella, eating this type of snack food may not be such a good idea. A bacterium called listeria can be found in prepared foods, particularly in deli meats, and pregnant women are up to twenty times more likely to become dangerously ill from exposure to these bacteria than non-pregnant women. Developing listeriosis can cause serious consequences, such as miscarriage or fetal death. If you're craving a deli sandwich, have fresh-carved roast beef or turkey instead. If you decide to purchase deli meat, re-heat it so that it is steaming before eating. Choose your prepared foods from a known source – avoid sandwiches at tiny stores where they may not be fresh and stay away from potato salad that's been warming in the sun at the company picnic.

Other foods that are high-risk for food-borne illnesses include soft cheeses (feta, brie, and camembert). Hard cheeses and pasteurized soft cheeses (cream cheese and cottage cheese) usually are safer to consume. Make sure that any you consume while pregnant are pasteurized.

Seems like everything good is off-limits! Don't worry, there are plenty of healthy, tasty foods available during pregnancy. Homemade foods prepared from fresh ingredients are the best, both in terms of safety and healthfulness. However, don't be surprised if, during the first and second trimester, all your favorite cooking smells are suddenly unappealing, if not downright nauseating.

THE DREADED NAUSEA

Morning sickness can be one of the most uncomfortable parts of your first trimester. For most women, it goes away after the first few months, although there are unfortunate women who feel nausea throughout their entire pregnancy. Morning sickness is really a misnomer – while nausea upon awakening is the most common form, many women feel nauseous at any time during the day or night.

There are hundreds of home remedies for morning sickness, which work to varying degrees for different people. Things to try include saltines and eating multiple small snacks rather than single, large meals. Emily found that "generic" anti-nausea foods helped the most. "Try gingersnaps, ginger ale, lemonade or just biting into a whole lemon. I have no idea why that works, but it does." Avoid heavy, greasy or spicy foods.

THE PREGNANT BUTCH

One aspect of pregnancy that is unique to lesbian couples has to do with stereotypical roles. Suppose, for whatever reason, one member of a couple is more "butch" than the other, and she decides to become pregnant. She may choose to carry a child for medical reasons, or reasons of age (if her partner is considerably older). Perhaps the more "femme" partner has tried unsuccessfully to get pregnant for some time, but having a family is still very important to the couple. Pregnancy can also be a part of life that any female may desire to take part in, regardless of how much she may reject typically-feminine roles.

For some women, especially those who adhere fairly strongly to butch/femme gender roles, the concept of the more butch partner becoming pregnant can be a difficult one to grasp. The mere idea of being inseminated and getting pregnant may not occur to butch women as a desirable choice. Once the idea is suggested as a possibility, though, the concept may become more and more appealing. As long as a woman is biologically female, pregnancy is always a possibility.

Considering a pregnancy can be a psychologically difficult concept for many butch women, who may feel uncomfortable with their female body or reject it completely. The process of attempting to become pregnant can be a physically and psychologically exposing one, in which all sorts of intimate areas of a woman's body are probed by various strangers. For many butch women, this may be extremely unappealing.

Ironically, the body's instinct to tense up can result in more discomfort than being relaxed about the whole thing. For women, butch or not, who experience fear or trauma with the thought of inseminations, it is vital to have a supportive partner present at all examinations and inseminations. The IUI process in a doctor's office involves many internal exams, from vaginal ultrasounds to track the process of ovulation to the actual insemination itself (which is similar to a Pap smear), and it can help immensely to have someone's hand to hold throughout these procedures. As difficult as it may be, this is a time to ask for help if you need it.

Be considerate of your partner. For couples where the more femme partner wished to become pregnant but was unable to, it may be particularly difficult for her to accept that her butch partner is willing and able to carry a child. She may feel that her role within the relationship has been supplanted, and may suffer from feelings of envy or even guilt at her own perceived shortcomings. She may find it difficult to relate to her new position as a support partner, rather than the one who is to be pampered and nurtured. Good communication and flexibility are essential to making a family work. If both partners can verbalize and discuss their feelings, there is a good chance that such a family unit can work out well. See Chapter 8 for more information on gender presentation and pregnancy.

HELPFUL PARTNERS

Morning sickness and pregnancy-related nausea caused by the hormonal surges your body is undergoing can render you virtually useless in the kitchen. If you are experiencing them, ask your partner to take over cooking duties.

Jasmine never did much cooking before Emily got pregnant, but she quickly learned that she'd have to step up and take over in the kitchen. "Man, Emily used to be the best cook! She made omelets, stir fries and other things. Once she got a couple weeks into her pregnancy, though, she couldn't stand to be in the kitchen anymore. So I had to learn, and fast!" Emily agrees that Jasmine was a quick study. "She started out burning toast," Emily laughs, "but now I think she's a better cook than I am."

A gay male couple using a surrogate can also help the woman to have a healthy pregnancy. David and Jack decided to ask Miriam, a woman David had known for years, if she would be willing to carry a child for them and Miriam agreed immediately. David wanted to be involved in the pregnancy, but he didn't want to be "in her face" or reading ingredient labels for her. So he chose to act as a supportive partner – he got involved in her daily exercise routine. He went for long walks with her every day, and bought her an exercise ball for home stretching.

Jack wasn't interested in participating in exercise with the surrogate, but he did love to cook. "One of my favorite parts of Miriam's pregnancy was all the cooking I got to do! It was a real challenge to make foods that were good-tasting and looked pretty, but healthy and low in salt. Sometimes we'd make a complete meal and bring it over to her house, complete with tablecloth and candlesticks. In retrospect, we probably went over the top, but it seemed like a good idea at the time." Remember that the mother may not feel like cooking or eating during parts of the pregnancy, but she and the baby both require nutrients. To the extent that all parties are willing, help with the cooking and other household chores. You can help the baby get off to a good start and will also be aiding the prospective mother in preparing her body for giving birth.

BIG NO-NOS

Another particularly important thing to avoid while pregnant is alcohol. Alcohol can severely damage a developing baby, especially early in the pregnancy. It is quickly metabolized and travels through the bloodstream to the placenta, so when you drink your baby drinks with you. While in some cultures moderate alcohol use is considered traditional and safe during pregnancy, it is not recommended. Recent statistics indicate that alcohol use during pregnancy is one of the leading causes of preventable mental retardation in children.

Smoking is also hazardous to a developing fetus. Second-hand smoke is just as dangerous for your baby. The same chemicals are inhaled and can pass through the birthmother's bloodstream to the baby and the fetus is getting less oxygen when the birth mother is around smoke. Smoking has been known to cause low birth weight, pre-term labor and miscarriage. Pregnant women should avoid places where people are smoking heavily, such as bars or clubs. These same rules apply to being around illegal drugs such as marijuana. While women who are trying to become pregnant should definitely quit smoking *before* trying to become pregnant, this habit absolutely needs to stop once pregnancy begins.

If a pregnant woman has cats, an important thing to avoid while pregnant is changing the litter box with bare hands. Cat feces can contain a parasite which causes toxoplasmosis. This health malady is normally mild in non-pregnant adults; for pregnant women, it can cause serious complications in the fetus, such as miscarriage or brain damage. Have your partner take on litter box duty until the baby is born or if you're single and must change the litter box yourself, wear disposable gloves and wash your hands well when you're done. Some providers will do a routine test to see if you have antibodies to toxoplasmosis, which would mean that you were previously exposed and are now immune. Many adults are immune, but if your test shows that you lack the immunity and you have cats, you'll want to be particularly careful about litter box duty. The toxoplasmosis parasite also can be found in raw meat and in outdoor dirt, so be careful and wear gloves while gardening and cooking.

LAMAZE

Once pregnancy is achieved, it is never too soon to start thinking about birth. The standard type of childbirth education class is often offered through a hospital or the pregnant woman's medical provider and usually includes the Lamaze method of patterned breathing. This is the famous "hee hee hooooo" approach to controlling breathing during contractions. The main goal of Lamaze is to help prevent the use of pain relieving drugs for as long as possible by focusing your attention outside your body in order to lessen the pain of giving birth. Many hospital childbirth education classes also focus on the use of various pain relief options, ranging from narcotics to epidural anesthetics. Hospital-sponsored classes can be particularly useful, because they will show you the standard of care at a particular facility, and can help you understand what to expect once you are at the hospital while you're in labor.

Hospital classes usually include a tour of the hospital's labor and delivery rooms, as well. Even if you decide not to take hospital-sponsored classes, it's a good idea to sign up for a separate tour of your hospital so you know what you can bring and what the procedures will be. Also make sure to pre-register at this time.

BRADLEY

There are many alternatives to the typical Lamaze method. Perhaps the most popular is the Bradley method, which focuses on long, measured breaths during and between contractions. The Bradley method focuses on natural childbirth and ways to avoid pain relieving medications altogether during the birth process. If a drug-free childbirth experience is important to you, a Bradley class may be a good choice. If you are more ambivalent about whether or not you want pain relief, however, you may find Bradley classes more difficult, because success is often measured by whether you are able to have a natural childbirth. If you think you might want pain relief, you won't want to set yourself up for a perceived failure.

ALTERNATE CLASSES

Other options for childbirth education classes include hypno-birthing and "birthing from within." In hypno-birthing, your support partner actually learns how to put you into a light hypnotic trance to help control the pain of contractions. This method may not work for everyone, because it depends on your ability to be hypnotized. It also requires a serious commitment to practice the exercises in the weeks leading up to birth. Other childbirth education options include more psychological-based programs such as "birthing from within," which focus on the emotional as well as the physical aspects of childbirth. You may also find independent classes which combine elements of multiple methods. These classes have the disadvantage of not going into any one method in as much detail as is possible in a more focused class, but the advantage can be that you have many more possible options for dealing with labor – if one method doesn't work, you can try another.

Childbirth classes teach you much more than how to breathe. A good course will show models or charts of how your baby is growing inside you and what changes your body is making to accommodate the growing fetus. Every class will teach some method for dealing with contractions, when to call the hospital, techniques for pushing, advice on your choices for medical pain relief and much more. There are also specialized childbirth classes for non-English speakers and teenage mothers, infant care for new mothers, breastfeeding techniques and others.

THE LOGISTICS

The most common source of childbirth preparation classes is your hospital or medical provider. In some areas, birthing centers or childbirth education centers sponsor classes of various types. Also check out your local town's recreation and adult education department – they may offer childbirth education classes. Another place to look for classes is online: try www.lamaze-childbirth.com and www.bradley-birth.com. One advantage of private classes it that they may be held at more convenient times. Some childbirth instructors will also come to your home for private classes, which can be very convenient if you already have small children and don't feel comfortable leaving them with a sitter.

With most childbirth education methods, it is assumed that the laboring woman will have a support partner who will attend all the classes with her and be present at the birth. For heterosexual couples this is usually the husband, though it can sometimes be a close female friend or relative. The usual mix in group classes, therefore, may make a lesbian couple feel, at least at first, uncomfortable. If you have any doubt about your comfort level in a class, you may want to talk to the instructor ahead of time to get a feel for her comfort level with non-traditional families. If a class full of heterosexual couples would make you feel too uncomfortable, you might feel better with a smaller class or private lessons.

The situation will vary for a gay male couple working with a surrogate or a couple in an open adoption working with a pregnant birth mother. Depending on the birth mother's individual preferences and comfort level, she may want one or both of the adoptive parents as her labor support partner(s). Some birthmothers and surrogates are comfortable with having the child's future parents with her in the delivery room, and if she doesn't have another source of support she might want to have one or both partners attend classes with her. If the birthmother or surrogate is uncomfortable with this arrangement or doesn't want the future parents in the delivery room, then she may choose a different labor support partner to help her in classes. Try not to feel too rejected if this is the case.

Other prenatal classes also can be very useful. Especially if this is your first child and you and your partner don't have much experience around newborns, include infant first aid and CPR classes. Inquire if your health insurance provider or town recreation/adult education department may offer such classes relatively inexpensively. Other classes you might want to sign up for include: newborn baby care, breastfeeding support and techniques, prenatal exercise classes such as yoga or water aerobics and sibling preparation classes which get older siblings ready for their new roles as big brothers and sisters. Classes such as mommy-and-me groups for women with newborns and post-natal exercise classes where babies are welcome are also good choices.

PARENTAL LEAVE, FAMILY LEAVE

While a pregnant woman is usually given some amount of paid time off from work, her partner may have no such privilege. The extent of family or maternity leave for partners depends almost entirely on their place of employment and state of residence. Some companies provide paid "parental leave," for some number of weeks for any partner. Others provide "paternity leave" only to a male spouse, while still others may have a "family leave" policy that could be extended to include a same-sex partner.

Some companies will grant family leave to a same-sex partner if the couple is legally registered. In California, for example, women would need to become registered domestic partners prior to the birth of the baby in order for some partners to take advantage of their companies' family leave policies. Find out the specifics of these policies well in advance of the birth of your child. Some companies, in states without DP benefits, may choose to have their own domestic partner registration and benefits. In this case, you may need to file a form, sometimes notarized, with your company's human resource department to be eligible for these benefits. This form may or may not be confidential, so be aware that your status as registered partners may become a matter of public record or at least part of your employee file.

Still other companies, even ones that grant a partner family leave time, may require proof that the child exists. Some will ask that you fax or email a preliminary birth certificate from the hospital before leave can be officially granted. If this is the case, be sure to bring all necessary contact information with you to the hospital, in order to get the process started a soon as possible.

Also check if your company has an official policy on leave for same-sex couples and if leave is granted to adoptive parents. Some companies and some states offer paid family leave for bonding with a newly born or newly adopted child. If you're planning a second-parent or domestic partner adoption after the child is born, you may be eligible for leave once that adoption takes place. However, this won't help you during the newborn's first few weeks. Some companies allow adoptive leave to take place once a child is placed for adoption, rather than requiring the adoption to be finalized. In the situation of a same-sex couple, this may allow leave to be taken from the first day a child comes home. In a larger company, work with the human resources director to determine you employer's exact policy on adoption leave.

STATE AND FEDERAL LEAVE

If the company the pregnant woman works for doesn't have any parental leave policy at all, she may still be eligible for at least some leave at either reduced pay or no pay, depending on your state of residence. Some states have a family leave program that is designed to allow workers to spend some time with their newborns or newly adopted children, or account for other family emergencies, without fear of losing their jobs. Depending on the state you live in, you may be allowed up to six weeks of leave at some percentage of your salary. To find out the specifics for your state, contact your company's human resources department or the state agency.

On a federal level, you may be eligible for up to twelve weeks of unpaid leave, courtesy of the Family and Medical Leave Act; see http://www.dol.gov/esa/whd/fmla/ for more information. The twelve weeks of federal FMLA leave can often be used after your six weeks of state leave are used up, if available. Try to work with your human resources to maximize the amount of leave you are able to take, while also minimizing the financial hardship for your family. Many families may not be able to afford to take twelve weeks of unpaid leave, but it's a good option to have just in case you need it.

CONCLUDING ADVICE:

Being pregnant can be the best nine months of your life… or not! Some pregnancies are more difficult and have more complications than others. You can improve your chances of having a good pregnancy by being healthy: eating well and exercising. Your choice of caregiver will also contribute to your general sense of well-being. Investigate midwives and obstetricians, and discuss the options with your partner. Pick a caregiver that you're both comfortable with, and whom you can trust if emergency situations arise. Whether your pregnancy is difficult or easy, the objective is the wonderful baby that will be yours.

QUESTIONS ABOUT AND DURING PREGNANCY:

1. Do you belong to a gym or fitness club? Do you have access to a swimming pool? Do you have a good pair of supportive athletic shoes?
2. Have you taken a good look at your diet and tried to incorporate healthy food choices for you and your baby?
3. Have you and your partner chosen a midwife or obstetrician? Have you taken your partner to prenatal appointments, and made sure that she also establishes a relationship with your caregiver?
4. Have you signed up for a birthing class? Have you and your partner talked about different labor and delivery options and picked one that works well for you?
5. If you are working with a surrogate or a birthmother for a child you plan to adopt, have you asked if you can be involved in the pregnancy? Have you found ways to be supportive without being intrusive?
6. Have you already quit smoking? If not, are you willing to?
7. Do your and/or your partner's companies offer good family leave policies? If not, have you arranged prenatal and child care for your baby?

chapter ten

DELIVERY AND BIRTH

The day is drawing closer and closer when your baby will be born. It's everything you've worked for, and you want the delivery to be as special as you've been dreaming. During the last few months before the actual birth, there are some important arrangements to be made.

Different arrangements may be necessary if you are a lesbian couple giving birth to your child, a gay couple using a surrogate or a couple doing an open adoption. Usually the woman giving birth has primary input into the circumstances of the birth, so much of this chapter will apply most directly to lesbian couples. However, couples using a surrogate or couples doing an open adoption may also want to have input into where and how the birth takes place, and/or be present for the actual event, and thus this chapter will be relevant for them as well.

GETTING READY! PREPARING FOR THE BIRTH

As we've discussed, your choices may depend on the laws of your particular state or county. Lay midwives are certified to attend home births in some states, but not all—research the laws in your state first. The options available to you may also depend on your medical history. If you're deemed high-risk, many times a midwife or a birthing center won't accept you, and you'll want to be under the care of an obstetrician and plan to give birth in a hospital.

Be aware, as we've discussed before, if you have had a previous C-section, midwives or standalone birthing centers may not accept you, because there is a risk of rupture and other serious complications. In that case you'll likely have to deliver in a hospital setting. Again, if you have been considering a VBAC, revisit your particular situation (including the factors that led to your C-section in the first place) with your midwife or obstetrician. You can then discuss final options for the location of your baby's birth.

FINAL DECISIONS ON A HOSPITAL

You are already aware that one of the major considerations for where to give birth is, for many people, financial. You've already looked into and are utilizing insurance policies which are specific in terms of what they cover and at what percentage. You have researched what coverage your particular insurance policy provides. Many HMOs, for example, only pay for you to give birth at one or two particular hospitals, while a PPO plan may be more flexible. The downside of some PPOs, of course, is that you may have more out-of-pocket costs.

You may have been pleasantly surprised to find that your insurance covers midwife care at your home in addition to, or instead of, obstetrician care at a hospital or medical office. Alternatively, you may have found that it only covers hospital care. (If possible, you have researched all of these options before becoming pregnant. Since pregnancy is sometimes considered a "pre-existing condition," it can be difficult to switch insurance plans or get insurance if you don't have any once you're pregnant.)

This is the time to take a tour of the labor and delivery facilities. Sometimes these tours have to be scheduled in advance, so make sure to schedule it well before the baby's anticipated birth; many babies come early, so don't wait until a week before the due date. Try to attend with your partner or other birthing support person and prepare a list of questions ahead of time.

Once you've narrowed down the list of possible hospitals to two or three, there are several things to consider. What's the driving distance from your home or office? Make sure to account for traffic at all hours of the day—it may be that hospitals further away in miles are actually closer in terms of time due to potential rush hour traffic. Also make sure to research the size of the hospital. A small hospital may have a more intimate setting, but may not have an anesthesiologist on call twenty-four hours a day. The implication is that, in the event of an emergency C-section, you may have to be transferred to a different hospital. In a hospital without an anesthesiologist on-call, epidural pain relief may also not be available at off-times.

Consider how many birthing rooms are available. Does the hospital have separate labor, delivery and recovery rooms, forcing you to change rooms both before and after delivery? Some hospitals perform all of these functions in the same place, but others do not. Ask the nursing staff how many labor and delivery rooms are typically free at any given time. How often are they all full, and what happens in that event? Are there an obstetrician and anesthesiologist on-call twenty-four hours? What level of neo-natal intensive care unit is available in the hospital, in the event of complications? It is far better to know the answers to all of these questions well in advance of the actual birth.

Other things to ask include whether most deliveries are performed by midwives or doctors (OBs). Some hospitals have midwives on-call twenty-four hours for standard deliveries, plus one OB on-call for complicated deliveries. Find out if your OB practices at that particular hospital, and what your chances are of getting him/her for the delivery. In many hospitals, OBs rotate through being on-call so even if you're seeing one particular doctor for prenatal care, there's no guarantee that your doctor will be there for your birth. For this reason, if your OB practices as part of a group, it's often a good idea to see all the OBs in the group throughout your pregnancy, so there's a higher chance that you will have met the doctor who will be delivering your baby.

When Ruth was pregnant, she and her partner Janice found that there was only one doctor in the group covered by Ruth's insurance that they liked. Janice recalls, "Some of the doctors were just horrible, and ignored me completely—there was no way I was going to let them deliver our child! Unfortunately, this was the only hospital in the area that our insurance covered, and there was no way to switch our insurance before Ruth was due to deliver. So we decided to be induced when the one doctor we liked was on call. Ruth was overdue anyway, so we figured we'd probably be induced in any case, so why not try to get the doctor we liked?"

When you're checking out hospitals and doctors, inquire as to what restrictions the hospital has on laboring women. When do they want the woman to come in? At the beginning of labor or when it's already well established? Do they allow eating or drinking during labor? What are the hospital's general policies and rates for episiotomies, epidurals and C-sections? You may find, for example, that one hospital has a much higher C-section rate than another; if this is something you want to avoid, you may wish to choose a different hospital. To make a fair comparison, though, take into consideration whether one hospital accepts more high-risk patients than another.

Learn about the hospital's security system for new babies and mothers. You will want to ensure that you, and only you, go home with your baby. Some hospitals have video monitoring of the pediatric floor, matching armbands worn by parents and babies and barcode-like devices that you and the baby must wear. Though these systems may pose a slight inconvenience, they are an effective way to prevent kidnapping and administrative mistakes.

SECURING PARTNER ACCESS

Make sure that the hospital staff is willing to identify both you and your partner as the parents of the child. Make an appointment with the hospital administrator to discuss the fact that you and your partner will be there for both the birth and the duration of your stay. If they announce something like, "Only spouses may be present" or "Only immediate family is welcome," then you may want to switch hospitals. Legal action may be a possibility, depending on your state anti-discrimination laws, but you may decide that the added stress isn't worth it.

If your hospital has security systems to make sure that babies are taken only by their actual parents, make sure that the hospital will get matching bracelets for you, your partner and your new child. In addition to securing access for a lesbian partner, similar circumstances apply to a male couple who wish to be present during their surrogate's labor and delivery or with a couple doing an open adoption who wants to be with the birthmother during delivery.

Some other questions to bring up: Can the adoptive couple or couple using a surrogate visit with the newborn without the birthmother's presence? Will they be permitted to sign the infant out of the hospital? Bring copies of all legal paperwork to the hospital with you, and be prepared to explain it to the nurses and other hospital staff. Most of the time, the hospital will be willing to work with you to make the childbirth experience a positive one for all involved.

You should also inquire as to post-delivery regulations. Learn the average hospital stay, both after a normal vaginal delivery and after a C-section. Ask if your partner can stay with you throughout the recovery and whether the baby can stay in the room with you at all times. Some hospitals may suggest that the newborn stay in the nursery whenever you're sleeping, but if you prefer, your partner should be able to stay with the child while you catch up on your sleep.

Another consideration in choosing a hospital is whether labor and delivery and recovery rooms are shared or private. Jeanne tried to request a private room for both labor and delivery, but she knew that it wasn't guaranteed. "My hospital had a first-come first-served policy, so I was told that if I was the only woman about to give birth, I'd have my first pick of the rooms. If I got there last, then I'd get whatever was left." Jeanne got lucky when it came time for recovery. "It turned out that while there were six women giving birth around the same time I was, somehow I ended up alone on the maternity floor and was given my own room with the baby."

If you do end up in a shared room, most couples will be too wrapped up in their own new family addition to pay much attention to their roommates. If you should encounter any problems with other mothers or families, speak up to the nursing staff and ask to be moved to a different room.

In Ruth and Janice's case, their hospital had a policy that if the maternity rooms were shared, husbands couldn't stay overnight because of "privacy concerns." Ruth says, "The maternity floor was crowded, and we had to share a room with another couple. When nighttime came, the nurses kicked out the husband, citing their policy. However, they let Janice stay with me and our new son, since she was female and they had no policy against female spouses staying!"

ADDITIONAL QUESTIONS TO CONSIDER

Remember that even after the birth, there are differences in hospital services that you should consider ahead of time. If you plan to breastfeed, for example, find out the hospital's policy on giving bottles and supplements. Are supplements necessary? Some women do not want to train their children to use bottles and prefer that supplements be administered via a dropper or spoon; make sure to inquire as to whether the nursing staff is prepared to honor this request. Is there a lactation consultant on staff and what hours is she available? Do the nurses have any training in breastfeeding support? If the child will be out of your care in the nursery, inquire as to whether the nursing staff will bring the child to you for feedings.

Circumcision presents another host of questions. If the child is a boy and you wish to circumcise, find out the hospital's policy. Can it be done while you're still in the hospital or do you have to bring the child back? If you wish to be in the room during the circumcision, ask if this will be allowed. What type of pain relief is available? What procedures are used? Is the procedure entirely covered by your health insurance? Most hospitals will have their own set of rules and you shouldn't expect them to deviate too much from their standard procedures. If you don't like their policies, consider having the circumcision done somewhere else.

HOSPITAL ALTERNATIVE: CHOOSING A HOME BIRTH

Home birth is not a decision to be taken lightly. In considering home birth as a viable option, there are several factors to take into account.

First, you may want to consider your proximity to a hospital in case problems arise during labor. If you live in a rural area, for example, your options will be much more limited if you encounter a serious medical problem while having a home birth.

The main advantage of a home birth is, for many women, the personal setting. You're free to labor at your own pace. While occupying a hospital bed, there is always some pressure because someone else may need the bed. Also, in a hospital birth, you're more likely to be offered drugs (such as Pitocin) to augment a slow or seemingly stalled labor. These interventions can often lead to other interventions, which can cumulatively increase your chance of having a C-section eventually. However, sometimes these interventions are required and absolutely necessary, so don't disregard the hospital option based solely on these criteria.

THE MISTRESS OF CEREMONIES

If you wish to do a homebirth, you should find a certified midwife whom you trust. Your relationship with the midwife will be much more intimate than that with an OB, mostly because you'll be seeing the same person for all of your prenatal care (and, of course, the delivery). Some midwives have an office where you can come for prenatal care, while others may come to your home to do basic checkups. Investigate the laws in your state concerning what types of midwives (direct entry midwife, lay midwife, certified nurse midwife) are certified to attend home births and get recommendations from hospitals and local birthing centers.

Some questions you should consider when choosing a midwife: What happens if your midwife is already attending a birth when you go into labor? What type of backup does she have? Most midwives practice in teams for this reason—someone should always be available. If this is the case, you should become familiar with everyone on your midwife's team (at least get to know her direct backup).

WHEN TO SKIP A HOME BIRTH

Home birth is not always possible. Take the case of Megan and Molly, a lesbian couple expecting their first child. Megan had her heart set on working with a midwife; her college roommate studied to become a midwife and Megan felt that the at-home setting would be better for her and the baby. However, it was not to be. Megan had gestational diabetes and her doctor recommended a hospital birth in order to monitor her condition more closely.

Generally speaking, it won't be feasible to deliver at home if you have certain medical conditions or if your pregnancy is deemed high-risk. Many of these conditions (such as a previous C-section) are pre-existing, while others (gestational diabetes, pregnancy-induced hypertension) may appear during the course of the pregnancy. Be prepared to be flexible; if you develop one of these conditions while pregnant, you may have no choice but to transfer to a hospital or birthing center.

GUSSY UP THE ROOM

Most midwives will ask you to have a variety of supplies on hand. These may include washable or disposable sheets and towels and a variety of sterile instruments that can be purchased as part of an at-home birthing kit. Beware that childbirth is not a clean process; properly protecting your home in advance will give you one less thing to worry about during the laboring and birthing process.

One option in doing a home birth is a water birth. This option may be appealing for a variety of reasons and is safe for most pregnancies. If you don't have a large enough bath tub, you can rent a birthing tub (which is basically an oversized, structurally-sound wading pool). Laboring in water can provide support and pain relief. If you choose this approach, make sure you have enough room for the birthing pool and that you have a large enough hot water heater to fill it with the required amount of warm water.

If you are considering a home birth, you should think about who you would like to have present for the birth. In a hospital, visitors or birth attendants are limited, but at home there are no such limitations other than the size of your home. You may think that it is natural to include your extended family (such as children and other relatives), but be prepared to eject certain people if you so choose. While hospital staff will remove any distracting or disruptive relatives, in your own home you and your partner will have to take that responsibility upon yourselves. If you choose to labor at home, consider hiring a doula (a labor support assistant) who can act as a buffer, if necessary, between the laboring woman and any other friends or family members invited to attend the birth.

If you have other children, consider whether you would like them to attend the birth. If so, you may want to arrange for a designated person to supervise them during labor and delivery. If you have pets, consider whether they need to be part of the process, or should be confined to another part of the house. Dogs in particular should be restrained so that they don't become upset over the strange sights, smells and sounds.

Be prepared for any potential problems that could arise. In the event that your labor fails to progress or if there are any unforeseen medical emergencies, you may need to be transported to a hospital. Discuss this possibility with the midwife ahead of time. What type of medical training does the midwife have, and what criteria are used to determine if you need to be transported to a hospital? Also consider whether your midwife has privileges at the hospital where you would be going and if she can still assist with the birth. If she does not, you will have to work with whichever obstetrician is available at the hospital at the time of your arrival. Even if your midwife doesn't have privileges at the particular hospital to which you are taken, she might be allowed to stay on as a labor-support assistant. Ask in advance about the hospitals policies in this type of situation.

CHOOSING A BIRTHING CENTER

Some women want the amenities of a home-birth, but are either worried about medical complications or have a pre-existing medical condition that won't allow for a home birth. In these situations, a birthing center may be a good compromise.

Birthing centers are not all the same. The two main varieties are stand-alone and those that are attached to a larger hospital complex. Stand-alone birthing centers are usually staffed by midwives, often have prenatal care visits available and may have amenities such as whirlpool tubs, birthing balls and other accessories to make labor progress more smoothly. In many, you can deliver and then continue your stay in the same room.

Some birthing centers may even offer simple forms of pain relief such as narcotics, although most will not offer full anesthetic relief such as an epidural. If you think you'll want an anesthesiologist, you should probably choose a hospital. And, of course, if you need a C-section, you will be transferred to a hospital as well.

Some birthing centers are affiliated with hospitals. With these centers, most or all "normal births" take place in the birthing center and only high-risk patients or those who need C-sections are moved to the hospital. This type of birthing center may be a good choice if you prefer to try for as natural a birth as possible, but want the added security of having a full hospital nearby.

EQUALITY BEFORE THE BIRTH

Once you've decided where to give birth, one of the most important things you'll need to do is ensure that your partner will have complete and equal access to all aspects of the process. For a lesbian couple, the woman in labor will probably want her partner with her every step of the way. Megan felt strongly that Molly needed to be there; not only was she her labor coach, but she relied on Molly for strength and support. However, their hospital gave them a hard time about it.

Megan had to be firm. "I had to call the hospital administrator three separate times to get her to understand," she says, "But finally they saw that I wasn't going to back down; my partner WILL be there for the birth, and that's final." She would have switched to another health insurance company if she had to, but fortunately the hospital staff agreed to accommodate them.

Generally, this particular issue shouldn't present a problem, because all hospitals allow the laboring woman to have at least one support person. However, if you're scheduled for a C-section, you'll need to verify that your partner can be there with you during the surgery, and that your partner can stay with the child after you've given birth (while you're in recovery).

In some hospitals, before a C-section, the woman is taken to a preparatory room and no one is allowed to accompany her. However, once this preparation is complete, the partner (wearing sterile attire) should be allowed into the operating room before the surgery is scheduled to start.

As a worst-case scenario, suppose your hospital balks at the idea of a female partner, and refuses to let her in. First, try not to let this be a surprise. If at all possible, find out your hospital's policy ahead of time. If necessary, meet with the hospital administrator to discuss whether having a female partner will be a problem. This is exactly what Megan had to do. "They'd just never gotten a request like this before, and I think they honestly didn't know what to do with us."

Work to get any problems with the hospital resolved long before you go into labor. Be polite and respectful, but emphasize that your partner has a right to be with you, and that you won't negotiate on this point.

If the hospital actually refuses to allow your partner, you may consider switching hospitals. If time and finances allow, you may choose to hire a lawyer and discuss legal action. Keep copies of any written documentation that denies your partner full access and compare this to state anti-discrimination laws (if they exist in your state).

When Molly and Megan arrived at the hospital for the delivery, the first thing Megan did was to introduce Molly. "I made it clear that Molly was my partner and that she was to be involved in all decisions." Discuss amongst yourselves what will happen if there is a medical emergency. Should your partner stay with you or your child? Every couple will have their own opinion on this important matter and it's a decision that should be reached in advance.

Once the child is born, both partners will need equal access to the baby and full responsibility in the eyes of the hospital. Insist that both parents' names are given to the hospital as guardians of the child.

When in the recovery room later, you'll be surrounded by other new mothers, many of them with their husbands, boyfriends and other family. If you fear that you may encounter unfriendliness or hostility, remember that you'll probably never see these people again in your life and there's no point in engaging in nastiness. Your new family is the important thing, so focus on your new child and your partner.

Two dads working with a surrogate may also want access to the birth mother, if she is willing. Don't feel obligated to explain your family to anyone; you have just as much right to be there as anyone else. If people ask, though, be prepared to answer politely with a line such as, "We're the proud new fathers! Wow, your new baby is adorable." The same is true for a gay or lesbian couple adopting from a woman giving birth. Arrangements will need to be made in advance so that the couple can be present for the birth if possible.

DEALING WITH THE BIRTH CERTIFICATE

Once you've given birth but before you're officially discharged, a hospital official will come by your room to record the birth. This step is necessary in order to register the birth with the state. This is the form that will ultimately be used to produce your child's birth certificate. Depending on your legal status and what method you used to conceive, you should think carefully (ahead of time) and perhaps consult an attorney about how to fill out the birth certificate. For example, say that you conceived the child using anonymous donor sperm and you and your partner petitioned under UPA before the birth to have both partners recognized as legal parents. In this case, you have every right to have both of you listed on the birth certificate.

However, even with a court judgment in hand, you may encounter problems from the hospital staff. They may refuse to add a partner as "Partner Two" – and most states still only have forms listing "Mother" and "Father," not "Parent" and "Parent." Expect that you may have to do some modification of the form to indicate "Parent" and "Parent." Rest assured that, though it may take up to a year or more, if you receive an erroneous birth certificate you can file a corrections report with your state; you'll eventually be rewarded with a correct birth certificate.

If a lesbian couple is planning a later second-parent or other adoption, it is important to consider what will be put in the "Father" slot on the birth certificate. Beware putting false information on this form, as it may be illegal and could cause trouble down the road when a partner attempts to legally adopt the baby.

If a lesbian couple uses a known sperm donor with whom they plan to co-parent, they may choose to list this man as the father on the birth certificate. If you use a known donor but don't plan to give him any legal parental rights, carefully consider whether or not he should be listed on the birth certificate. Putting his name as "Father" may be legally required in some states, but listing a known sperm donor can also give him full paternal rights and responsibilities. Listing a known donor on the birth certificate, even when he hasn't planned to be a co-parent, can have drawbacks.

In some states, if you conceived using anonymous donor sperm, you should leave the "Father" slot blank. In other states, the correct response is "unknown" and in still other states, the correct answer is two dashes in the "Father" space. To find out what your state requires, talk to an attorney or a sperm bank in your state. It's important to discover the legal implications of these decisions ahead of time and have a well researched plan for filling out the birth certificate before the birth takes place.

If you're a gay male couple working with a surrogate, you'll also want to consult a lawyer in your state to see what you can legally fill out on the birth certificate. If you are not able to list both fathers, you may be able to list just the biological father and then do a second-parent or other adoption later to get the second father added. Some states may give you trouble with trying to create a birth certificate with the "mother" spot blank, so find out what you can put there ahead of time.

CONCLUDING ADVICE FOR BIRTH:

Choosing a good birth environment is essential to a good labor and delivery. Find a place that's comfortable for you, and one that is covered by your insurance if cost is an issue. Speak to the hospital administrator ahead of time about allowing your partner full access to you and the baby. Get their agreement in writing, if at all possible. If you qualify for a home birth, consider all the available options. Talk to friends who've done a home birth, and see what they liked (and didn't like) about their own experiences. Perhaps a birthing center is the compromise you've been looking for; in that case, follow up on what's available in your area. Once you've picked where you want to give birth, make sure you've done your best to remove any obstacles that might make it difficult for your partner to participate fully in the whole birthing experience, and think about what you plan to fill out on the birth certificate.

QUESTIONS:

1. Do you want a home birth, or a hospital birth? Which is right for you?
2. Are home births legal in your state?
3. Are there any birthing centers in your area? Are they covered by your insurance?
4. Have you spoken with the hospital administrator to make sure that your partner will be respected in the labor and delivery room?
5. Have you found out about your chosen hospital's security policies and made sure that your partner will have equal access to your child?
6. If you are working with a surrogate or birthmother, have you asked her if you can be present at the delivery? If not, make sure to have a plan for how she will contact you once the child is delivered, and how and when you will be able to take your new baby home.
7. Do you have a plan for how to fill out the birth certificate? Have you talked to a lawyer to find out what your options are, and what your best bet is given your future plans to legalize parental relationships?

chapter eleven

THE FIRST TWO YEARS

Parenthood is one of those things you can never really prepare for – you can do all the research in the world before your child is born or adopted, but there's really no comparison to the real event. Many parents, especially if they go through a long wait for an adoption or a lengthy period of infertility, have plenty of time to build up preconceived notions about how they plan to parent their child. Perhaps they will only breastfeed, with no bottles, or feed only organic formula and use cloth diapers. Their child will eat only homemade baby food, and will never watch television.

These ideals may seem like a good idea pre-baby. Once the child actually arrives, though, one of the most important attributes of good parenting is flexibility. Phyllis and Susan, for example, are a lesbian couple living in Maine. They recently gave birth to their first child. Before the baby arrived, they talked extensively about how they wanted to raise her. "She's only going to play with wooden toys because we HATE plastic baby toys. She's never going to have those horrible noisy electronic beeping toys—you know those things? And we're going to vacuum her nursery every day so she doesn't get allergies."

Many parents are critical of themselves if they cannot live up to unattainable standards. Find what works best for your particular family and accept that parenting is an evolving skill.

FEEDING, BREASTFEEDING AND CO-LACTATION

One of the major activities of a newborn baby will be eating. For a lesbian couple, one of whom has just give birth, there is one mother who is biologically better able to nurse, but this does not mean that the other partner is not ready or eager to take on her share of feeding duties.

Lesbian or gay couples who have just adopted a child or had one using a surrogate often find there is even less of a biological advantage or position that gives one partner preference in terms of feeding. If the baby is being fed formula, this makes it easy for both partners to feed the child. It's important to consider who will be home with the baby, while of course taking into account that both partners may want to feed her! Of course, if one partner gets more family leave than the other, or works from home or has chosen to be a stay-at-home parent, then the equal dynamic may shift to one parent doing the bulk of the feeding (as well as other baby-care duties). In this case, however, the parent working outside of the home may wish to do the bulk of the evening feedings, so he can reconnect with his daughter after a long day away. The most important thing to consider, of course, is balance, as well as the desires of the two parents.

When one partner in a lesbian couple has given birth, there can be some tension about who feeds the baby. If the couple chooses to breastfeed, the one who gave birth obviously has an inherent advantage since she has readily available breastmilk for the baby on demand. However, she should make sure not to discount the feelings of her partner, who likely feels just as strongly that she needs (and deserves) an equal chance to feed their child.

Sharing experiences such as feeding can be accomplished in many different ways. Some women, especially those who have given birth before, induce lactation so that they can feed a child they have not given birth to. Some adoptive mothers are also successful in this endeavor. Inducing lactation is a non-trivial undertaking, however. It usually requires months of dedicated pumping before the birth of the child to stimulate lactation, and sometimes various herbs or other medications can be taken to help stimulate milk production. Induced lactation is more commonly successful in women who have previously given birth and produced milk, since in that case the woman's body has already lactated.

Not every woman will want to induce lactation. For those who do not want to go through the required pumping of breast milk, but still want to share some of the breastfeeding experience, a device called a "supplemental nursing system" (SNS) or a "Lact-aid" may be used. These can even be used by men who want the experience of nursing their child. A SNS includes a container that can be filled with expressed breast milk or formula and a small tube which is attached near the adult's nipple. As the baby suckles, the tube drips milk into the baby's mouth. This system allows the baby to get the experience of nursing and gain nourishment at the same time. The SNS is sometimes used to train babies who have difficulty in nursing, to get them used to sucking on a real nipple.

If your partner doesn't want to use such a device, however, the simplest alternative is also the most widely used—bottles. "Nipple confusion," which happens when the baby has difficulty switching between the breast and bottle is occasionally a problem, but in most cases babies can learn to accept both kinds of nipples. Some doctors recommend waiting at least four to six weeks before introducing a bottle. In practice, though, based on what we've learned, waiting that long will get the baby used to only breastfeeding, and he or she may be more likely to reject a bottle when it is finally offered. A different strategy is to start out with alternating between breast and bottle feeding from the beginning. An advantage of this method is that your partner can feed the child right from the start.

While putting breast milk in the bottle has many advantages, including being readily available and passing on important immunities to the baby, formula also gives needed nutrients. In the case of adopted babies, you may have to feed the baby a formula. If you end up using formula, or combining both formula and breast milk, for whatever reason, don't feel guilty – many healthy babies have been raised on formula alone and it provides more than adequate nourishment.

Infant formulas have become more and more sophisticated over the years and include many ingredients and compounds that are found in breast milk. They come in milk-based and soy-based varieties and in an array of options in terms of both formulations and formats. Ready-to-serve, concentrated or powdered formulas are available. Formula comes in types ranging from organic to high-tech, with some formulas now containing ingredients such as DHA.

PUMPING

Of course, research shows that breastfeeding is the best option for feeding a baby if possible. Once the woman's milk has come in and breastfeeding is well established, a woman may start pumping her breasts if she and her partner wish to feed the baby with expressed breast milk instead of formula. Some women have trouble breastfeeding, some have trouble pumping, while others have no difficulty with either. There are many options in breast pumps, ranging from single handheld ones to double electric ones that allow a woman to pump both breasts at once. For women who plan to return to working outside of the house while the baby is only a few weeks or months old, a double electric pump can be a valuable investment. Milk can also be frozen to be used as needed at a future date.

Women who return to working outside the home after the birth of a child should negotiate time to pump milk with their employer. Some companies provide private rooms where a lactating mother can plug in the pump. If you have a private office you should just be able to pump breast milk at your desk. A hands-free attachment can allow you to read e-mail or catch up on other reading while pumping. There are car adapters for your breast pump and you may use them in the car, though it isn't recommended to pump while driving.

Laura, a lesbian mother in Delaware, returned to work eight weeks after son Jason was born. Her partner Jenny stayed home with their son and works part-time from their home. Luckily, Laura works only a few miles from their house and so was able to come home on her lunch break to see Jenny and nurse Jason. Laura also pumped breast milk for the baby in the morning, before leaving for work. She found that she got the most milk during this morning session.

Laura was able to get by with only two pumping sessions at work, one in the morning and one in the afternoon. Since she had a private office, she was able to shut the door and blinds and put a "do not disturb" sign on her door so co-workers would not interrupt her. She got a mini-fridge for her office to store the pumped milk so she could bring it home later in a refrigerated bag. Laura rinsed the pump parts out in the office kitchen. Laura says, "This was extremely embarrassing at first, but fortunately once people figured out what I was doing they got used to it, so I quickly got over my embarrassment." At night she ran the parts through the dishwasher at home.

This arrangement worked well for Jenny and Laura, allowing Laura to pump enough milk to keep their baby Jason satisfied most days. On weekends, Laura tried to get an extra pumping session or two in between feeds to help build up the stash of milk that she stored in the freezer. On the days when Laura wasn't able to pump enough milk, Jenny supplemented the baby's feedings with formula. They found that as Jason got older Jenny had to do this less and less – he was able to wait until Laura got home to be fed and then sometimes would have a long nursing session in the evening. Jenny and Laura also co-sleep with Jason, so that he can nurse during the night while allowing them both to get some rest at intervals.

THE ART OF BONDING

When considering feeding options, remember that babies do not just bond with whoever feeds them. They also bond with the person who gives them love and attention. In fact, some birthmothers with whom we spoke reported that their partners developed more sophisticated means of calming and soothing their children than they did, since they did not have the breast as a pacifying option.

If you and your partner have any conflicts or concerns about who will feed the baby, who is bonding with the baby and who is feeling left out of the process, it is very important to address them as soon as possible. Ideally, major decisions should be talked out before the child is born or adopted. Is one parent planning to stay at home? Is one giving birth? Do both partners feel strongly about trying to lactate or does one partner not really have any interest in feeding the child? Do one or both partners feel strongly about using formula vs. breast milk, or bottles vs. breast? These are complicated and important issues, and you can address many of them before a child is born rather than in the confusing first month of life with a newborn. However, be flexible and accept that though you can talk out issues before a child's birth, afterwards you may have to modify or change pre-birth decisions.

CONTINUED RESPECT AND NURTURING FOR THE PARENTS

While it is important to address the role of the non-lactating partner in the feeding of a child, we also need to ask how the lactating partner feels about this. Some women enjoy breastfeeding, but others may resent being turned into a "feeding machine." Remember that even when a woman is a breastfeeding mother, she is still a woman and undoubtedly wants to be treated as such. Take her out for a nice dinner or other adult activity. Greeting her at the door each evening with a screaming, ravenous baby is probably not the best way to welcome her home. And if she's at all sensitive about using the breast pump, refrain from making comments about "milking time."

Remember that the couple is still a couple, and have roles as individuals and partners as well as parents. Two partners who learned this are Phyllis and Susan. In the first three months after their daughter's birth, the multiple responsibilities of parenting a newborn completely exhausted them. Susan was staying home and breast feeding, and Phyllis helped out with bottle feedings in the evening when she got home from work. Their schedule had become fairly standard: comfort the crying baby, feed the baby, change the baby.

After a couple of months, Phyllis and Susan realized that they had had no adult conversation with each other since their baby was born. "All we talked about was the baby. We were so tired in the evenings that by Sally's last feeding, we both just crashed into bed. Of course, she's the most important thing in both of our lives, but after a while we realized that we'd sort of forgotten about each other."

Make a point of remembering that you and your partner had a child *because* you love each other. Continuing respect and nurturing for both parents is vital, and these issues should be addressed and brought out into the open as soon as possible before they fester and turn into much bigger deals over time. Phyllis and Susan have come up with a workable solution: they have one of their neighbors stay with Sally every Wednesday evening, while they get some much-needed "grown up time" alone. Sometimes they go to a movie, to a bookstore or even just to the grocery store. What they do isn't important, as long as two loving adult partners do it together.

NEGOTIATING ROLES: STAY AT HOME PARENTS VS. WORK OUTSIDE OF HOME PARENTS

One of the most important things to consider, even before a couple decides to have or adopt a child, is that child needs to be cared for. Among the issues to be discussed are: Will one partner quit her job to stay home full-time? Will both partners continue to work, using day-care and other child-care options as needed? Will they find an in-between solution, such as one or both partners working part-time or working from home?

These are decisions that should be discussed and mutually agreed upon well before actually having a child, but again partners need to be flexible. If one parent finds out that he thought he wanted to stay home with the new baby, but after a few months he's going crazy without being around other adults all day, then maybe it's time to reconsider. Or maybe one parent intends to return to work after the baby is born, but once she works for a few months realizes that she's miserable and barely earning enough to cover child care expenses. Then she might reconsider and decide to stay home.

Financial considerations are often one of the largest factors to take into account. Many couples simply do not have the luxury of having one parent stay at home, and need to have two incomes to survive financially. When making a decision based on finances, however, be sure to consider all the hidden costs of working. In addition to balancing salary with the cost of child care, think about things like the cost of commuting, work clothes, dry cleaning, house cleaning and restaurant takeout meals. With one parent staying at home, these expenses can be reduced or eliminated completely.

If finances allow, and if one parent is interested in staying home, it's important to make this a decision that can be reconsidered on a periodic basis. Perhaps one parent will decide that he wants to stay home until their youngest child is in school, and then return to work either full-time or part-time. Or a parent might commit to staying home for his child's first year, doing some consulting work from home during that period to stay current with his field, then return to work after the first year. Such arrangements can keep a stay-at-home parent from feeling trapped, especially if he has a job waiting for him at some point in the future.

For a lesbian couple, one of whom has just given birth, it might seem to make sense that the one who gave birth be the stay-at-home mom so that this partner can breastfeed the child more easily. This is what Susan and Phyllis chose to do. "I wasn't that thrilled with my job anyway, so staying home felt like the right thing to do," Susan says. "I know we're lucky that Phyllis earns enough so that we can afford for me to stay home." However, don't assume that you have to do it this way. If the biological mother has a higher-paying job or simply doesn't want to stay at home, there are other options that you can discuss.

For gay male couples who have just adopted a child or had one using a surrogate, there may be some resistance to the thought of a stay-at-home father. Stay-at-home dads are still relatively rare, though the situation is starting to become more common. A stay-at-home dad may feel uncomfortable or even scorned when he feels like he is infiltrating the mostly-female world of stay-at-home mothers, whether they're on the playground or in mother-child classes. However, once he is accepted by the community, such adult contact will probably be regarded as welcome and necessary.

Some couples, especially in technical fields that make working at home a possibility, have found unique solutions to the problem of working and caring for children. Beth and Sylvia are a couple in California with three small children. They both work in the computer industry, and both work for companies that allow them to telecommute part-time. They trade off working at home and working at the office – Beth goes to her office on Tuesday and Thursday, and Sylvia goes to her office on Monday, Wednesday and Friday. On the days they work at home, they have to balance emails, phone meetings, feedings, snacks and naps.

To get uninterrupted work time, Beth works for a few hours early in the morning before the kids and Sylvia are awake, and Sylvia works for a few hours in the evening once the rest of the family is asleep. This arrangement allows one parent always to be home with the kids, while keeping two full-time salaries coming into the house. Sylvia says, "It can be hard to work at home with small children, but we have a childproofed office/playroom that allows the kids to play safely while we work. I love being able to be with my children all day on the days I work at home, and it's great to be able to drop everything and read a story to my two-year-old occasionally. Of course, this setup requires discipline, and some days I get more accomplished than others. Still, I feel lucky that my company allows telecommuting, and plan to stick with this schedule as long as I can!"

LOCATING AN ACCEPTING PEDIATRICIAN

You'll be amazed at how many visits your child will need in the first two years of his life. It is very important to find a pediatrician who is comfortable with your same sex family and treats you as a "real" family, taking into account the concerns of both partners when necessary.

The best way to find a good pediatrician is by referral. Before the birth or adoption of your child, talk to some of your friends with children, especially ones who have similar philosophies about child-rearing. Once you've gotten a few suggestions, make an appointment to interview them. Most offices will allow you to book a brief appointment to meet with a pediatrician or other doctor to see if you think they are compatible with your needs.

Sylvia says, "We went through three pediatricians before finding one that we both liked. The earlier ones we had, we just felt like they were ignoring one of us at appointments, or never seemed to return our calls." Beth agrees. "When we chose the doctor we have now, we were really aware of the doctor's office itself. The front office staff was helpful, and they never tried to rush us off the phone. The waiting room had lots of toys and other distractions for the kids, and they didn't have a television – we liked that the kids weren't all sitting there staring at a TV."

Take a good look around. Is the waiting area clean and large enough, with plenty of places to sit? Do they have a separate sick child waiting area? Do other patients seem to be waiting a long time to be seen? Do the nurses greet any of the kids by name? Do they and the doctors seem to get to know their patients?

Once you get in to see a potential pediatrician, have a list of questions to ask. These can range from questions about potential parenting practices, such as extended breastfeeding, co-sleeping and vaccinating to general parenting philosophy. You may also want to find out if the doctor has any children of her own, and how old they are, if that's important to you. If possible, both partners should attend the visit, but if not, the one who does attend should explain that he has a same-sex partner ("our future child's other dad") who couldn't be there today. Ask outright if the doctor has any problems with gay or lesbian parents, or if she has any other gay families in her practice. If you have any questions or feel uncertain about the doctor's comfort level with your family, find another doctor—the last thing you want is someone in a position of authority, like your doctor, potentially undermining your parental status.

THE GAY-FRIENDLY DAYCARE

A similar issue in the first years of life may be finding a gay-friendly daycare situation. Again, recommendations from gay and lesbian friends with children in your area can be the best way to start. If you don't have any friends to offer recommendations, see if your town or area has any sort of daycare provider fair; your town recreation department might sponsor an open house where various providers can come and give out information. You can also see if your town has a list of accredited daycare providers.

Once you have found some possible options, make sure to take a look at all the important factors like staff-to-child ratios (do they meet state guidelines?), staff turnover, facilities (clean with age-appropriate toys?), snacks provided (do you bring your own? Can they deal with pumped breast milk if applicable?), diapers (will they take cloth diapers if you supply them?), etc. Also explain to the staff that you are a lesbian or gay family, and see how they respond. Ask if there are any other gay or lesbian families using the facility that you could talk to. If you sense any hesitation or hostility, keep looking.

Another option that can be useful to consider, if you're having trouble finding a suitable daycare center, can be smaller situations such as small in-home care centers or a nanny or childcare person who comes to your own house. A smaller daycare center can provide advantages and disadvantages – a major advantage is that usually it is very small, with just a few kids and a provider who runs it out of her home. Make sure the practice is certified by the state, where required. A disadvantage can be a lack of backup if your daycare provider gets sick.

Having a nanny come to your home to provide daycare may seem expensive, but there are various options to reduce the cost. Rather than a live-in nanny like Mary Poppins, you can instead look for a younger exchange student or au pair. Another choice is a childcare provider who does not live with you, but who comes to your house to care for your child or children on a specific schedule. Still another option is to negotiate a "nanny-share" agreement with a friend or neighbor, where one nanny agrees to watch the children from both families, either at the same time in one house or on alternating days. An advantage of a nanny is that you can screen her carefully in advance and make sure she is completely comfortable with your family situation.

USE THOSE NAMES!

As your baby learns to talk, start using those names for you and your partner that you decided on (see Chapter Six). This is the time to get used to calling each other "Daddy" and "Papa," so you can get your names straight before your baby picks up on any confusion. Give yourself time to try out the names, since they may not work out as well as you'd thought. One parent might decide that he wants to be called by his first name before the child comes, but once the baby is adopted, he might realize that he wants to be called "Daddy Rick" or "Pops" instead of just "Rick." As with all things, be flexible: if your child can't say "Mommy Josephine," consider shortening it to "Mommy Jo."

Make sure you talk about "all kinds of families" early on so that your children don't get used to the idea that families need to be a certain way. Even before your child can really understand what you're saying, start talking about families. Look for baby books you can read about families that are inclusive – they don't have to be just about gay families, but more and more books these days are starting to include all different sorts of families as incidental background to an unrelated story. It's never too early to start building up a library of these sorts of books. For more information on specific titles, see Chapter Eleven and Appendix 3.

RECORD-KEEPING

Finally, you'll want to keep a record of all the special moments in your new baby's first year. Baby books abound, full of places to put precious photos and place keepsakes like a lock of the baby's hair, as well as record important dates such as your baby's first smile or first step. But it can be difficult finding one that reflects your actual family.

Baby books geared to lesbian and gay families, as well as adoptive families, are starting to appear. One great option is *And Then There Was Me,* which includes pages to deal with all sorts of situations, such as "my sperm donor," "my birth mother," "how my parents met" and other traditional and non-traditional topics. This book is particularly innovative because its binding allows parents to remove or reorganize pages as desired, to truly customize the book to their particular situations. The book is available online from various sites such as http://www.2moms2dads.com Another option, of course, is to make your own baby book using a blank photo album, book or scrapbook.

CONCLUDING ADVICE:

Most of what newborns do involves eating and sleeping, and how you choose to feed your child is probably your first major parenting decision. You'll also need to figure out if your child will go to daycare or if one parent will stay home with the baby. Try to resolve these issues before the baby's born, since you'll have trouble making decisions when in a sleep-deprived state, but be flexible as real life parenting may require you to reconsider earlier decisions.

QUESTIONS FOR PROSPECTIVE PARENTS:

1. Have you and your partner talked about breastfeeding versus formula feeding? How do you both feel about it?
2. If you choose to breastfeed, are you willing to pump so that your partner can also feed the baby?
3. If your baby will be breastfed and also eat from the other partner, have you thought about whether you want to use bottles, or if you plan to use a supplemental nurser or other bottle replacement?
4. If you plan to use formula, have you decided which one to use?
5. Will both you and your partner continue to work after the baby arrives? Can one of you afford to stay home?
6. Have you looked into finding a gay-friendly pediatrician?
7. Have you decided on daycare options, if necessary? Have you found a gay or lesbian-friendly daycare or nanny?
8. Have you decided on what names you would each like to be called by your child? Have you practiced using them so that you're ready for the day the baby starts talking?

chapter twelve

THE TODDLER PERIOD

Parenting a toddler is a challenge. When a child is no longer a baby, but not yet able to understand and reason at an elementary level this can make for a lot of frustration! Most parents experiment with different activities, finding their own coping mechanisms for engaging their rapidly-developing children in interests that give the children satisfaction.

EXPLAINING DIFFERENT KINDS OF FAMILIES

Toddlers who are surrounded by loving parents, whether their parents are two mommies or daddies or one mommy and a daddy, will grow up happy and well-adjusted. However, many external influences will eventually make your child aware that his family is different from others.

For example, most children's books feature families with a mommy and a daddy. Picture books for children usually feature stories about families (since most toddlers are interested in them). Most of these books have a male-female family structure, even those that involve animal families. If your child has two mommies, then hears stories about families with a mommy and a daddy, she will probably start to ask questions such as "Where is my Daddy?" or "Do I have a Daddy?"

These questions are perfectly normal and if you explain your family make up simple and forthrightly this will help your child to understand and feel secure with her family. Accept her curiosity as an opportunity to teach your child that there are different kinds of families. Explain that some families have two Mommies; others have two Daddies. Some have a Mommy and a Daddy, and some children live with a grandmother or a grandmother and grandfather. Show her that children may live with many different configurations of grown-ups. Communicate that a loving family is the important thing and is not limited to a certain family structure.

To make your children more secure, locate books that specifically have gay families in them. *Heather Has Two Mommies* by Leslea Newman is a good example of a children's book for families in which there are two mothers. Others choices include *The Generous Jefferson Bartleby Jones* by Forman Brown and *Jenny lives with Eric and Martin* by Susanne Bosche. (See Appendix 3 for more books for children with gay and lesbian parents.)

One creative method, if you're reading a story in which there are a Mommy and a Daddy to your toddler, is to change the language so that it will reflect your family's makeup. If you can't find books that specifically include gay and lesbian families, you might change the names of characters in the book to suit your family situation. For example, if you're reading a book with a Mommy and a Daddy and your family has two Daddies, change the Mommy to 'Grandma' or 'Auntie' or make it two Daddies if this is reflective of your family.

Children under four years old probably won't pick up on the traditional gendered roles depicted in many children's picture books. Once your child is a bit older, in order to understand his thought processes ask him who he thinks the characters in the pictures are. Some gay fathers have been surprised to find themselves identified with the bear in the dress. This makes sense, however, when you realize that the dress-wearing bear may be cooking lunch just as the father does every day. Be forewarned, though, that once your child learns how to read, he may object to the practice of adapting the story. Or he may not! Most kids like to read about themselves and people like them. Just remember that to your child, his or her family is the example against which all other families are measured. It is your job as parents to make sure that the child is completely comfortable with your family's structure.

Grandparents or other caregivers should also be acquainted with your reading philosophy. For example, if your practice in reading a book is substituting "Grandpa" for Daddy, make sure that your other caregivers are consistent when they read the same book. Explain your reading habits to your child's daycare provider, and any other who may be reading to him.

When you're reading books, watching television or just out and about in the neighborhood with your child, make a point of noting different kinds of families. If you're at the playground for example, you could say, "Look, Sam is playing with his grandmother!" or "Look, John's Daddy is pushing him on the swing." Emphasize that there are all kinds of loving families.

Once you've been talking to your child about different kinds of families, you may find the child repeating what you have explained like a mantra. "Some kids have two Mommies; some kids have a Mommy and a Daddy," etc. You may also find that once your child starts to encounter friends with different types of families than hers, she probably will be very curious about the type(s) of parents that she does not have. Encourage this curiosity, but also keep reminding her that her own particular family structure is perfectly okay.

TODDLER QUESTIONS AND ANSWERS

Don't be surprised if kids in your preschooler's class ask your child (or you) where her Mommy is, if she lives in a house with two Daddies. Remember that questions from a child this age are asked purely out of curiosity. Teach your child the best way to respond to such questions is to be truthful and matter-of-fact. If you hear the question you might explain that Madison doesn't have a Mommy, but she does have two Daddies. "Our family is different from yours, but we're still a family." This answer will satisfy most preschoolers.

If you encounter attitudes from a friend of your child that seem more hostile or disbelieving, it is possible that the child has picked up her parents' attitudes and prejudices. You may want to chat with the child's parents or teachers about tolerance for different kinds of families. Maybe the child's parents simply haven't met any gay couples before, and are unsure of how to explain this family structure to their child. In this case, it can be a good opportunity to talk to the parents. Perhaps you could say, "I noticed that your son Sam seemed confused because Madison has two Dads. Since we were there when Sam made some comments about our family to Madison, we explained that some families are different from others, but you might want to talk to him a bit more about this."

It's also possible that some parents are either uncomfortable or openly hostile toward your family. If you run into these negative attitudes in your child's preschool situation, it is probably best not to encourage a friendship between your child and these children. If the parents' attitudes are affecting your child in school, this is the time to talk to the teachers or principal about how they plan to address the problem.

With these measures the parents of some children your child befriends who may have had or have negative attitudes toward same sex families may be helped to see that a gay family is every bit as loving and nurturing as theirs hopefully is. A good example, especially that of your own child, can be the best way to change prejudice.

VOICES OF INEXPERIENCE AND IGNORANCE

Jill and Claire had been together for years before deciding to have children. When their daughter was eighteen months old, both women had to go back to work full-time. They didn't have any family in their town to help with babysitting, so they went through a long screening process to find the "perfect" daycare for the baby. They attended sample sessions at the daycare, met with the staff and felt they had made a good choice.

What they weren't expecting, though, were the reactions of some of the other parents. One mother at the daycare walked up to them on the first day of school and said, "Are you sisters? You look so much alike!" (both women were short in stature with dark hair, but the resemblance ended there). Another mother came up to introduce herself and then Jill introduced herself and said, "This is my partner." The woman smiled in obvious confusion. "Your partner? Was your husband tied up at work today?"

Claire and Jill were baffled. They weren't ignorant, of course, but they'd been together so long that they'd simply forgotten the fact that, to many people, their relationship was outside of the norm. After they'd explained that they were, in fact, a lesbian couple, most of the other parents in the daycare acknowledged them and there were few problems.

However, one father in the group was particularly uncomfortable having the child of lesbians in his son's class. "We overheard him talking to his wife about how his son would never grow up to be a real man if he was surrounded by lesbians. Number one, his son was seven months old! Number two, we only worked in the daycare one morning a week. And number three. . .lesbians are no better or worse than anyone else."

Depending on your child's age, to further acceptance of your family it might be appropriate to ask the preschool about having a session on different types of families. If the school doesn't have a counselor or can't afford to bring in outside speakers, offer to come in and lead a session yourself. Kids this age will not understand anything abstract or lessons that go into too much detail, so focus on simple explanations and information, such as: some families have a Mommy and Daddy, but other families have other types of parents.

One simple way to illustrate the different kinds of families is to read the children at the daycare center a picture book, designed for this age group. We've cited several good ones in Appendix 3, which you may check out of your local library. Bring the book in to the center to read or buy one and donate it to the school. Look for books with simple text and illustrations, and remember that the book you pick doesn't need to focus specifically on gay families.

Choose a book that discusses how different families are made up of different people who love each other. This is the kind of simple message that a toddler or preschooler will understand and children will hopefully carry this idea with them as they grow and get ready for elementary school. Another good example is *The Family Book* by Todd Parr. This books talks about all different kinds of families, including ones with two Moms and two Dads, in a matter-of-fact, humorous way. Preschool children will respond to this type of fun book, especially when it's incorporated into their regular play and reading schedule. Another good book is *Who's in a Family?* by Robert Skutch. Skutch also illustrates different kinds of families, including single families, gay/lesbian families, mixed race and divorced families.

ARRANGING PLAY DATES WITH OTHER GAY FAMILIES

Playing casually with the other families from the playground is a great way for your child to be exposed to a variety of backgrounds; it can also be a good opportunity to meet other parents in your area. Your kids can have the chance to meet children of other races and religions and may also meet kids who speak other languages. They'll learn to play cooperatively with kids of different ages and in settings that are less structured than the usual preschool or daycare environment.

However, for gay families, especially as your children become older and more aware, it also can be very helpful for them to meet other families that resemble theirs. If all their friends come from heterosexual families, even if you reinforce that all kinds of families are okay, your child won't see this modeled in real life.

Of course, if you live in a small area where you're the only or one of a few gay families in town, this may not be possible. However, if you live in an area with other gay families, try to seek out other gay families with kids about the same ages as your own.

Locating other gay families may be difficult. Parenthood tends to tone down some of the "signs" that you may have relied on in your dating days, so don't rely exclusively on "gaydar." If you see a family that seems to be a candidate, a playground or other public setting is a good place to chat them up, especially if your children are already playing together. If you and your partner are there as a couple, make sure that both of you show your parental status in case they are also looking for a gay family with which to connect.

If you're at a playground without your partner, you might take the opportunity to include references to your partner, along with the appropriate pronouns, in your conversation and see if the other parents will respond in kind. If you don't run into any other gay families at the playground, another great way to meet other same sex parents is to check out whether your area has a gay and lesbian community center. If so, see if they offer any parenting groups, classes or other programs. The center may have community bulletin boards where you could post that you're a gay family looking to interact with other gay families.

If your community center doesn't offer any same sex family-oriented programming, ask them why not. You might even volunteer to coordinate such a program yourself. It'll be worth it, because your children will have the chance to make new friends. Some areas of the country also have independent gay family groups; your community center may be able to refer you to an appropriate group in your area.

And don't forget the Internet. Online community lists such as craigslist.org and meetup.com usually offer opportunities to meet other gay parents. Read current postings and see if any other gay families in your area are looking for new friends. If you don't see any such postings, add some yourself! (See Appendix 3 for a listing of groups for gay families.)

If you do find other gay and lesbian families in your neighborhood, try arranging the first play date at a neutral location. Choose something fun for the kids, such as a park or playground. Ideally, give your children a chance to play while the adults have an opportunity to talk and start getting to know each other. You may meet some new friends this way, but don't expect your families to click instantly just because they're both same-sex.

You may arrive at your long-awaited play date to find that your kids either have no interest in playing with the other couple's kids, or that they take an instant dislike to each other. Don't force the kids to play with each other if it's clear that they really don't want to. You may also find that you have absolutely nothing in common with the other couple, aside from your sexuality; that alone certainly is not enough to sustain a friendship. However, if your children get along well, it may be worth keeping up the friendship just for the occasional outing to a park or restaurant.

MEETING OTHER GAY FAMILIES

Claire and Jill were elated to find what appeared to be another lesbian family at their baby music class. It was an interactive class where the parents and teachers worked together to expose the children to different types of sounds and rhythms. Claire, in particular, had noticed the other female couple and had made an effort to set up her station next to theirs. "We thought they might be a lesbian family, not just two sisters, so we tried to get to know them. But it sure wasn't easy."

They'd spoken casually with the other family a few times, trying to form a relationship that might result in a play date for their daughter. Once they knew for sure that the other women were lesbians, Claire went out of her way to be friendly, but usually had to make the first move in starting up a conversation. "We were really trying to make friends with another gay family because we wanted Darah to have friends with lesbian parents. We didn't want to be the only lesbians in her life!"

However, this particular relationship never caught on. The other family never responded to Claire and Jill's overtures, other than casual conversations in class, and expressed no interested in getting together on a weekend. "Either they just didn't like us, or they already had enough friends, because we were never able to get friendlier with them. We tried asking them out to dinner—they said they were busy. Suggested a trip to the park after class—again they said they had other plans. They just weren't interested."

Some people are simply not destined to be friends with each other. Claire and Jill kept looking for gay families to interact with and they ended up meeting several new friends in their area through a gay email list.

THE IMPORTANCE OF EXTENDED FAMILY IN RAISING CHILDREN

Family relationships can be wonderful, especially if you have supportive family members close by who can help out with babysitting as needed. However, if there are any uncomfortable feelings or tension on the part of the extended family members, toddlers and preschoolers are old enough to understand these feelings.

Extended family can work wonders in terms of broadening a child's horizons and range of experiences. It can also do wonders for a parent's sanity. All couples need some "together" time, especially after having children, and an extended family can provide a safe way for you and your partner temporarily to escape.

One of the most important things to remember about grandparents, when a gay family is involved, is that they need to consider your children as their grandchildren. Unfortunately, in many cases, grandparents will only consider a grandchild truly theirs if the child was born to their own child.

Jen and Drew adopted their first child from a Ukrainian orphanage, and were upset when Jen's parents refused to recognize the child as their grandchild. "They just didn't think of our new baby as theirs, because I hadn't physically given birth. They were never comfortable with my sexuality, and never approved of my relationship with Drew, but somehow I thought that adopting a baby would legitimize us in their eyes. They were happy for us, I think, but I know they don't consider Jenna their granddaughter."

A similar situation can result when one partner gives birth to a child; her partner's parents may refuse to accept the new baby as their own grandchild. Drew gave birth to the couple's second child, and once again Jen had trouble with her parents. "I guess we threw them for a double-whammy, in a way, by adopting the first, then Drew carrying the second. They can't bring themselves to call my kids 'theirs'—and that hurts."

Especially in families where a couple has two or more children with different biological origins, different treatment from the grandparents can be particularly obvious and hurtful. Raoul and Thomas have two children via a surrogate—Raoul donated the sperm for their son, and Thomas for their daughter. Thomas has noticed that his parents treat their two children differently; he sometimes hears them talking to their friends about Gloria, but never about Luis. "All I want is for my parents to acknowledge both of our children as ours, and therefore as their grandchildren," says Thomas. "After all, they're part of our family, and they're growing up as brother and sister – that's all that matters. It's so painful when I hear them mention their granddaughter, but ignore their grandson. Luis is just a baby now, so he doesn't care, but when he's older he's going to notice."

On the other hand, if your parents are supportive of your relationship, they're likely to embrace your children with open arms.

If your parents do have trouble acknowledging your children, that's definitely an issue that you'll want to discuss with them—immediately and openly. While babies probably won't know that they're being slighted, or that the "real" grandchildren are getting better birthday presents and more visits, a toddler will start to understand these sorts of inequalities. Even if the grandparents are not outwardly dismissive, a toddler will pick up on any hesitation. Whether it's in the sound of the grandparents' voices or the lack of physical contact, any disapproval will be noticed.

Especially if you or your partner have siblings with children living nearby, any differences in treatment will quickly become apparent. Your kids may ask why their cousins get to have sleepovers at Grandma and Grandpa's house while they don't. Or they may notice if they're at their cousin's birthday party and he gets lots of new toys from their grandparents, but your child remembers that she only got a new box of crayons from Grandma and Grandpa for her birthday. During the toddler years kids start learning about fair treatment, so expect them to point out every inequality.

If your siblings live in other parts of the country, differences in treatment may be less apparent to your kids. Still, they're bound to pick up on the differences in treatment eventually, and in the meantime they're missing out on a close relationship with their grandparents.

The best way to alleviate this situation: talk to the grandparents. Let them know how much it hurts you that they can't seem to appreciate your children the way that they deserve to be appreciated. Tell them that whatever they think of your relationship, they need to respect it if they want to be a part of your children's lives. Kids need their grandparents' attention and approval and should not be made to feel slighted or unworthy. Make sure your parents are acquainted with and accept your philosophy before inviting them for a visit or making a trip out to see them.

Part of making the grandparents comfortable with your family, of course, is treating both sets of grandparents equally. Don't favor the biological grandparents. And in the case of an adopted child, make sure that both sets of grandparents know that this child is a real part of your family now and that you expect him to be treated as such. If you set the tone by sending out adoption announcements, inviting relatives to visit and keeping your extended family updated on the new addition, your family will in most cases accept the new family member as part of its own.

INTERRACIAL FAMILIES

Issues of family acceptance can be complicated even further by issues of race. Suppose you have adopted a child whose ethnicity is different from your own or used a sperm or egg donor whose race matches your partner's but not your own. Your family will not only have to deal with the fact that you are a gay or lesbian couple raising a child, but that the child does not look like or have the ethnic background of the rest of the family.

While babies don't notice skin color, as toddlers learn more about the world around them, they will begin to notice things such as race and ethnicity. If your child comes from a different ethnic group than either or both of his parents, the toddler years are when you should expect the first questions, such as "Why do I look different from you, Daddy?" or "Why is my skin so much darker?"

Raoul and Thomas addressed this situation very matter-of-factly. Raoul's skin is much darker than Thomas's and their son Luis has skin which is darker than their daughter Gloria's. They have explained to their children, "Papa's skin is black, and Daddy's skin is white. Together, we all make brown!" Their young children are satisfied with this explanation.

Especially in cases where the child doesn't resemble either of the partners, it is important to have some answers thought out and explained ahead of time. The social worker for your home study can help you to prepare, and can offer advice if you're beginning to consider transracial adoption. He'll discuss the issues with you and help decide if transracial adoption will really work out for your family. He can also provide suggestions on ways to discuss race and ethnicity with your child.

One good approach is to start with the discussion about how families come in different configurations. Just as some families have two Mommies and others have two Daddies, some families have children who look like them, while others may not. Emphasize that all children are beautiful and make sure to surround your child with multi-ethnic baby books and pictures. Make sure he understands that there *are* other kids out there who look like him.

Try to expose your child to other members of his ethnic group, so that he can see other children and adults who look the same way he does. For Thomas and Raoul, this was particularly easy; Raoul's family is dark-skinned and Thomas's is light, so the kids had equal exposure to adults of both backgrounds. Be careful not to imply that your child *must* identify with any particular group, and do not limit your child's friends to children who happen to share his skin color.

As some grandparents may reject grandchildren that aren't biologically related to them, some grandparents may have difficulty accepting grandchildren who are of a different race or ethnic group than they are. Again, this is the kind of thing that kids will begin to pick up on in the toddler years, and it is something that should be addressed sooner rather than later.

Thomas says, "At first, I just thought my parents were standoffish, because they weren't used to people of other ethnic groups." He tried inviting them over for dinner when Raoul's family was also visiting, and tried to arrange outings with both families. "In our case, nothing really helped. My parents still haven't come around."

Try to slowly acclimatize the parents to the idea that a child who looks different from them will soon be joining the family. If you're doing an transracial adoption that requires a waiting period, such as an international adoption, try and get photographs ahead of time. Share these with the grandparents and coo over how adorable the child is. If your parents make any comments that could be considered offensive, such as remarking on how light or dark your soon-to-be-daughter's skin is, or how slanted her eyes are, the best response may be to deflect them with a comment such as, "Yes, isn't she adorable?"

If grandparents are still having trouble with a child's race once the child is two or three years old, it's probably time for a serious talk. Let them know that they won't be allowed to be part of your child's life if they don't get over their racism. Explain to them that your child is now old enough to hear and understand any inappropriate comments, and that even innocuous ones (such as suggesting that your African American son will make a great basketball player) are unacceptable in your house. Be firm, since your child's self-esteem is at stake.

For some grandparents, all it may take is one reminder. Others may need continued, gentle (or not-so-subtle) hints. If they do continue to make inappropriate remarks in your child's presence, talk to them about these comments. But do it outside of your child's hearing. In most cases, if the grandparents want to be a part of your child's life, they'll change their behaviors.

CONCLUDING ADVICE:

Toddlers get into anything and everything, and aren't shy about voicing their opinions. If you and your partner aren't out as a gay couple, expect your children to do the "outing" for you. Most gay families will want to interact with other gay families and it's a great way to give your children a sense of belonging. Arrange play dates, take classes together, enjoy an evening at a restaurant with other local same sex families. Extended family can play a big role in your toddler's life, so try to make sure relatives are on board with your sexuality. Ensure that your kids are treated fairly and surround them with love from all sides.

QUESTIONS:

1. Are your kids old enough to understand that, while they have two mommies, some other families have a mommy and a daddy instead? If so, have you talked to them about it?
2. Have you read books to your children that include different kinds of families and different ethnic groups?
3. Have you thought about an answer to give if you get casual inquiries about your family?
4. Have you talked to the other children at your child's daycare about different kinds of families?
5. Are there other gay families that you can invite over for a play date? Are there any groups for gay families in your area that you can join?
6. How do your parents feel about your children? Are they as loving and accepting as you want them to be?
7. If your parents treat your children differently from other grandchildren, have you talked to them about it?
8. If your children don't match your ethnic group, have you thought about how to explain the differences to them and to other family members?

chapter thirteen

YOUR CHILD'S MIDDLE YEARS

While many children attend some sort of preschool or daycare when they're younger, elementary school may be your child's first encounter with the formal educational system. To successfully navigate the school system, take advantage of the easy spots, while having patience as you gather information to get through the tough ones.

One of the best ways to get to know your school system and the teachers, administrators and staff is by volunteering at your child's school. Most schools and teachers want parents to help out, whether it's inside or outside the classroom. If you become an involved parent, you'll have a first-hand view of your child's classroom and the school.

BEING OUT WITH THE SCHOOL

One of the first steps to take when registering your child for public or private school is to list yourself and your partner as the parents of your child. In most places, to register a child in the public school system, you'll need to prove that you are a resident of the town where the school is located, and that at least one of you is a legal parent or guardian of your child. Such proof should take the form of a birth certificate or adoption decree. Make sure to bring one of these documents with you to the school.

If both parents are not legal guardians of the child, you may not legally be able to list both adults as parents. It may be tempting to go ahead and list both parents in the slots for Mother and Father. In many jurisdictions, the school system may not hassle you over because two women or two men are the parents of record. In some states, two women or two men can be equal parents under the law.

However, if you live in a particularly conservative area, you may run into difficulty without (or even with) proper documentation. As a last resort, list the second parent as an emergency contact. If this becomes necessary, make sure that both parents meet the principal and teacher well before classes start; establish yourselves as the child's de facto parents, even if you're not permitted to be officially listed. Demonstrate your equal parental status to the professionals who actually are involved – mainly, your child's teachers.

If you present yourselves as equal parents to teachers and other administrators, most will accept you as your child's parents. They probably won't even ask for your documentation. Assume the best about people but if you have problems deal with them in the best way possible for your child's education.

GET INVOLVED AND STAY VISIBLE

Volunteering at your child's school may not be possible for all parents, especially those who work full-time jobs or take care of younger siblings. However, a day or two per month can make a big difference in both your level of comfort with the school system and your child's education.

Some schools have formal parent participation programs. They may require a certain number of parent volunteer hours per year; if so, you'll likely have to sign a form agreeing to fulfill these hours before your child can attend that particular school. There will be a variety of ways in which you can put in your hours, ranging from chaperoning field trips and in-class work with the teacher to supervising lunch recess or working on the school's garden on the weekends.

There will also be many ways that you can volunteer time outside of your child's classroom; these may range from cutting out paper shapes for the next day's lesson, to soliciting donations for classroom supplies, to working on the class website. Getting involved will not only help your child and the rest of her class get familiar with your family structure, it will bring you closer to other parents. This will help ensure that your child and her family are respected; if other parents see you there, working with the kids and devoting your time to the classroom, they'll probably become more comfortable with the idea of a gay family.

Other schools don't have such a formal program. For these, the best way to become involved in your child's class is to ask the teachers how you can help. Some questions you might ask yourself and your partner are: Can you volunteer during lunch recess? Can you drive for the next field trip? Can you do a presentation on music or an interesting cultural holiday? There are many ways to help teachers in your child's classroom. Doing these things will provide opportunities to get to know other kids and their parents.

Coaching a sports team is another great way to become involved in your child's curriculum. Many elementary schools don't have after-school sports, but you can offer to set up and coach a team. Talk with school officials first to resolve any legal issues. You can also volunteer as a coach for many national sports programs, such as AYSO (American Youth Soccer Organization) or youth teeball/baseball. One of the best ways to convince other people that your gay family is perfectly "normal" is to participate in the same activities: eat the same food, play the same games and kiss the same boo-boos.

The more you offer to help, the more you're likely to be seen as "just another parent." By being involved in your child's education, you'll not only be more likely to see potential problems before they become real ones, but you'll be modeling the legitimacy of your family.

DEALING WITH TEASING

For many parents and students elementary school can be their first time meeting a child with same-sex parents. Children's reactions will probably be varied. Maria, who has two moms (Gloria and Susana), was the only child in her kindergarten who had gay parents and most of the other kids were just fascinated. "Wow, you have two moms? You're so lucky! I want two moms!" A boy in the class, David, was full of questions about how Maria ended up with two mothers. "What about your dad? Do you have two dads too?" Another boy in the class, Juan, expressed some amount of disbelief. "No way, you can't have two moms. Everybody has a mom and a dad. Teacher, Maria's lying!"

However, the vast majority of the kids in the class didn't really care how many mothers Maria had. Once she explained that she had two mothers, most of the kids nodded and then moved on to crayons, glue and the rest of their kindergarten lives. Kids of this age usually have matter-of-fact reactions to new situations, and tend to accept explanations if given honestly.

Sarah, a five-year-old student, saw Maria's shorthaired mother Gloria and said, "Is that your dad?" Maria replied simply, "No, I have two moms." Maria's mothers had done a good job of preparing Maria for school by giving her examples of what to say, in case other kids asked about her family. "We told Maria to just be honest and explain that she has two moms. She could also tell them she has three cats, a turtle and a baby brother!" remarked Gloria. "Most of the kids in her class were much more interested in the turtle than in Maria's parents, anyway."

Arming your child with simple explanations can diffuse most of the curiosity of elementary-age classmates. However, with older kids who aren't familiar with same sex family situations, your child might encounter hostility toward her family. Maria never experienced this personally, but Gloria and Susana were aware of problems experienced by a third-grade boy who had two dads. "They moved to Texas recently, and their son Henry was in third grade when he started at our school. From the beginning, most of the kids were fine with his two dads but a couple of other boys gave him a hard time. They teased him, and said that he must be gay if he had two fathers."

Fortunately, the boy in this case told his teacher about the teasing and the bullies were quickly reprimanded. The teacher then led the class discussion in a unit on different family structures and Henry's dads came to school to talk to the other students. They explained that they were a family, just like any other, except Henry happened to have two fathers. The class then did a project where each child drew family pictures. They learned that most families had some minor differences.

At school your child may be the victim of unwitting slang. In the older elementary grades, many of the kids use slang expressions, such as "Cool!" to describe something they like or "Nasty!" to describe something they don't. Sometimes the word "gay" is unfortunately used to describe something that is disliked. Teach your child to ignore these sorts of slurs when he hears them and to ask his friends not to use words in derogatory ways, because he doesn't like it. Many kids won't even know what "gay" means and will probably stop using the expression when asked.

If your child tells you that he's being teased by other students, your first line of defense should be to talk to the classroom teachers. If the teacher is on your side, she should be able to intervene; she should speak directly to the students involved, and use the incident as a chance to teach the class about diversity. If you encounter problems with the teacher, though, you'll need to take the situation up a level and talk to the principal. If you don't get results there, keep moving up – talk to the school district about their harassment policy.

Sometimes, hostility may be found in unlikely places. For example, Megan, a second grader, was overheard on the playground telling some other kids that her moms were lesbians. The teacher who overheard her immediately gave her a three-day suspension for using "unacceptable language." When her mothers found out why she had been suspended, they appealed to the principal, who explained that "lesbian" was deemed unacceptable language for elementary school students to be using. When the two mothers explained that Megan was simply using the word to describe her family, the principal remained unimpressed. Megan's mothers took the fight all the way to the school district and eventually hired a lawyer to sue the district itself. Their lawsuit succeeded, but by this time, they had moved Megan to a private school tolerant of different family compositions.

Changing schools may be a last resort if your child encounters hostility. Don't think of it as giving in; think of it as giving your child the education she needs and deserves in a safe environment where she can thrive.

TEACHER TRAINING MATERIALS

If you become involved in your local school district, you might find that teachers have many questions and very little training in how to deal with nontraditional families. Fortunately, a number of groups have come up with training material on this subject for teachers.

One good resource is a film called *It's Elementary*. This hour-long production, which originally aired on public television, is aimed at teachers and other educators. It gives real-life examples of children in grades from kindergarten through eighth grade, and models ways to discuss family diversity, stereotypes and to prevent discrimination. This film can be purchased from a variety of online sources and costs less than one hundred dollars. You may also be able to check the film out at your local public library. If you think your child's teachers would be interested in viewing the movie and perhaps discussing some of the lessons with you, you might get a copy or suggest that they do.

Another effective educational resource is a traveling photo exhibit and an accompanying book, called *Love Makes a Family*. The exhibit includes high-quality photographs of gay and lesbian individuals and their children. It's appropriate for display at a local school library or other public location. The book that compliments the exhibit contains interviews with some of the people shown in the photographs. You can find out more about this project at http://lovemakesafamily.org

Don't expect all teachers to welcome criticism, even when it's constructive. Teachers are people and we all have some prejudices and areas about which we know little. Their self-esteem (as well as possibly their jobs) depends on the school administrators' and parents' satisfaction with their teaching skills. Your child's teacher may see your suggestions as threatening, so you need to make sure to approach him or her with a positive attitude. Offer such material only as a supplement to his regular curriculum. This will probably work best if you already have an established relationship with your teacher and school system.

MOTHER'S DAY AND FATHER'S DAY

Most kindergartens celebrate lots of holidays, including Mother's Day and Father's Day. These holidays may cause some consternation to gay families that have two fathers or two mothers. One common question for new same sex parents is, "Should I let my daughter make a Father's Day card?" or "What should our son do for Mother's Day?"

The best way to deal with these holidays is to talk to the teacher ahead of time. Explain that while your family structure doesn't involve a mother, your family does have two fathers. Therefore, you'd like the teacher to offer adjustments to any Mother's Day projects that she might be planning. Susana, one of our interviewees, talked to her daughter Maria's teacher about making cards for Mother's Day. The arrangement they came up with was to have Maria make two cards. On Father's day, she made a card for her grandfather. Communication with your children's teachers can go a long way to smoothing such situations.

Observing Mother's Day and Father's Day practices doesn't just affect gay and lesbian families. These holidays can also be awkward for single parents or children in divorced families who may have a mother and a stepmother. Being proactive could help out several other children in the class, in addition to your own.

MODELING FAMILY PRIDE

Elementary-age children learn by example. It's one thing to expect your child to be open and proud of her family at school, but if you and your partner are closeted in the rest of your life, she'll soon notice the contradiction.

In general, if you expect your children to be proud of their family, you shouldn't be closeted around your children unless absolutely necessary. Otherwise, they'll learn that there's something secretive about their family and they may come to the conclusion that there's something wrong with them or the way they live. Young children need a solid foundation upon which to base their growing self-esteem and they need your honesty, openness and pride in their family.

If you're not already out, expect your children to do it for you. Jeannie was at the park one afternoon with one of her dads, when a mother sitting on the next bench started chatting with Jeannie's dad, Steve. "And what does your wife do?" the woman asked. Steve fumbled for a minute, but Jeannie piped right up, "My other daddy works in a big office with lots of windows. He takes the elevator to the fourth floor every morning!" Clearly, Jeannie's dads taught her to be proud of her family, but they need a bit of work on their own level of comfort when talking about their relationship. The more open you are about yourself and your partner, the more comfortable you'll be when your children decide to speak for you.

Children are naturally open to talking about themselves (and everything around them). They won't understand how to keep secrets without a lot of explanation and practice. In the long run, teaching your children how to hide their families will not do them any good. On the contrary – children need to know that you're proud of them, in order for them to be proud of themselves.

Marching in gay pride parades is not the only way for your children to know that their family is okay. Simple acts will tell your children that you're proud of who you are. Holding hands at the grocery store, opening the door for your partner to get into the car or giving a kiss as you're running out are all ways in which you may already demonstrate your affection for each other. Don't be afraid to do these things in front of your children, especially once they're old enough for school. You won't embarrass them simply by being who you are.

Being out at work is another way that you can teach your children about family pride. Most people keep photographs of their children on their desks at work. You should do the same, putting pictures of your kids next to that photo of your partner. Talk about your children to your co-workers, to the extent that the other parents do, and never feel that you don't have a "right" to participate when your friends start bragging about their kids. Your children are every bit as legitimate as theirs, and you put in the same amount of work: the long nights of bottle-feeding, endless walks trying to elicit a burp, hours spent in the car driving back and forth to soccer games.

COMPASSION, EMPATHY AND CHARITY

Most children are naturally empathetic. As kids learn to have appropriate responses to situations that come up, they rely on both their growing knowledge and their emotions. As with just about everything else, kids learn appropriate emotional reactions from their parents. If your daughter sees you crying at a sad movie, for example, she's likely to burst into tears as well, even if she doesn't understand what the movie was about.

As your children grow, they'll also model other behaviors on you. Most five-year-olds want to be just like Mommy or Daddy. For example, Maria went through a phase where she wanted to do everything that Mama Gloria did. "She started wanting to take showers with me in the morning, which was brand-new for her. She wanted to use mouthwash because she saw me using it, and started wanting to floss her teeth because I did – it was great!"

Now is the perfect time to start encouraging your children to become tolerant, active and charitable. Take your children with you if you volunteer at the local soup kitchen, if the administration there will allow it. There are many opportunities to teach your child about getting involved in the community. Join a "Meals on Wheels" program or have your child help you in preparing meals for AIDS patients.

Being charitable is an important concept to instill in any child. One couple with whom we spoke, Steve and Rob, felt strongly that they wanted their daughter, Jeannie, to understand that many people in the world are less fortunate than she is and that she needs to try to help them. "We decided to get her directly involved," Steve says, "because she just didn't understand what we were getting at. The problem is, a lot of organizations won't let you bring young kids with you when you volunteer because of legal reasons." Steve and Rob decided to have Jeannie collect pennies to donate to a homeless shelter. She came with us to drop the money off, and it really made her understand what her parents had been talking about.

Let your child know that giving back to the community can also be fun! Sign up for AIDSWALK, the March of Dimes or other charitable activities, and have your daughter or son participate. They'll probably enjoy the occasion. Wherever possible, lead by example. If your children see you regularly involved in making donations or personally helping out less fortunate people, they'll learn to do the same.

INTEGRATING RELIGIOUS EDUCATION

Religion plays an important role for many gay families. Regardless of the religion, prayer and devotion often play large roles in people's lives. Many people become more religious when children enter the picture; most of us want to teach our children something about our religious beliefs. When your children reach school age, the subject of religious education inevitably comes up as well.

In the United States, almost all religious schools are private, so they involve a separate cost for parents. Some private schools also incorporate religious classes. For many people, though, their children attend a public school during the week and then take religious classes either after school or on a weekend.

Gay families need to do research before choosing a religious school for their children. One good way to go about locating a school is by word-of-mouth. When Elias and Tzvi wanted to find a Hebrew school for their son Tal, they talked to another family who already had children attending a nearby Hebrew school. "In our case," said Elias, "there was only one other Jewish kid in Tal's class, so we talked with her parents and found out where she was starting school. We visited the school and sat in on some sample classes. We liked it and it worked out."

If you don't have any personal recommendations to go on, call the church, mosque or temple directly. If you cold-call religious schools, ask if they're gay-friendly and tolerant; if not, then you'll need to look at other choices. Tzvi said, "We called the temple directly, but the person who answered the phone didn't know anything about the school. Seemed strange, but okay, so we asked to talk to their religious education department. I just asked outright how they'd feel about having a gay family join their congregation." If they express any hesitation, or seem uncertain, keep looking.

When trying to find an accepting religious institution, the more liberal end of the spectrum is usually more accepting. If you'd like a general Christian congregation, for example, the MCC (Metropolitan Community Church) or UU (Unitarian Universalist) may be good choices. In Judaism, Reform or Reconstructionist congregations are most likely to be accepting. However, don't dismiss investigating the most mainstream denominations. You may find that the church or synagogue down the street is a warm and welcoming place for all different types of people.

PLAY DATES AND SLEEPOVERS

As your child becomes friendly with other kids in elementary school, you will probably begin to get requests for play dates. If your school isn't a parent-participation school or you haven't gotten a chance to meet the parents of your child's friends, such dates are good ways to get to know them. Be aware, though, that you may need to explain your family makeup. Unfortunately, some people might worry about leaving their child in the hands of homosexuals.

When first making contact with the parents of one of your child's schoolmates, be upfront and matter-of-fact about your family structure. If the friend's mother suggests that your child come over Thursday after school, you might say, "Well, I'll be working then, but Maria's other mother should be home and can bring her by around 3:00. Is that okay?" If you want to get to know the other family a bit better before dropping your child off for a play date, try inviting the parents to come along on a family outing to a local park or restaurant. Or, you can invite them all to come to your house one afternoon, so parents can socialize while the children are playing.

Be honest about explaining your family. Be friendly, and try to avoid getting defensive if it's not warranted. Most families like to swap parenting stories, so feel free to share yours. "Gloria and I actually met about fifteen years ago, but we weren't ready for kids until Maria came along. How about you and your husband?"

Expect questions, some of which may not be tactful, from the other parents. "Which one of you is the real mom?" or "How did two men end up with a baby?" are common ones. Remember that most questions are probably asked out of curiosity rather than malice, so give answers that you feel comfortable with – and then move on. Don't dwell on their questions, but if they keep probing you or seem blatantly homophobic, don't push the issue. Avoid getting into an argument. That won't help your child to adapt to her school, other families and teachers. Eventually, if some parents don't accept gay families, then you will want to encourage your child to expand their group of friends.

For older elementary-aged kids, you'll probably find that not only do they want to have play dates with their classmates, but they may also want to have sleepovers. You might encounter some hesitation on the part of some other parents who may not want to allow their children to sleep over at your house.

Usually, the best way to handle this situation is for you and your partner to get to know your child's friends' parents as well as possible. Once the parents get to know you, most will accept that you are loving, responsible parents, as they are, and there's no need to worry about leaving their children in your care.

Tim and Morrie, one couple we interviewed, had twin girls, Tina and Gina, who were in fourth grade at the local public school. The girls wanted two of their best friends to sleep over on the twins' birthday, and they were very excited about sending out the invitations. Jennifer, the mother of one friend, seemed very hesitant about allowing her child to attend, so Tim phoned to reassure her that everything would be fine and the girls would have a lot of fun. Jennifer didn't know any other gay men, though, and she didn't feel comfortable leaving her daughter "alone" in a house with two men, so she refused to allow her daughter to go.

Tim came up with a solution that seemed to please her: he invited his sister to spend the night, ensuring that there would be a female adult present. Tim and Morrie's primary concern was having a happy sleepover for their children, so they did what they could to make this party a reality. "Jennifer, Macy's mother, wouldn't let her come otherwise. Morrie and I just had to handle our own feelings – what mattered was giving the twins the best birthday we could. And they had a great time! The girls made popcorn, watched movies, and giggled most of the night."

CONCLUDING ADVICE:

Many gay parents worry: How is my child being treated at school? Are the other kids teasing him, because he has two mothers? You can help make sure the answer is "no" by talking to your child's teachers and making your positive presence known to the administration. Be proactive: provide your teacher with training materials that deal positively with gay families and think about ways your kids can be creative when it comes to making parent-specific holiday cards. Give your children the confidence they need to feel secure in their family structure; they'll exude that confidence both on the playground and in the classroom.

QUESTIONS FOR INFORMING AND ENRICHING YOUR CHILD'S ENVIRONMENT:

1. Does your school know that your child has same-sex parents?
2. Have you ensured that your school considers both you and your partner equal parents of your child? Are you both listed on her school documentation?
3. Are you setting a good example for your child by being out at work, at the playground, etc?
4. Are your children's friends' parents comfortable with your sexuality?
5. Has your child ever been teased at school? What would you do if your child were teased?
6. Has your church, temple or mosque made you feel awkward about joining their congregation? Have you talked to them about how to make your family feel accepted?
7. Have you gotten involved in your child's education?
8. Have you thought about ways for your child to be involved in the community and help out others who might be less fortunate?
9. Have you talked with your child's teacher about how to handle Mother's Day and Father's Day?

chapter fourteen

TEENAGERS

The teenage years usually are full of adventure, misadventure, success and failure. All parents, including gay parents, are kept mighty busy while their children navigate this rite of passage. A few things for gay parents to concern themselves with as teenagers become aware of their own sexuality are: is the teen gay? Is he straight? How can I be the right kind of role model if he chooses a path different from my own?

"ARE MY CHILDREN EMBARRASSED BY ME?"

Every parent of teenagers, in every part of the world, has embarrassed his or her children at some point. Most of the time, parents do this accidentally; walking too close, giving a good-bye kiss or tucking a strand of hair behind an ear can all be lethal offenses for a teenager. High-school-age kids have a burning need to assert their independence, and most of the time, they don't want Mom or Dad hanging around them.

Helen, the daughter of two lesbians (Jamie and Lynn), can confirm an occasional level of annoyance with her parents. "My moms are usually pretty cool, but they have their awkward moments. Mom likes to wait for me after school, which is okay, but she pulls up the car right in front, and waves out the window when she sees me coming! She doesn't get that it's just not cool for someone to have their mommy waiting for them. But at least she cares... more than I can say for some parents."

Has Helen ever been embarrassed that her parents are gay? "I've been in school with the same kids for most of my life, and everyone knows I have two moms." But what about new students, or ones that don't know her? "Sometimes I get stupid questions, like 'What's it like having two moms?' It's like... DUH! They're my parents. We eat dinner, they tell me to get off the phone and do my homework...regular parent stuff."

Most kids who grow up in a gay or lesbian household are used to their parents being gay. If you've taught your children self-respect and they've learned that your family is a loving and legitimate one, they will grow in maturity though they may question your authority, etc.

ADOPTING OLDER CHILDREN

Adopting older children will be challenging for all parents, but gay parents will have their own set of issues. Many heterosexual adoptive parents are looking for healthy newborns, not pre-teens or teenagers; for this reason, gay parents often find more children available in these ages. Some states are even placing children for adoption with gay families. There are a huge number of older children throughout the world who need homes – and gay households can be part of the solution.

If an older child has recently entered your household, as parents you need to take a strong lead from the very beginning. Older children have probably been through the foster or adoption system for years and may be hardened against the idea of finally having a family. They may rebel against anything and everything – including the idea of a gay family.

As with most aspects of parenting, consistency is the golden rule. Establish yourselves as good parents before attempting to tackle any other issues; build up a layer of trust. Provide consistent love and nurturing, while meeting the child's needs to the best of your abilities. Listen to what the child needs and respond so that he knows that you're not just hearing him, but also listening. Make it clear that you expect your child to respect you as both a person and a parent.

GETTING USED TO EACH OTHER

Once your children are intertwined in your homes and lives, expect some questions about your lifestyle. Every older child comes into an adoption with preconceived ideas; he may have heard things from other children, good or bad, about gay people, and he may use slang expressions that aren't appropriate. Also, you might run into these problems when accepting a foster child into your house.

At times your reaction may be anger or defensiveness, but remember that you chose to adopt or foster this child and you chose to welcome him into your home. It's your responsibility to enforce positive language and be firm on the rule that derogatory words about all people simply aren't allowed. Explain to your child that your family is made up of adults who love each other and also love him; despite what he may have heard, there is nothing wrong about your sexual orientation or the love of you and your partner for each other. If the child continues to be resentful, fearful and angry about being placed in your home despite your best efforts over time, re-placement may be necessary.

If you already have biological or adopted children living in your home, be sure that they understand that an older child will soon be joining the family. Knowing that you already have children who accept your sexuality will probably help the new child tremendously; your kids will help affirm that your family is loving and stable.

Marie and Colleen, a lesbian couple to whom we talked, have two children who were born to Marie and decided to apply for a foster child. Their first placement was a thirteen-year-old girl. At first, things were a bit rocky. "Emma knew she was coming to stay with a lesbian family, but I don't think she really knew what that meant. She wasn't uncomfortable with us, but you could tell it wasn't what she was used to. She kept asking our girls, "Where's your dad?" but she eventually accepted that our family just didn't have a father figure. She'd been abused by men in her life for years, so I think she was actually relieved not to have to deal with them."

Colleen hadn't been expecting the backlash from Emma's friends at school. "For the first year, Emma went to school in a different district, because that's where she had lived before coming to us. Her friends there gave her a pretty hard time, I think... it was a tough school, and there wasn't a lot of support for gay kids there, let alone gay families." Colleen made a point of giving Emma plenty of love and affection and tried to offset the negative things Emma was hearing at school. "We went out for dinner with other gay families, and showed her that we're just as normal – for better or for worse! – as anyone else. We were lucky because she's a very bright girl, and she figured things out on her own."

Once Emma's adoption was finalized, she transferred schools to attend the one where with Marie and Colleen's other girls went. "She was a freshman in high school at the same time our daughter Nan was a junior and our daughter Maisie was a senior. They just took Emma under their wing, it was a really great thing to see. Emma felt very at-home at her new school. And the girls were thrilled to have a younger sister."

Marie and Colleen knew they were lucky, though. "Some friends of ours, also gay, chose to be foster-parents as well. They had a really hard time; first, they couldn't get a placement. Then when they finally did, the fourteen-year-old boy refused to go live with them, saying he didn't want to live with 'fags.' That really hurt them. In this case, the placement did not work. "Bill ended up doing an international adoption and they got a cute little girl. For them, adopting an older child just didn't work out."

Be optimistic, however – kids are amazingly resilient and adaptable, even in situations that would be difficult for the most well-adjusted adult. Laura and Wei-Lin had just adopted an older child from an Asian country, and were worried about what she would think when she realized that she was not only coming to live in a new country, but that she would have two mothers as well. Grace was escorted to the United States, so her mothers met her for the first time at the airport.

When Grace realized, through the help of her translator, that she had not just one but two mothers waiting for her with open arms, she was elated. Laura describes: "Grace had the look of a child who was just offered cake AND ice cream, and realized that she didn't have to choose between them – she could have both!" Going from having no moms at all to not just one, but two, was beyond Grace's wildest dreams. Despite coming from a culture where families headed by two women were almost unheard of, Grace blossomed in her new home and hasn't shown any problems in adjusting. While not all stories of adoption of older children are this easy, neither are they all as hard as the worst-case scenarios that many potential adoptive parents fear.

ADOPTING A GAY OR LESBIAN TEENAGER

Gay and lesbian teenagers, and gender-variant teens, have particularly difficult times in foster care and are at a higher risk of running away or turning to drugs and alcohol. A supportive and understanding gay or lesbian single parent or couple can make all the difference in helping a confused or questioning teenager understand his sexual orientation and realize that there's nothing wrong with being gay.

As with adopting any older child, it can be a good idea to start the process as a temporary foster care placement, to see if the child and the others in your household can adjust well. Remember, too, if the child is a lesbian and you are one, this doesn't mean that there will instantly be any sort of bond or understanding between the two of you. Take the time to get to know one another and try to develop a positive relationship.

SEXUAL ORIENTATION AND CHILDREN OF GAY PARENTS

Are children who grow up with gay or lesbian parents more likely themselves to be gay or lesbian? The answer is no. Careful studies have been done to try to determine if these children are more likely to be gay. The results of these studies have shown that they are statistically no more likely to identify themselves as gay or lesbian adults than children who grew up in heterosexual families.

One interesting difference did show up in some studies, however. While the final sexual orientation of such children appears statistically indistinguishable from the rest of the population, children who grow up in gay or lesbian families are more likely to have considered a same sex relationship at some point during their teenage and adult years.

So what does this mean? One interpretation is that children who grew up with gay or lesbian parents are more comfortable with the idea of same-sex relationships than their peers. In addition, children who were gay or lesbian and raised by same-sex parents tended to come out earlier than their peers from heterosexual families. The most likely explanation is that these children don't fear the rejection and hostility that is unfortunately common in many heterosexual households. Perhaps they are simply more aware of different kinds of sexuality and are able to identify such feelings in themselves earlier than their counterparts.

IS MY CHILD GAY?

Most heterosexual parents tend to assume that their child will also be heterosexual; their son will end up marrying a wonderful woman and their daughter will find a great man to settle down with. These relationships can be celebrated in a traditional wedding with flowers and dancing, or through the act of simply obtaining a marriage license from a Justice of the Peace.

Gay and lesbian parents, however, are aware of a greater variety of future relationship possibilities for their children. Their son may end up living with another man, and their daughter could well be on her way to starting her own lesbian family. While gays and lesbians currently cannot be married in most states in the US, if they grew up in heterosexual families, they may have come to expect that a big wedding is an eventual part of everyone's life.

While many parents may joke about their toddler daughter one day marrying the cute little blond-haired girl down the street, some parents (even gay or lesbian ones) may not be prepared to deal with their daughter actually being gay when she reaches the teenage years. On the other hand, some parents may secretly hope for their child to be gay. Most parents, at some level, want their children to be like them; there is a distinct pride in having someone carry on the family name, or be the guardian of other family traditions.

If your child is gay, you might expect that he would be interested in the same community events and organizations that you enjoy—such as Gay Pride, a gay film festival or a women's music weekend. He's probably attended these events for all of his life, and you might expect him to continue seeking out such activities.

However, don't be surprised if your child isn't interested when he or she becomes a teenager. Children at these points commonly rebel against their parents as they attempt to forge their own identities. He'll need to find his own ways to express his sexuality.

As gay or lesbian parents, dealing with your child if he or she is coming out as gay will likely be a lot easier than it would be for heterosexual parents. After all, you've had the same (or similar) experiences; he can count on you not to be completely horrified or cast him out of the family because of his sexual orientation. On the other hand, don't expect everything to be completely smooth either. Older parents, especially ones who may have come out at a less-accepting time, may have to deal with their own internalized homophobia.

Parents who have experienced significant discrimination for being gay or lesbian may find that they want to protect their children from this experience. They may find themselves less than thrilled to discover that their son is also gay, because they think they know what he's in for. The key thing to remember here is that you trust your children's decisions; they've been around you for your entire life, and the odds are good that they understand the impact of their choices. Remember also that society is becoming more and more accepting of lesbians and gay men, and it's less likely that your child will experience the amount of discrimination that you did during your coming-out period.

However, it might be appropriate to arm your child with enough information. Let him know that not everyone is as open and accepting as your family and friends, and that not every community is as tolerant as the one in which he was raised. It can be harsh to learn that this acceptance does not extend to every part of the country, let alone the world. If your child is considering going far from home for college, make sure she takes into account the surrounding political climate, as well as attitudes she may run into from her freshman peers.

MY CHILD ISN'T GAY!

If your child is gay or lesbian like you, you're probably on familiar territory. But what do you do if your child decides he or she is heterosexual? Marie and Colleen's older daughter, Maisie, came home from eighth grade saying that she met the cutest boy at school.

The most important thing any parent of a teenager can do is show support for the child's choices, while giving gentle guidance as necessary. Colleen says, "If we were straight, we'd want to support her being gay... so we felt that though we're gay, we wanted to support her choice to date boys."

Being open and accepting of people of all sexual orientations is good advice for everyone. Trina and Linda, another couple with whom we spoke, realized that their daughter might grow up and want to date men. They discussed the situation and resolved that they wanted their girl growing up with positive impressions of men, even though they personally were lesbians.

Remember that your child is much more likely to be straight than gay, given that gay and lesbian people make up just a small percentage of society as a whole. If your children decide not to follow in your footsteps here, don't take it personally and don't see it as a rejection of you or your family. Your children will become whoever they are destined to become and your parenting style is not going to make them either gay or straight.

A factor to consider, especially for parents raising children predominantly in gay and lesbian culture, is that if your child grows up to be heterosexual, he may have trouble fitting in or relating to other straight people. Casey, a woman in her twenties raised by lesbian moms, has definitely noticed this problem. "My sister Carla is a lesbian and fits into the culture we were raised in just fine. As a kid, I never realized that growing up going to lesbian protests wasn't the norm. When I went to college, I was away from my moms and the whole environment I grew up in for the first time. I realized that I didn't really know how to relate to straight people! It would be a lot easier if I were attracted to women like Carla is, but I'm not–I like men." Casey wishes that her moms had exposed her to more of straight culture when she was growing up.

LOOSENING THE REINS

It's important to make sure that you don't put undue restrictions on boys that your daughter wants to date, while giving her free rein to date girls; both genders should be treated equally.

Make sure your daughter understands that one date does not determine her sexuality for the rest of her life. She should know that she's free to date people of either gender and you'll support her both ways. Allow her some latitude, and enough space to come to her own decisions. Try not to be judgmental of her choices and you'll retain the loving relationship you've always had with her.

DOES A LESBIAN HOUSEHOLD NEED A MALE ROLE MODEL?

One issue that can come up at any age, with families parented by gay or lesbian couples, is whether their opposite-sex or even same-sex children need opposite-gender role models. Well-meaning friends or relatives might say that the son of a lesbian couple clearly needs the influence of a man in his life; similarly, a gay couple raising a daughter may hear comments about the girl's lack of a mother. Especially in the teenage years, when puberty hits and hormones start raging at an uncontrollable pace, gay parents and/or their children should discuss whether or not other role models are necessary.

When your children are young, assure your friends and relatives that studies have shown that most children, who grow up in families with two mothers or two fathers are perfectly well-adjusted. They are able to relate to both women and men, once they become adults.

For younger children, arranging for friends or relatives of the opposite sex to be part of their lives is a good idea to get your child used to adults of the opposite sex early on. Usually, a grandparent, aunt or uncle or close friend can meet this need. Marie and Colleen, for example, invited Marie's parents to come and visit at least twice a year. As a preschooler, their younger daughter Callie was fascinated with a few things about Grandpa that she'd never noticed with her mothers. "Callie learned, for the first time, that men were people with facial hair and belts. She'd never seen either of us wearing a belt. Also, she pointed at Grandpa's scratchy face and was fascinated by the hair on his hands and arms. Gradually she learned what men's physical appearances are like."

After getting familiar with Grandpa, Callie started to classify the adults that she saw when she was out shopping or running errands with her mothers. "She'd say, 'That's Grandpa!' whenever she saw a tall man with grey hair. Eventually she figured out that there were other men in the world who were *not* Grandpa."

Once your children start school, they'll be exposed to adults of both genders. They'll learn about the physical differences as they become pubescent, through sex education classes in school or when you choose to teach them. Teenage children in particular, though, may benefit from having a close relationship with a role model or confidante of their own gender.

When Bob and Steve's daughter Kaylie was about twelve years old, she started asking questions that neither man felt well-prepared to answer. "She was asking us all these really detailed questions about breasts and her menstrual cycle," reported Bill. "While we obviously had all the technical answers, we couldn't speak from experience about any of these things that she was genuinely concerned with." They checked several books out of the library for her, but felt like that hadn't really sufficed. "It seemed cold to make her learn about being a woman from books."

They arranged for Bob's sister, Julie, to come and visit for a weekend. Julie had known Kaylie since she'd been adopted, so the two were already good friends. Julie did an entire "becoming a woman" weekend with Kaylie – she took her shopping for her first brassiere, treated her to a manicure and pedicure and left time for plenty of girl talk in between outings. Kaylie warmed up to Julie and asked her lots of questions about womanhood and puberty, and Julie left Kaylie with her cell phone number, encouraging her to call whenever she needed to. Julie also made a point of calling Kaylie once a week, just to chat.

BIRTH CONTROL

While gay and lesbian couples don't generally need to worry about birth control, if you have a teenage son or daughter, this is an issue that you need to address. Hopefully you've already had the discussion about sex, and your children understand the importance of safe sex. However, once your children approach puberty and teenage-hood, it's a good idea to have periodic reminders.

If your children are dating members of the opposite sex and they've decided to embark upon a sexual relationship, make sure that both your child and her partner are fully equipped with both knowledge and sexual protection. If your son or daughter decides to engage in a physical same-sex relationship, birth control won't be an issue, but protection will still be important. Explain to your children and then remind them about how sexually-transmitted diseases can be prevented.

It may be uncomfortable for a lesbian couple to provide condoms to their teenage son; if you decide to do this the best way to accomplish it is matter-of-factly. Buy a box of condoms, show your son where it is, explain how they're used and make sure to explain the consequences of NOT using them. Tell him that protection will always be available if he needs it. Reassure him that you're not trying to keep tabs on every aspect of his life, but want him to stay healthy and safe.

CONCLUDING ADVICE:

Teenagers are a challenge for any parent. They're much more savvy and independent than they were as toddlers. They suddenly present new demands: Car keys! First dates! Prom night! As a gay parent, accept that your children may or may not be gay. If you adopt a teenager, expect the same issues. Be sure the older child you're adopting wants to be placed with a gay family and make sure you can deal with your child's sexuality. As you prepare your children to enter the adult world on their own be tolerant and accepting.

QUESTIONS:

1. Have your teenagers ever expressed any embarrassment about having gay parents? If so, are you discreet but honest?
2. Have you considered adopting a gay teen?
3. Will you be comfortable if your teenagers are heterosexual?
4. Will you be comfortable if your teenagers are gay or lesbian?
5. Will you allow your children to experiment with dating other teens of both sexes, if they want to?
6. Have you made sure not to denigrate the members of the opposite sex, even if you don't have much contact with them?
7. If you're gay male parents of teenager daughters, do you have any close female friends or relatives who might be able to talk candidly to them?
8. If you're lesbian parents of teenage sons, do you have any close male friends or relatives who might be able to talk candidly to them?

chapter fifteen

COMING OUT LATER IN LIFE

For the most part, we have focused so far on gays and lesbians who come to terms with their sexuality before having children. This is, of course, not the case for all parents. In fact, while the number of children in planned same-sex families is increasing every year, the majority of children in same-sex families still are from previous heterosexual relationships.

BEING TRUE TO YOURSELF AND YOUR SPOUSE

For many people, sexual orientation is something that they begin to realize early in their lives, usually in their teen years as they first begin considering the idea of sexuality. In other cases, early adulthood is the time in which sexuality becomes a burgeoning issue with a clear resolution: either you're gay, or you're not.

For still others, though, discovering one's true sexual orientation is a journey that takes much longer. Some people might grow up in conservative towns and might not encounter the concept of gay or lesbian relationships until later in life. People in these circumstances might get married at a young age, often unaware that they have any other options.

FIGURING OUT SEXUAL IDENTITY

Shane, a man from a small Midwestern town, was born and raised in a small farming community. As expected, he got married to a local girl when he graduated from high school and continued working on his parents' farm. Shane says, "Getting married was what I was supposed to do. I never even thought about it. Everyone else was doing it. I'd never even left the county – and didn't know that there WAS anything else. Betty and I married young, she was eighteen and I was nineteen. I love her, that's for sure; but I never really felt attracted to her. Or any girl, for that matter."

Several years went by and the couple had two children. As his father's farming business was booming, Shane decided to expand by computerizing the family's billing process. He knew something about computers from his high school classes, and was a very quick study. His new computer came with Internet access, and Shane, who had begun questioning his sexual orientation, eventually found his way to online chat rooms. There, a whole new world opened up to him - that of other men who felt the same as he did. "I was embarrassed at first, and always turned the computer off when someone came into the office. But it was something I'd never seen before. For the first time, I felt like I wasn't alone."

Men and women who come out later in life have a complicated situation to face – more so than those who realize their sexual orientation before they marry and have children. In addition to having to deal with the emotions and physical complications of a marriage, general confusion and anxiety often accompany one's realization of homosexuality. These feelings are compounded by being involved in a heterosexual relationship.

If you're married, with or without children, how do you start to think about telling your partner that you're no longer heterosexual? It may be tempting to continue keeping your sexuality a secret. But for most people, finding a more compatible life partner is a strong desire. It also might be temping to stay married and have a discreet affair on the side; however, these types of secrets have a way of being found out. The stress of keeping such a secret will be hard on both you and your marriage, not to mention your children. As difficult as it can be to contemplate coming out to your family, in the long run everyone will probably be happier.

If you're married and have realized that you're gay, talk to your husband or wife. The talk could go very well. Your mate could have been suspecting that you're homosexual for years and the discussion could be a great relief. Be open and honest and express gratitude for support. Many partners who come out remain great friends with their former husbands or wives.

If you fear reprisal from an angry spouse, make sure you have a safe place to go with your children. The police will enforce restraining orders where necessary. It is important to have some money and other assets in your name. Some spouses will take your coming out personally, as if you are rejecting them. Explain your feelings honestly and try to describe how you came to determine your homosexuality.

WHAT WILL MY KIDS THINK?

If you come out while your children are still babies, there will be little adjustment required, since they haven't been taught to be biased, racist or homophobic. They'll adapt to your new partner as they would to an opposite-sex spouse if you were to divorce and remarry.

Toddlers will require a simple, clear explanation. If your two-year-old has been around a mommy and daddy for all of his life, explain that he will have two mommies. Present the idea in terms of your child's being lucky he will have not just one mother, but two! Similarly, play up the advantages of two daddies if that will be your new situation. Make sure to focus on the advantages, rather than dwelling on any potential negatives.

Expect the child to ask where Daddy is, if your husband has left the family home (or if you've moved out and taken your children with you). As with any situation in which parents have divorced or split up, children need time to adjust to seeing both parents on schedules.

Help your children adjust by remaining friendly with your former spouse whenever possible. Your ex-husband may date other women, and you also may be dating other women. Talk to your ex ahead of time, and let him know that you won't judge the women he chooses to date; make it clear that you expect the same level of respect from him. Your feelings about each other's future partners are less important than maintaining a level of peace and consistency for your children, and you'll need to make sure your ex is on board with this philosophy.

Coming out to grade-school children is a slightly different proposition. Honesty is still the best policy, so sit down with them and have a simple, matter-of-fact talk. "This has nothing to do with your father; he and I love each other very much, and we love you more than anything in the world. I'm not leaving your father for another man, or another woman for that matter; I just need some freedom to explore some things about my life, including what I need to do to be happy." If your child asks questions, answer them. Don't be ashamed of who you are, or your children will learn to be ashamed as well.

If you've raised your children in a respectful home where slurs and pejorative language about others are not allowed, the odds are good that your children will treat your announcement with respect. If they haven't yet learned what it means to be gay or lesbian, explain that while you used to be married to Daddy, you may want to date other women now. Make sure they understand that your sexuality has nothing to do with your love for them and that they will always be of primary importance in your life.

Acquaint your own parents with your decision. In many cases this will be easier said than done, but it's important to remind them to respect your choices. It is important that your children not have grandparents speaking badly of you behind your back. Speak to both your parents and your former spouse's parents. Even if they don't approve of your sexuality, they owe it to you and your children to be civil and polite around their grandchildren.

When you come out you may be on the receiving end of some hostility from other family members, especially those related to your spouse. Your children may be taunted or teased by their cousins. This is another reason why it's a good idea to be open and honest with all relatives; explain that your kids come first and even if the relatives don't approve of your lifestyle, your children have done nothing wrong. They deserve to be treated as they were before your announcement.

COMING OUT TO TEENS

If you come out as gay or lesbian when your children are teenagers, you'll need to approach the situation differently. Most teens are aware of what it means to be homosexual; if they haven't already experimented sexually with a partner, they've learned enough in health class (and from their friends) to know the basics of sex. Your child may already suspect your sexual orientation, perhaps even before you admitted it to yourself.

Your children are likely to be tolerant and their relationship with you probably won't change any more than it would between "normal" divorced parents. The biggest change they're likely to go through is getting used to Mom and Dad living in separate houses, not Mom dating a woman. Most teens want their parents to be happy, even if that means that they have to go their separate ways.

However, be prepared for the possibility that your child may not approve of your coming out as gay. Some children may have an outright dislike of gay people. This often will depend on the community you're living in, as well as their exposure to anti-gay sentiments. If you're aware that your children feel this way, it could make it all the more difficult for you to come out.

Even if your children are not outwardly homophobic, expect some level of discomfort. Teenage boys, for example, may feel embarrassed by a gay father.

Don, an interviewee with whom we spoke, has a father who came out of the closet when Don was a junior in high school. "It was really awkward for me. My friends started thinking that I was gay, that my dad and I were having sex... it was awful. They didn't understand that my dad's being gay had nothing to do with me."

Kids can be cruel to each other. "It got so bad that I had to ask my dad to stop dropping me off at school," Don said. "The jocks on the football team just wouldn't let it go. I had to start eating lunch inside, just so they'd leave me alone. Eventually, they forgot about it when they found someone else to make miserable." Did this experience make Don resent his father? "Not really, no. He can't help being who he is. I just wish he'd decided it after I left for college."

Timing is important. Is it possible to delay your coming out until your child reaches some major milestone? In some cases, that may be advisable. Your children's reactions will probably be emotional, so try to plan the announcement so that it doesn't conflict with final exams, or any other major event in a child's life. You don't need to wait an eternity, but you also don't need to give your children more to deal with than they can handle.

WILL I LOSE MY CHILDREN IN THE DIVORCE IF MY EX-WIFE KNOWS I'M GAY?

Most people who come out while married will eventually want to divorce the partner to whom they are currently married. This frees them for dating or possibly a domestic partnership, with someone of the same gender. Depending on your particular situation, however, remaining married is an option – you and your wife may agree to stay married for financial reasons or for the sake of the children, but have an open marriage where both you and your wife can see other people on the side. Such relationships are rare, but can work as long as there is honesty and good communication between all parties.

If you do decide to divorce, make sure that you and your spouse come to an agreement that divorcing is best for the two of you and for the family. Blindsiding your wife with divorce papers is not a great start to an amicable split. Before beginning the legal proceedings, consult a lawyer to ensure that you leave the marriage with your fair share of the assets. Especially if you have been a stay-at-home parent, you may be financially vulnerable in a divorce. If you visualize a divorce in your future, start making sure that some financial assets are in your name or at least are joint, and try to save up a little money of your own.

Become familiar with the laws for divorce in your state. Grounds for divorce vary in different states, but most states have what is called a "no-fault divorce." This allows a married couple to dissolve the marriage without having to provide a reason such as infidelity. Requirements for division of property, financial support and child custody also vary from state to state.

If your relationship with your spouse is still friendly, talk to your to-be-ex about a custody arrangement for the children. If you fear that your spouse will try to keep the children completely away from you because you're gay or lesbian, find an experienced lawyer who will argue your side during the divorce proceedings. Depending on the state you live in, it's unfortunate but possible that a straight spouse could use the fact that you are gay as a reason to bar you completely from seeing your children. Document your involvement in your children's lives and gear up friends and family to make positive statements on your behalf.

THE DANGERS OF DIVORCE

Emily, a thirty-five-year-old woman, was married to Duncan for ten years before Emily came out as a lesbian. The couple had two school-aged children. Emily had been secretly involved with Lisa (a woman from work) for two years, before she finally got up the courage to tell her husband. At that point she told him that she was gay. The couple divorced, and Duncan agreed that Emily could have primary custody of the children.

However, Duncan became involved with a new woman, who started pushing him to seek full custody. A court decision eventually forced Lisa to move out of the house that she and Emily had shared with the children for three years. Lisa had to buy a house down the street in order to stay close to her partner and new family.

Fortunately for Emily, Duncan's new relationship floundered, the lawsuit was dropped and Lisa was again allowed to move back in with Emily and the children. Even so, this true story is a chilling reminder of the power the court system can have over you and your family. If at all possible, maintain at least a civil relationship with your ex. Try to work things out informally, rather than involve the courts.

WILL THE WOMAN ALWAYS GET THE KIDS?

Custody laws have historically favored women when deciding custody after a divorce. Traditionally, after a divorce, the woman has received full custody of the children (with the father visiting them on weekends), child support and alimony payments from the ex-husband. However, more recently courts have begun to recognize the more equal role that many fathers play in their children's lives. Thus the courts have awarded equally shared custody to divorcing parents. In some cases, the father may be able to receive full custody of his children.

Shane, the Midwestern dad who came out after having two children, got divorced from his high school sweetheart, Betty, and moved to the city. His two children remained with their mother. Shane says, "I assumed that there was no way I could get custody of my children, so I didn't even fight for them in the divorce. I mean, who was going to let two little girls live with a gay man?" After a few years of occasional weekend and summer visits, however, Shane met Carlos and the relationship became serious. "Carlos loved kids, and he was great with Megan and Melinda. He was real supportive about my going back home to spend more time with them. Eventually I got a great job working for an insurance company in the city. Carlos and I bought a big house near the lake with plenty of room for the girls, so that we could have them stay with us more."

Shane's ex-wife, Betty, was taking care of her elderly parents and running their farm. She was willing to try letting the girls spend the school year with their Dad in the city. The understanding was that the girls would spend the summer with her on the farm. Shane says, "Betty was pretty mad at me when I first told her I was gay, but we've both calmed down and matured a lot over the years. We realize that we got married too young for either of us to know what we really wanted out of life." Shane reports that the girls love living with him and Carlos during the school year, and spending the summer helping their mother on the farm.

In another situation, suppose that you're already divorced once you come out as gay. What if your spouse tries to take away your children because you're homosexual? Sadly, in some jurisdictions, homosexuality can be considered grounds for losing custody of your children. In most places, though, your sexual orientation doesn't have any bearing on your fitness as a parent and the courts recognize this. If you have a good (or at least non-hostile) relationship with your ex spouse she or he will want you to be part of your children's lives.

If, however, you fear that you ex could use your coming out as a way to gain custody or at least avoid paying child support, be cautious. You can still be true to yourself, without offering full disclosure to your entire family. In the long run it's better to be open and honest with everyone, but if you're indanger of losing custody, it might be best to avoid a major coming-out announcement until your children reach legal age.

YOUR FIRST GAY DATE

Dating after a divorce is always complicated and is especially so when there are children involved. It may be even more complicated, though, when you are suddenly dating a man instead of a woman.

As with dating of any sort when you're a parent, the best advice is to take it slow. If you have shared custody with your ex, it may be best to first date on nights when your children are with your former spouse. Protect your kids' feelings as well, and don't bring home every single love interest. Remember that kids, especially younger ones who have just "lost" a parent, may be eagerly looking for a replacement parent; that's a lot of responsibility to place on someone you just met. Alternatively, older children may be resentful of anyone who seems to take the role that Mom or Dad used to have. Let your kids know that you're dating, but don't bring your date home to meet them until the relationship has gotten serious.

Elementary-age children probably won't care about the sexual orientation of your potential dates. Older kids, though, may become intensely curious about the whole dating process. Before bringing home another man for the first time as a date, make sure that you have a conversation with your children. Let them know that he is a special friend, one with whom you may be spending some "alone time." Even if you've previously had a general talk with your kids about the fact that Daddy will be dating men instead of women, you should have this discussion again once the abstract becomes a concrete reality.

Be wary of where you choose to look for new dates. While online matchmaking sites can be convenient, be careful not to leave anything even vaguely explicit on a computer screen where your children might see it. Let discretion be your guide. Also, don't give out any information online that might reveal the identities of your children. Be safe rather than sorry, especially in an era where so many people (including pedophiles) have access to the Internet.

MEET MOM AND STEP-MOM

Those who come out later in life often will find themselves single or dating with children. As relationships blossom and follow their natural course, it's possible that your children will eventually have a new stepparent: your new partner. Generally speaking, having a gay stepmother or stepfather will probably be a major adjustment, but not necessarily any more so than if you'd remarried someone of the opposite gender.

The first question that many gay people have in this situation: how can you convince your children to accept your new partner as a parent? If you are a new stepparent, you can best enter a child's life by being her friend and not her parent; she already has parents to fulfill that role. If you have children, advise your new partner to be a buddy first to your children: listen to their problems, help with their homework and generally establish himself as a consistent, caring force in your children's lives.

As the relationship gets more serious and it becomes clear that your new partner is going to be around for the long haul, the first big change in your children's lives will be when you and your partner move in together. Make sure your children understand that they still occupy the most important role in your life while, at the same time, you're making room for someone else to love (and who will love them, in turn). Involve your children in all aspects of this new change; if you're moving, for example, let them help decorate their new rooms. If your partner ends up moving into your house, let your children help carry boxes and get your partner situated into your home, and your lives.

One advantage of a having gay partner-turned-parent is that you're not trying to directly replace your ex-spouse with another parent, at least not in your children's eyes. After all, if a gay woman divorces her husband and partners with another woman, her children now live with two mothers – not a mother and a "new" father. This arrangement may help children accept their new parent, and give her a special role to fill in their lives.

If you are a stepparent who enters a child's life after his birth and the relationship breaks up, you may find yourself without any legal standing toward your former partner's children. Even if you raised them for most of your lives, you may have no rights toward them if you didn't give birth or legally adopt them. Unfortunately not much can be done in this situation, aside from attempting to reason with your former partner. If a stepparent adoption is a possibility in your situation, by all means consider doing one – they're relatively inexpensive, fast and easy compared to other adoption proceedings. Keep in mind that legal rights come with responsibilities - once you become a legal parent, you are legally responsible for the children you adopt until they reach age eighteen.

COMING OUT BISEXUAL

Some adults may conclude that they have a sexual preference, but not an exclusive one, for partners of the same gender. If your primary relationship ends for whatever reason, you might choose to date either men or women (or both).

While some people realize they are bisexual while they're already married, their sexual orientation may be purely theoretical. Michaela is a woman who has been married to a man for ten years. She eventually realized that she is also attracted to women. However, her marriage to her husband Yves is a good one and she has no intention of getting divorced. Since her marriage is monogamous, her sexual orientation as bisexual may remain theoretical. While sometimes Michaela is attracted to women, she doesn't actually act on those attractions.

Some people in this situation embrace their bisexuality and become politically active in the LGBT movement, working at rallies and appearing at protests. Coming out as bisexual is very similar to coming out as gay or lesbian, except for the invisibility that tends to come with bisexuality. Being bisexual isn't always clear or apparent. People in same-sex relationships are usually perceived as gay or lesbian, while people in straight relationships generally are assumed to be heterosexual. Most bisexuals do not date both men and women at the same time; bisexuality simply indicates a willingness to form relationships with either gender.

Explaining to your children or spouse that you are bisexual may cause some confusion. Children tend to see the world in black and white—either you're straight or you're gay. Children may have difficulty understanding that sometimes Daddy dates men, but sometimes he dates women. They may also have a hard time explaining this to their peers. On the other hand, young children are quite flexible, and may simply accept your sexuality as a matter of course.

Older children will probably have questions about your being bisexual. They may not understand; they may think you're just undecided, and will eventually come out as gay or return to being straight. Their confusion is understandable. Be patient and give them time to adjust.

JAYE AND HER DAD

Jaye is a ten-year-old girl from Alaska, whose parents divorced when her father came out as bisexual. Dan had full custody of his daughter, and a few months after the divorce was finalized, started occasionally dating both men and women. After his first few dates with men, Jaye sat down at the breakfast table and confronted her dad. "She said," Dan recalls, "if I was bisexual and could choose to date both boys and girls, why couldn't I just choose girls and go back to being married to her mom? I explained that her mother and I had other differences, and it wasn't just my sexuality that led to the divorce. She then asked me why I couldn't at least date only women. I realized that she must have been getting some flack from her friends at school, once they found out that her dad was bi."

If your child is confused about what it means to be bisexual, it's best to keep the explanations simple. Tell her that you're attracted to people, regardless of whether they're male or female. Explain that gay people can't help being gay, and straight people can't help being straight. Dan says, "I asked Jaye if she'd like it if every kid in her class had the same backpack. Every single kid. She looked horrified and said no, of course not. I asked if she thought everyone should have the same exact haircut. And if everyone should bring the same lunch to school every day. She started getting the message that, sometimes, it's okay to be a little different from the herd."

The bottom line is, teach your children that your sexuality, whatever it may be, has nothing to do with your love for them. Make it clear that your children will always come first in your life, regardless of who you choose to date. If your children are secure in their relationship with you, they're much more likely to be secure with your other relationships.

CONCLUDING ADVICE:

For many people, the realization of being gay or lesbian doesn't come until they've already been married and had children. While you may want to take certain precautions when discussing your sexuality with your current spouse, with children, be clear and honest. Allow your children every opportunity to ask questions. If you start dating, always make sure your child knows that he comes first, and that you have his interests at heart. Give everyone time to get used to each other, and trust that you've raised your children to respect you.

QUESTIONS FOR ADULTS COMING OUT:

1. However you come to the realization, do you feel like you'd be happier in a homosexual relationship?
2. Do you think your teenagers already know that you're gay?
3. Have you spoken to your current spouse about your feelings? How do you think he or she would react?
4. Would you and your heterosexual spouse consider remaining married, while you date people of your own sex? Do you think this would be easier for you or for the kids?
5. Would your spouse be easily receptive to the idea of shared custody, were you to enter into a homosexual relationship?
6. How do you think your children would deal with you dating members of the same sex as yourself?
7. Would your children accept your new partner as their step-mother or step-father?
8. If you are bisexual, do you want to remain in a heterosexual marriage with your spouse and not act on your attraction to the same gender?

chapter sixteen

THE FUTURE OF GAY AND LESBIAN PARENTING

While homosexuality is far from being universally accepted today, people in most parts of the world are aware of lesbians and gay men raising families. A generation ago, gay and lesbian parenting was essentially invisible. Today, more and more gay and lesbian couples are choosing to have children in planned gay or lesbian families. In the early days of gay parenting, children from previous heterosexual relationships were the most prevalent. Today, it's becoming more common to see gays who are intentionally planning children into their lives. In some places, gay and lesbian families are even commonplace. Some states and countries have legalized gay marriage, and more and more cities, counties and countries are following suit.

While conception of a child still requires one egg and one sperm, who knows what the future may hold? Perhaps one day, two women may be able to fuse their eggs and create a child that is genetically related to both women.

INCREASING ACCEPTANCE WHERE IT MATTERS

Gay people have existed throughout history (as well as all over the animal kingdom). Modern gay rights movements, however, have allowed gay and lesbian people to live openly, without the secrecy that was required in the past. This increased visibility has come about due to an increasing acceptance of gay and lesbian relationships, and these relationships are now seen in the context of larger society. Gay relationships generally are no longer considered deviant, wrong or to be carried out behind closed doors.

With this increased visibility comes a chance to participate in one of life's most public (and important) roles: becoming parents. Many people who came out twenty years ago would never have considered that being a parent could be compatible with a gay sexual orientation. They may have lived their lives according to this societal misconception, thereby missing out on the chance to raise families with their partners.

Fortunately for those gay and lesbian people who do want children, raising a family is entirely possible today. It's interesting to note that parenthood has actually promoted the further integration of gay and lesbian couples into mainstream society as a whole. Parenting often requires that gay couples venture into areas of society that are dominated by heterosexual couples. These include the public school system, local playgrounds, Baby and Me classes and visits to the pediatrician.

Increased inclusion in "straight society" usually brings about a heightened acceptance of gay families. While parents in your Mom-Child swim class may first look askance at the two dads helping their toddler learn to float, most will soon accept your family as simply another family raising a child. Recent polls consistently show that most people tend to be more tolerant and accepting of gays and lesbians if they actually know them personally. Participating in activities that require inclusion in the greater heterosexual society can only increase this exposure (and, therefore, tolerance). While gay and lesbian parenting has been made possible by society's tolerance, gay parenting itself has also helped to create acceptance through visibility.

Gay and lesbian parenting is certainly growing. The 2000 United States census, the first to ask about same-sex unmarried partners, showed that about 25 percent of gay and lesbian couples were raising children. That's a huge number for a population that used to be invisible. The majority of those children were from previous heterosexual relationships, but the number of children in planned gay and lesbian families is increasing every year.

Jacopo and Paolo, a gay couple in their early forties living in a large metropolitan area, have definitely noticed homosexual family structures being more accepted as the years have passed. Paolo explains, "It seems like most of my friends have paired off, settled down, have a house in the suburbs and a couple of kids! It's really a transformation." Jacopo agreed. "Our favorite park in the neighborhood used to be a hangout for talking with friends, catching up on news . . . and now I see guys taking their babies out."

"We'd never even thought seriously about having kids," Paolo continued. "It always seemed out of our reach, something that only the straight people could do.

But once we saw some of our friends with babies, we really started thinking about it. We're actually in the process of adopting right now. How the tables have turned!"

"NORMALCY"

In areas of the United States such as New York City, San Francisco, Provincetown and Key West, as more and more gays and lesbians have children, areas of the country start to have a high concentration of gay families. In places like the San Francisco Bay Area, for example, gay and lesbian families are common.

While gay people without children tend to congregate in urban areas, gay and lesbian families often spread out to the suburbs, so they will have a house with a yard, a decent school system and pediatricians available. Gay and lesbian families can often be found living near major metropolitan areas all over the country, increasing both visibility and acceptance in regions that might not otherwise be sites of activism.

In areas with large concentrations of gay and lesbian families, there is often enough of a critical mass to sustain specialized gay parenting groups, plus other resources. There are gay-friendly doctors and help in dealing with the public school systems. Such help is becoming more and more available.

In regions where gay and lesbian families are common, you may find that curricula in preschools and elementary schools have been revised to reflect the true diversity of families. Such education usually includes gay and lesbian families as a matter of course, but also includes other family structures. You may also find that public libraries include books that reflect alternative families. Local bookstores, both small independents and also large chain stores, are more likely to carry books that portray gay families.

If you live in a gay-friendly area but don't find these types of resources available, get information and in places where gay families are a normal part of everyday society, make requests to include gay-related literature in school and library book offerings. If you encounter resistance, you may be supported in your endeavors by a gay-friendly school system or a non-discrimination clause in the library's contract or in the town's charter.

If your town isn't overflowing with gay families, most importantly, be yourself. Be proud of the fact that you are a visible gay or lesbian family. Sometimes all it takes is one out family to form a nucleus of change. For example, if your family is profiled in a local or regional newspaper, people in other areas will read the article. Even if the focus of the article is your love of gardening, and not your gay family, other gays might think that your town is a good place to live. You and your family might pave the way for the acceptance and integration of future gay families in your region. The discussions that you have today with your daughter's school system or with a town librarian, may institute policies that can help next year's students feel more comfortable.

GAY AND LESBIAN MARRIAGE

What's the future of marriage for same-sex couples? In the United States, in earlier years, no state specifically allowed for marriage between two people of the same gender. A law in 1996, called the Defense of Marriage Act (DOMA), spelled out for the first time how marriage should be defined, on a federal level. This law was subtitled "An act to define and protect the institution of marriage" and was succinct in its two main points. By law, no state has to respect a same-sex marriage issued from another state. Also by law, marriage consists of a union between one man and one woman.

The Defense of Marriage Act was clearly a major blow to gay and lesbian couples everywhere. Yet, due to lawsuits by gay couples in Massachusetts, Vermont and Hawaii, the wheels of change have begun to turn. Massachusetts is currently the one and only state to offer legal gay marriage, but more and more are beginning to consider it. Marriage should be a fundamental right for any consenting adults who wish to marry, and in the future, sexual orientation should play no role in their ability to wed.

The United States definitely trails behind some other countries when it comes to equal marriage rights. For example, partner registration between gays and lesbians has been legal in Holland since the mid-1990s, and same-sex couples have been given full rights as married couples since 2001. Denmark has also allowed same-sex marriage for years. Some Canadian provinces (such as Ottawa) allow gay marriage, due to a decision by the Supreme Court of Canada. It was recently ruled there that excluding gays from marriage was discriminatory.

Other countries give same-sex couples some, but not all, of the rights of marriage. Iceland and Finland are two such countries. France has a domestic partnership law that offers gays many of the protections they would otherwise have under marriage; Norway, Germany and Hungary offer similar rights. Spain recently changed its laws.

CHILDREN OF THE FUTURE

Producing children today, whether the old-fashioned way or using more advanced reproductive technology, is still fundamentally based on genetic material from one egg and one sperm. Two men who want to have a child together must use a donor egg as well as a surrogate womb. Two women need donated sperm. In each of these cases, the resulting child will be the union of genetic material from one member of the couple, plus a (sometimes anonymous) third party.

The fact that two men or two women can't have a child without the help of a third party may be a gay couple's greatest obstacle to parenting. Having to choose which parent will be the biological one is a difficult and sometimes heart-wrenching decision, since it automatically excludes one partner from the process.

Lesbians also have an option to allow both women to share in a pregnancy. Some women choose to implant a fertilized egg from one woman into her partner. In this method, one woman is essentially serving as an egg donor for the other. This still requires the use of a sperm donor, but allows both women to participate in the creation of their child. It's an expensive way to go, since this method requires using IVF rather than a simple insemination, and it also requires both women to take hormones to synchronize their cycles. But if a more shared experience is a priority, this method may be the only acceptable one.

So what can we expect from the future of medical science? One technique that has been studied involves the merging of two eggs from two different women. "Egg fusion" is not a widely-accepted idea, nor does it appear to be widely advertised, but the concept holds enormous potential for two women who want to create a child without the use of a third party. Another futuristic technique that has been suggested is to take a donated egg and remove all the genetic material from it, replacing it with genetic material from one man. This "male egg" could then be fertilized with sperm from the other man, resulting in a child whose genetic material comes from two men alone. These techniques sound futuristic because they are – but more options probably will be available in the future.

In the future, perhaps legal parenthood won't be limited by the number of parents and their respective genders. Once people expand their notions of gender to realize that parenthood should consist of the adults who love and commit to raising a child, perhaps our current restrictions on marriage and parenthood will become relaxed.

CONCLUDING ADVICE:

This book has covered a lot of ground. We've discussed gay parenting for all stages of your child's development: pre-conception, labor and delivery, raising a toddler and surviving with teenagers. We've looked at dealing with in-laws, coming out later in life and getting your child the best education possible. Once you embark on the road of parenting, you'll find that the path is full of surprises, most of all, we believe, you will discover that raising a family is the most beautiful adventure you'll ever have.

APPENDIX 1

State-by-state table of information about adoption, second parent adoption, domestic partnerships, surrogacy and donor insemination, as of April 2005.

State	State recognition of gay / lesbian couples?	State recognition of gay / lesbian couples?	Surrogacy legal?	Donor Insemination Legal? Other?	Other?
Alabama	Some counties	No; state law bans same-sex marriage	Laws do not specifically prohibit	Laws don't specifically prohibit donor insemination for unmarried women	Laws generally hostile to gay/lesbian parents; custody denied based solely on sexual orientation
Alaska	Some counties	No; ballot initiative bans same-sex marriage	No laws on surrogacy	Laws don't specifically prohibit donor insemination for unmarried women	Laws tolerant
Arizona	Some single parent adoptions to gay / lesbian individuals	No; state law bans same-sex marriage	Laws currently unclear; law criminalizing surrogacy overruled by AZ supreme court	No laws on donor insemination	Bisexuality cited as a reason to deny adoption certification
Arkansas	No	No; state law bans same-sex marriage	Yes; favorable surrogacy laws	Yes; unmarried women can undergo donor insemination	Gay/lesbians cannot be foster parents
California	Yes (statewide); registered domestic partners can do step-parent (domestic partner) adoptions; joint adoptions also permitted	Domestic partnership; gives most rights of marriage; but ballot initiative bans same-sex marriage	Yes; favorable surrogacy laws, good climate for gays / lesbians	Yes; unmarried women can undergo donor insemination; must be done by a doctor in the case of a known donor to remove parental rights	Laws generally very tolerant; law bans discrimination against prospective GLBT foster/ adoptive parents

State	***State recognition of gay / lesbian couples?***	***State recognition of gay / lesbian couples?***	***Surrogacy legal?***	***Donor Insemination Legal? Other?***	***Other?***
Colorado	*No; second-parent adoptions struck down by appeals court; Some single parent adoptions to gay / lesbian individuals*	*No; state law bans same-sex marriage*	*No laws on surrogacy*	*Yes; unmarried women can undergo donor insemination; must explicitly agree no parental rights for donor*	*Generally favorable*
Connecticut	*Yes (statewide)*	*Civil unions offer all state-level benefits of marriage*	*Yes; no state-wide regulation, but court case put two men's names on birth certificate*	*Laws seem to state only okay for married women, but may be ignored*	*Generally favorable*
Delaware	*Yes*	*No; state law bans same-sex marriage*	*Unclear, but lower court found it invalid*	*No laws on donor insemination*	
District of Columbia	*Yes; joint adoptions also permitted*	*Domestic partnership*	*No; surrogacy prohibited, but may be able to use surrogate in another state*	*Yes; appears unmarried women can undergo donor insemination*	
Florida	*No; Gays/lesbians cannot adopt*	*No; state law bans same-sex marriage*	*Yes; surrogacy is legal and well-regulated, but for married couples only*	*Yes; unmarried women can undergo donor insemination; court case explicitly removes legal rights*	*Adoption ban on appeal*

State	State recognition of gay / lesbian couples?	State recognition of gay / lesbian couples?	Surrogacy legal?	Donor Insemination Legal? Other?	Other?
Georgia	Yes	No; state law bans same-sex marriage	Maybe; laws unclear but surrogacy possible	Law does not mention unmarried women; must be performed by doctor	
Hawaii	A few approved	Domestic partnership (reciprocal beneficiaries); but ballot initiative bans same-sex marriage	No laws on surrogacy	No laws on donor insemination	Generally tolerant
Idaho	No	No; state law bans same-sex marriage	No laws, but appears to be permitted	Law appears to allow unmarried women; must be performed by doctor	
Illinois	Yes: individual, joint, and second parent adoptions all approved	No; state law bans same-sex marriage	Yes; favorable laws mean no adoption required in gestational surrogacy cases	Yes; unmarried women can undergo donor insemination	
Indiana	Yes	No; state law bans same-sex marriage	Yes; law a bit confusing but possible	No laws on donor insemination	

State	**State recognition of gay / lesbian couples?**	**State recognition of gay / lesbian couples?**	**Surrogacy legal?**	**Donor Insemination Legal? Other?**	**Other?**
Iowa	*Some counties*	*No; state law bans same-sex marriage*	*No laws on surrogacy*	*Laws unclear on donor insemination for unmarried women*	
Kansas	*No*	*No; state law bans same-sex marriage; Constitutional amendment bans gay marriage*	*Maybe; laws do not prohibit but also do not regulate, unclear if contracts would be enforcable*	*Donor insemination laws do not mention unmarried women*	
Kentucky	*No*	*No; state law bans same-sex marriage*	*Maybe; no direct laws but court decisions would seem to support uncompensated*	*Yes; unmarried women can undergo donor insemination*	
Louisiana	*No*	*No; state law bans same-sex marriage*	*Maybe; traditional surrogacy prohibited, but uncompensated gestational may be okay*	*Yes; appears unmarried women can undergo donor insemination; doctor supervision required*	*Relatively unfriendly*
Maine	*Some single parent adoptions to gay / lesbian individuals*	*Domestic partnership; but state law bans same-sex marriage*	*No laws on surrogacy*	*No laws on donor insemination; seems to be allowed for unmarried women*	*Fairly tolerant*

State	***State recognition of gay / lesbian couples?***	***State recognition of gay / lesbian couples?***	***Surrogacy legal?***	***Donor Insemination Legal? Other?***	***Other?***
Maryland	*Some counties*	*No; state law bans same-sex marriage*	*Yes; bound by surrogacy contract only (no laws)*	*Laws unclear for unmarried women*	*Fairly tolerant*
Massachusetts	*State-wide; joint adoptions also permitted*	*Gay marriage legal*	*Yes; well-regulated, but some court decisions favor surrogate in traditional surrogacy custody*	*Laws don't address unmarried women*	*Very tolerant*
Michigan	*Some counties; discontinued in others*	*No; state law bans same-sex marriage*	*No; surrogacy contracts illegal and unenforceable*	*Laws appear to allow unmarried women*	
Minnesota	*Some counties*	*No; state law bans same-sex marriage*	*No laws on surrogacy*	*Yes; laws allow unmarried women*	
Mississippi	*No; Same-sex couples can't adopt*	*No; state law bans same-sex marriage*	*No laws on surrogacy*	*No laws on donor insemination*	*Custody denied based solely on sexual orientation*
Missouri	*Some counties*	*No; state law bans same-sex marriage*	*No laws on surrogacy, but compensated surrogacy may be*	*Laws do not mention unmarried women*	*Relatively unfriendly*

State	State recognition of gay / lesbian couples?	State recognition of gay / lesbian couples?	Surrogacy legal?	Donor Insemination Legal? Other?	Other?
Montana	No	No; state law bans same-sex marriage	No laws on surrogacy	Laws do not mention unmarried women	Uncertain
Nebraska	No	No; ballot initiative bans same-sex marriage	No; contracts unenforceable, but uncompensated may be okay	No laws on donor insemination	Gay / lesbian foster parents banned
Nevada	Some counties	No; ballot initiative bans same-sex marriage	Yes; but only for married couples Laws do not mention unmarried women	Laws do not mention unmarried women	
New Hampshire	Some counties	No; state law bans same-sex marriage	Yes; but only for married couples	Yes; laws permit unmarried women	Statute banning gay/lesbian adoptions repealed in 1999
New Jersey	State-wide second parent adoption and joint adoptions	Domestic partnership	Yes; uncompensated gestational only	Yes; laws permit unmarried women	Tolerant
New Mexico	Some counties	No explicit laws prohibiting same-sex marriage	Yes; uncompensated only	Yes; laws permit unmarried women	Some agreements between bio parents and partners upheld by courts

State	State recognition of gay / lesbian couples?	State recognition of gay / lesbian couples?	Surrogacy legal?	Donor Insemination Legal? Other?	Other?
New York	State-wide	No explicit laws prohibiting same-sex marriage	No; but may be able to work with surrogate from outside the state	Laws do not mention unmarried women, but appears to be okay	Friendly
North Carolina	No	No; state law bans same-sex marriage	No laws on surrogacy; may be ok but can pay expenses only	Laws do not mention unmarried women	Custody denied based solely on sexual orientation
North Dakota	No	No; state law bans same-sex marriage	No	Yes; laws appear to permit unmarried	Gradual improvement
Ohio	Second parent disapproved by appellate court; adoptions by gay / lesbian individuals specifically allowed	No; state law bans same-sex marriage	Maybe; court decisions are unclear on this issue, but should be possible	Yes; laws appear to permit unmarried women; physician supervision required for known donors	
Oklahoma	Gays / lesbians may not adopt	No; state law bans same-sex marriage	Maybe; requires consent from surrogate's husband, could nullify agreement	Laws do not mention unmarried women	New adoption law states that no office, court, or municipality will legally recognize a joint same-sex adoption from another

State	***State recognition of gay / lesbian couples?***	***State recognition of gay / lesbian couples?***	***Surrogacy legal?***	***Donor Insemination Legal? Other?***	***Other?***
Oregon	*Some counties*	*No; constitutional amendment bans same-sex marriage*	*Yes; uncompensated only*	*Yes; laws appear to permit unmarried women*	*Favorable*
Pennsylvania	*State-wide*	*No; state law bans same-sex marriage*	*No state-wide laws; generally favorable*	*No laws on donor insemination*	
Rhode Island	*Some counties*	*No explicit laws prohibiting same-sex marriage*	*No laws on surrogacy; probably okay*	*No laws on donor insemination*	*Courts upheld lesbian visitation agreement after breakup*
South Carolina	*No*	*No; state law bans same-sex marriage*	*Maybe; no laws specifically prohibit or regulate*	*No laws on donor insemination*	*Conservative, but some favorable decisions regarding*
South Dakota	*No*	*No; state law bans same-sex marriage*	*No laws on surrogacy*	*No laws on donor insemination*	
Tennessee	*No second parent; adoption by single lesbian approved*	*No; state law bans same-sex marriage*	*Maybe; no laws specifically prohibit or regulate, but married couples only*	*Laws do not mention unmarried women*	*Growing tolerance shown by visitation agreements upheld*
Texas	*Some counties*	*No; state law bans same-sex marriage*	*Yes; legal and well-regulated, but married couples only*	*Yes; laws appear to allow unmarried women*	*Tolerance varies*

State	State recognition of gay / lesbian couples?	State recognition of gay / lesbian couples?	Surrogacy legal?	Donor Insemination Legal? Other?	Other?
Utah	No; unmarried couples can't adopt; joint adoption and gay/lesbian foster parents expressly forbidden	No; state law bans same-sex marriage	No	Laws do not directly address donor insemination	Generally hostile
Vermont	State-wide; some stepparent adoptions also allowed; joint adoptions also	Civil unions offer all state-wide marriage benefits	Probably yes, including for same-sex couples, but no official laws	No laws on donor insemination	Partners in civil unions have spousal status for adoptions
Virginia	No	No; state law bans same-sex marriage	Yes; uncompensated ok, but appears to be for married couples only	Laws do not clearly address unmarried women	Generally hostile; custody denied based solely on sexual orientation
Washington	Some counties	No; state law bans same-sex marriage	Yes; but can't pay surrogate (not even living expenses)	No laws on donor insemination	Generally tolerant
West Virginia	No	No; state law bans same-sex marriage	Yes; but must adopt in state courts (so only available to WV residents)	No laws on donor insemination	

State	***State recognition of gay / lesbian couples?***	***State recognition of gay / lesbian couples?***	***Surrogacy legal?***	***Donor Insemination Legal? Other?***	***Other?***
Wisconsin	*Specifically disapproved by appeals court*	*No; state law bans same-sex marriage*	*No laws on surrogacy*	*Yes; laws appear to allow unmarried women*	*Tolerant in some regions*
Wyoming	*No*	*No; state law bans same-sex marriage*	*No laws on surrogacy*	*Yes; laws appear to allow unmarried women*	*Generally conservative*

APPENDIX 2

Domestic adoption agencies reported to be friendly to single and coupled gay / lesbian adoptive parents

State	Agency Name	City	Website
Calilfornia	Across the World Adoptions	Pleasant Hill	www.atwakids.org
	Adopt a Special Kid (AASK)	Oakland	www.adoptaspecialkid.org
	Adopt-link - Lil Snee, Facilitator	Los Gatos	www.adoptlink.com
	Adoption Network Law Center (facilitator)	Orange County	adoptionnetwork.com
	Adopt-now - Nancy Hurwitz Kors, facilitator	Walnut Creek	adopt-now.com
	Family Builders by Adoption	Oakland	www.familybuilders.org
	FamiliesFirst	Oakland	www.familiesfirstinc.org
	Independent Adoption Center	Pleasant Hill, Los Angeles	www.adoptionhelp.org
	Kinship Center	Salinas and Santa Ana	www.kinshipcenter.org
	Pact	Oakland	www.pactadopt.org
	SF Child Project	Oakland	www.sfchild.org
Delaware	Adoptions from the Heart	Wilmington	www.adoptionsfromtheheart.org
Georgia	Independent Adoption Center	Atlanta	www.adoptionhelp.org
Illinois	Adoption-Link	Chicago	www.adoptionlinkillinois.com
	Chances by Choice: HIV+ children	Oak Park	www.chancesbychoice.org
	The Cradle	Evanston	www.cradle.org
	Family Resource Center	Chicago	www.f-r-c.org

State	Agency Name	City	Website
Indiana	Independent Adoption Center	Indianapolis	www.adoptionhelp.org
Maine	Sharing in Adoption	Falmouth	(207) 781-3092
Maryland	Adoptions Forever	Rockville	www.adoptionsforever.com
Massachusetts	A Red Thread Adoption Service (homestudies in MA and RI)	Norwood	www.redthreadadopt.org
	Wide Horizons for Children	Waltham (and other New England states)	www.whfc.org
New Jersey	Adoptions from the Heart	Cherry Hill	www.adoptionsfromtheheart.org
	Family Options Adoptions	Red Bank	www.adoptionsbyfamilyoptions.org
New York	AdoptionSTAR	Amherst	www.adoptionstar.com
North Carolina	Independent Adoption Center	Raleigh	www.adoptionhelp.org
Oregon	Open Adoption and Family Services	Portland	www.openadopt.org
Pennsylvania	Adoption ARC	Philadelphia	www.adoptionarc.com
	Adoptions from the Heart	Allentown	www.adoptionsfromtheheart.org
	Adoption Unlimited	Lancaster	www.adoptionunlimited.org
Texas	Adoption Advisory	Dallas	www.adoptadvisory.com
Vermont	Friends in Adoption	Middletown Springs	www.friendsinadoption.com
Virginia	Adoptions from the Heart	Chesapeake	www.adoptionsfromtheheart.org
Washington	Amara Parenting and Adoption Services	Seattle	www.amaraparenting.org
	Open Adoption and Family Services	Seattle	www.openadopt.org

Reproductive technology centers friendly to gay/lesbian clients

State	*Agency Name*	*City*	*Website*
California	*California Cryobank (sperm bank)*	*Los Angeles and Palo Alto*	*www.cryobank.com*
	The Sperm Bank of California (lesbian-run sperm bank)	*Berkeley*	*www.spermbankofca.org*
	Pacific Reproductive Services (sperm bank)	*San Francisco and Pasadena*	*www.hellobaby.com*
	Rainbow Flag Health Services (sperm bank with gay donors)	*Alameda*	*www.gayspermbank.com*
	Growing Generations (surrogacy)	*Los Angeles*	*www.growinggenerations.com*
	Ova the Rainbow (surrogacy and egg donation)	*Stevinson*	*www.ovatherainbow.com*
Massachusetts	*California Cryobank (sperm bank)*	*Cambridge*	*www.cryobank.com*
	Circle Surrogacy	*Boston*	*www.circlesurrogacy.com*
New Jersey	*Biogenetics (sperm bank)*	*Mountainside*	*www.sperm1.com*

APPENDIX 3

Gay Parenting Organizations and other Resources for Gay Families

Gay Parenting Websites:
Families Like Ours
http://familieslikeours.org/
Provides support to gay and lesbian adoptive families.

National Center for Lesbian Rights
www.nclrights.org
Legal resource site for lesbians across the country, focusing on legal rights for lesbians and their families. Also provides legal representation and resources for gay men, bisexual and transgender individuals.

Our Family
http://www.ourfamily.org
Organization in the San Francisco Bay area, furthers the rights of families with gay, lesbian, bisexual and transgender members.

Proud Parenting
http://www.proudparenting.com
Gay and lesbian family and parenting site.

2moms2dads
http://2moms2dads.com/
Resources for lesbians and gays who are parents or want to become parents.

PFLAG - Parents, Families and Friends of Lesbians and Gays
http://www.pflag.org
National support group for gay friends and family members

Mailing Lists For Gay Families:
Gay-Aparent
http://maelstrom.stjohns.edu/
Mailing list for gay and lesbian adoptive parents and prospective adoptive parents

Moms
http://groups.queernet.org
Lesbian/bisexual mothers, co-mothers, and wanna-be mothers

Glbt-Parents
http://groups.queernet.org
GLBT parents who are raising a child in a GLBT home.

Pqp - Prospective Queer Parents
http://groups.queernet.org
Queer child-raising.

Queerdads
https://www.milepost1.com
Mailing list for gay fathers

Pregnant Lesbians
http://groups.yahoo.com
Pregnant lesbians and their partners can share ideas, information and support about pregnancy, childbirth and children.

ShesHavingOurBaby
http://groups.yahoo.com
Lesbians trying to conceive.

Gay Family Support Groups:
Family Pride
http://www.familypride.org/index.php
Equality for lesbian, gay, bisexual and transgender parents and their families; sponsors family weeks in Provincetown and elsewhere for families with LGBT parents.

COLAGE - children of lesbians and gays everywhere
http://www.colage.org
Support for young people with gay, lesbian, bisexual, and transgender parents.

Our Family Coalition
http://www.ourfamily.org
San Francisco Bay area LGBT family group.

List of local GLBT parenting groups
http://www.familypride.org/groups.htm

Mountain Meadow Summer Camp
http://www.mountainmeadow.org
A feminist camp for kids with lesbian, gay, bisexual or transgender parents and their allies. Mountain Meadow is a two week sleep over camp held in Southern New Jersey.

Family-Related Gay and Lesbian Literature
Gay Parent magazine
www.gayparentmag.com
Magazine for LGBT parenting. Has been in print and online since 1998.

In The Family magazine
http://www.inthefamily.com
Website and magazine covering love, intimacy and family issues for gays and lesbians

Two Lives Publishing
http://www.twolives.com/ -, a publisher of children's books for kids in LGBT-parented families

Children's Books For Gay And Lesbian Families:

A Mother For Choco
Author: Keiko Kasza

ABC A Family Alphabet Book
Author: Bobbie Combs

Asha's Mums
Author: Rosamund Elwin

Celebrating Families
Author: Rosmarie Hausherr

Daddy's Roommate
Author: Michael Willhoite

Heather Has Two Mommies
Author: Leslea Newman

Molly's Family
Author: Nancy Garden

One Dad, Two Dads, Brown Dads, Blue Dads
Author: Johnny Valentine

The Family Book
Author: Todd Parr

The Generous Jefferson Bartleby Jones
Author: Forman George Brown

Two Moms, the Zark, and Me
Author: Johnny Valentine

Who's in a Family?
Author: Robert Skutch

APPENDIX 4

Sample Contracts for Sperm Donation and Surrogacy

Note: these are only sample documents, to use for reference. Please consult an experienced lawyer in your state who can create a contract for your particular circumstances, taking into account the legal requirements in your jurisdiction.

SAMPLE KNOWN SPERM DONOR AGREEMENT

This AGREEMENT is made this ______ day of ______________________, 20__, by and between ____, hereafter DONOR, and ____, hereafter RECIPIENT, who may also be referred to herein as the parties.

NOW, THEREFORE, in consideration of the promises of each other, DONOR and RECIPIENT agree as follows:

1. Each clause of the AGREEMENT is separate and divisible from the others, and, should a court refuse to enforce one or more clauses of this AGREEMENT, the others are still valid and in full force.

2. DONOR has agreed to provide his semen to RECIPIENT for the purpose of artificial insemination.

3. In exchange, DONOR has received from RECIPIENT ____________.

4. Each party acknowledges and agrees that, through the procedure of artificial insemination, the RECIPIENT is attempting to become pregnant. It is our intent that such inseminations shall continue until conception occurs.

5. Each party acknowledges and agrees that DONOR provided his semen for the purposes of said artificial insemination, and did so with the clear understanding that he would not demand, request, or compel any guardianship, custody or visitation rights with any child born from the artificial insemination procedure. Further, DONOR acknowledges that he fully understands that he would have no paternal rights whatsoever with said child.

6. Each party acknowledges and agrees that RECIPIENT has relinquished any and all rights that she might otherwise have to hold DONOR legally, financially, or emotionally responsible for any child that results from the artificial insemination procedure.

7. Each part acknowledges and agrees that the sole authority to name any child resulting from the artificial insemination procedure shall rest with RECIPIENT.

8. Each party acknowledges and agrees that there shall be no father named on the birth certificate of any child born from the artificial insemination procedure.

9. Each party relinquishes and releases any and all rights he or she may have to bring a suit to establish paternity.

10. Each party covenants and agrees that, in light of the expectations of each party, as stated above, RECIPIENT shall have absolute authority and power to appoint a guardian for her child, and that the mother and guardian may act with sole discretion as to all legal financial, medical and emotional needs of said child without any involvement with or demands of authority from DONOR.

11. Each party covenants and agrees that the identity of the DONOR shall be made known to the child at a time and in a manner to be determined solely by the RECIPIENT. Each party reserves the right not to disclose his identity to any others, and RECIPIENT agrees not to disclose DONOR's identity to any specific persons upon his written request including full names.

12. Each party acknowledges and agrees that the relinquishment of all rights, as stated above, is final and irrevocable. DONOR further understands that his waivers shall prohibit any action on his part for custody, guardianship, or visitation in any future situations, including the event of RECIPIENT's disability or death.

13. Each party acknowledges and understands that any future contact the DONOR may have with any child(ren) that result(s) from the artificial insemination procedure in no way alters the effect of this agreement. Any such contact will be at the discretion of the RECIPIENT and/or appointed guardian, and will be consistent with the intent of both parties to sever any and all parental rights and responsibilities of the DONOR.

14. Each party covenants and agrees that any dispute pertaining to this AGREEMENT which arises between them shall be submitted to binding arbitration according to the following procedures:

i. The request for arbitration may be made by either party and shall be in writing and delivered to the other party;

ii. Pending the outcome of arbitration, there shall be no change made in the language of this AGREEMENT;

iii. The arbitration panel that will resolve any disputes regarding this AGREEMENT shall consist of three persons; one person chosen by DONOR, one person chosen by RECIPIENT; and on person chosen by the other two panel members;

iv. Within fourteen calendar days following the written arbitration request, the arbitrators shall be chosen;

v. Within fourteen days following the selection of all members of the arbitration panel, the panel will hear the dispute between parties;

vi. Within seven days subsequent to the hearing, the arbitration panel will make a decision and communicate it in writing to each party.

15. Each party acknowledges and understands that there are legal questions raised by the issues involved in this AGREEMENT which have not been settled by stature or prior court decisions. Notwithstanding the knowledge that certain of the clauses stated herein may not be enforced in a court of law, the parties choose to enter into this AGREEMENT and clarify their intent that existed at the time the artificial insemination procedure was implemented by them.

16. Each party acknowledges and agrees that she or he signed this AGREEMENT voluntarily and freely, of his or her own choice, without any duress of any kind whatsoever. It is further acknowledged that each party has been advised to secure the advice and consent of an attorney of his or her own choosing, and that each party understands the meaning and significance of each provision of this AGREEMENT.

17. Each party acknowledges and agrees that any changes made in the terms and conditions of the AGREEMENT shall be made in writing and signed by both parties.

18. This AGREEMENT contains the entire understanding of the parties. There are no promises, understandings, agreements or representations between the parties other than those expressly stated in this AGREEMENT.

IN WITNESS WHEREOF, the parties hereunto have executed this AGREEMENT, in the City of ____________________, and State of ____________________, on the day and year first above written.

______________________________ ______________________________

Donor Print Name

______________________________ ______________________________

Recipient Print Name

______________________________ ______________________________

Notary Print Name

(Used with permission from Gay Family Options; www.gayfamilyoptions.org)

SAMPLE SURROGATE AGREEMENT

Note: this sample agreement is geared toward a state where only living expense reimbursement is allowed. Those amounts should be factored into the contract. In other states or countries, different financial arrangements may be permitted. Please consult a lawyer to draft a contract that will be legally sound in your particular jurisdiction.

This Agreement is made this date between SURROGATE, Ms. XXXXX and NATURAL FATHER, Mr. XXXXXX.

RECITALS

This Agreement is made with reference to the following facts:

(1) Whereas the NATURAL FATHER is over the age eighteen (18) years, and desirous of entering into the following Agreement. The NATURAL FATHER desires to take into his home the child or children as his own which is/are born to the SURROGATE and is/are biologically related to him. The SURROGATE wishes to facilitate the child's placement with the NATURAL FATHER and will fully cooperate to obtain this goal.

(2) Whereas the SURROGATE is over the age of eighteen (18) years and is desirous of entering into this Agreement.

(3) Whereas the decision of SURROGATE, to enter into a Surrogate Parenting Agreement, is a fully informed one, made after a careful and unemotional reflection of all aspects of this arrangement. SURROGATE has come forward voluntarily, without economic or emotional duress of any kind, and has freely chosen, to participate as a surrogate.

(4) Whereas the SURROGATE is aware of the religion, sexual orientation and preference of the NATURAL FATHER and is willing to work with him to assist him in having a child. SURROGATE believes the CHILD conceived pursuant to this Agreement is morally and contractually that of the NATURAL FATHER, and should be raised by the NATURAL FATHER without any interference by SURROGATE, and without any retention or assertion by her of any parental rights. The SURROGATE wishes to facilitate the child's placement with the NATURAL FATHER and will fully cooperate to obtain this goal. The SURROGATE does not desire to have a parental relationship with the child or children born pursuant to this Agreement. It is the intent of the SURROGATE to have any and all legal rights to the child legally terminated, to the degree legally possible.

(5) Whereas the SURROGATE has personal knowledge regarding the NATURAL FATHER, including but not limited to his full legal name, age, religion, race/ethnicity, employment, conditions of the home environment, knowledge of all persons who reside in the home, conditions of his health and area of residence. SURROGATE declares that she is fully satisfied that the best interests of the child will be served by consenting to the permanent placement of the child with the NATURAL FATHER and the relinquishment of all rights that she may have.

(6) Whereas the parties desire to maintain confidentialities between themselves and the public. In so stating, neither party will commit a breach of this agreement if they were to tell his or her family or closest friends about the circumstances of the pregnancy that is intended to occur here.

NOW , THEREFORE, notwithstanding the recitals stated above, in consideration of the mutual promises contained herein, and with the intentions of being legally bound thereby, the parties agree as follows:

SURROGATE, based on her information and belief, represents that she knows of no reason that she would not be capable of bearing healthy, normal children. Pursuant to this representation, the NATURAL FATHER is hereby entering into a written Agreement with the SURROGATE, whereby the SURROGATE shall be artificially inseminated with fresh sperm, frozen sperm, or sperm prepared in a preservative of the NATURAL FATHER, so that SURROGATE may bear a child biologically related to the NATURAL FATHER. The child is to be taken into the home of the NATURAL FATHER and raised by him without interference by the SURROGATE, and without retention or assertion by her of any parental rights. The birth of the child is intended to take place in XXXXXXXXX, unless SURROGATE is unable to get there in time, in which case it shall take place in XXXXXXXXXX.

II

Any party may withdraw his or her consent to artificial insemination and terminate this Agreement at any time prior to conception without consequence.

III

"CHILD" as referred to in this Agreement, shall include all children born pursuant to the insemination as defined in the terms and provisions of this Agreement.

IZ

NATURAL FATHER will assume responsibility for any child which may possess congenital abnormalities or defects, and the parties to this Agreement acknowledge that they have been advised and are aware of the risks of such abnormalities and/or defects.

SURROGATE represents that she will not form nor attempt to form a parent-child relationship with any child or children she may conceive and bear pursuant to the provisions of this Agreement. SURROGATE further represents that she will terminate all of her parental rights by way of consenting to an Adoption and/or stipulation to Entry of Judgment, and/or signing a surrender form terminating her parental rights to said child within four days after the birth of the child. The SURROGATE will immediately relinquish said child into the sole custody and control of NATURAL FATHER following the birth. SURROGATE will fully cooperate at NATURAL FATHER'S request, in signing any and all documents necessary to obtain a court order granting the NATURAL FATHER immediate and sole physical custody, if necessary, and adoption of the child prior to the birth of the child, if possible, and if not possible, within four days after the birth of the CHILD.

In so stating, NATURAL FATHER wishes SURROGATE to have a more substantial involvement with the CHILD than the average surrogate. This would mean that the SURROGATE would act as a sort of godmother to the child, seeing the child from time to time, and participating in the CHILD's life. Such involvement, however, would not alter the custody arrangement set forth above or entitle SURROGATE to any formal schedule of visitation that might be enforced in a court of law.

V

If SURROGATE violates this Agreement by asserting all or part of her parental rights, NATURAL FATHER may elect to respond in one of several ways. He may elect to terminate this Agreement forthwith, waive his parental rights and sever his connection to the CHILD by invoking all legal and equitable protections available, and SURROGATE agrees not to seek any child support from NATURAL FATHER. SURROGATE acknowledges and accepts NATURAL FATHER'S right to make such an election, and warrants that she will not object, and will not attempt to use this Agreement to assert the parental obligations of NATURAL FATHER.

In the alternative, NATURAL FATHER may elect to accept a shared parenting arrangement, with all rights and obligations of the parties to be legally established.

In the alternative, NATURAL FATHER may elect, after consideration of all available options, to seek a best interest of the child determination or a judicial enforcement of this Agreement in XXXXXXX and to assert all available remedies.

VI

SURROGATE agrees to submit herself and the child to H.L.A. testing, or any other legally recognized test to determine paternity around fourteen(14) weeks into the pregnancy. NATURAL FATHER may, if necessary, petition a court of law to establish his paternity. In such case, except as provided in Section VI of this Agreement, the issue of paternity shall be resolved pursuant to paternity blood testing (H.L.A. and/or any other legally recognized paternity test) through blood testing shall be binding on the parties to this Agreement.

SURROGATE will take any and all necessary action to facilitate the NATURAL FATHER obtaining a court order establishing his paternity.

VII

Except as provided in paragraph VI above, any material violation of any of the provisions contained herein, including but not limited to covenants, representations, warranties and promises, by either party, without legal excuse, shall constitute a breach, and, in addition to all other remedies available at law or equity, this Agreement may be terminated forthwith at the option of the aggrieved party.

As a precondition to any violation constituting a breach, the party committing said violation shall be given written notice of such alleged violation, within a reasonable time after discovery, and shall have a reasonable opportunity to cure said alleged violation, if possible. The continued performance of an aggrieved party following a breach, shall not constitute a waiver of said breach, in the absence of an express written notice to that effect given to the breaching party.

VIII

The SURROGATE has undergone psychological evaluation and screening interviews by a Social Worker and Psychologist (collectively the "Psychologist") designated by the NATURAL FATHER. The NATURAL FATHER has paid for the cost of said psychological review and/or evaluation. The SURROGATE shall sign, prior to her psychological evaluation, a medical release form authorizing the NATURAL FATHER to secure the release of the portions of this psychological evaluation/review, which discuss the SURROGATE's ability/intent to release the CHILD to the NATURAL FATHER following the birth of the CHILD, and the evaluation/review shall be submitted to the NATURAL FATHER or his representative for his approval. The SURROGATE agrees to undergo any psychological counseling or therapy designated by said Psychologist, prior to, during or for a reasonable period of time after the pregnancy (as determined by Psychologist), and while this Agreement is in effect.

The SURROGATE furthermore warrants that prior to the execution of this Agreement, she has signed a comprehensive medical release form allowing the Psychologist to disclose to NATURAL FATHER those communications, verbal or non-verbal, made by the SURROGATE, during the course of her therapy or counseling, or any opinions, perceptions or conclusions found by the Psychologist, which could reasonably relate to the SURROGATE'S performance of this Agreement.

The SURROGATE is not precluded from, and is encouraged to, seek and receive psychological counseling in conjunction with the conduct underlying this Agreement from any other source/person.

The SURROGATE warrants that she will consult or has consulted with a psychologist (which may be the same Psychologist and/or Social Worker as in paragraph first of this Section IX) about the psychological risks associated with performance under the surrogate contract and agrees to assume all risks associated thereby. The SURROGATE specifically consents to the medical and psychological risks associated with performance under this Agreement. Prior to insemination, the SURROGATE and the NATURAL FATHER shall undergo a physical examination under the direction of, and to the extent determined, in the sole discretion of a physician designated by the NATURAL FATHER, to determine whether the physical health and well-being of each are satisfactory. Said physical examination shall include testing for venereal diseases, including AIDS, in order to protect the health of the SURROGATE and the CHILD.

IX
The SURROGATE and the NATURAL FATHER agree to undergo any medical testing that the above mentioned physician deems necessary while this Agreement is in effect. Both the SURROGATE and the NATURAL FATHER agree to waive any privileges of confidentiality between the parties to this agreement as to any and all medical information either obtained or received by the physician designated by the NATURAL FATHER and/or any treating physician providing services in conjunction with or related to the conduct of the parties contemplated pursuant to this Agreement. Confirmation that the NATURAL FATHER is free of AIDS and of HIV will be provided to SURROGATE prior to the first insemination.

X
The SURROGATE agrees to and promises that she will not have any sexual intercourse with a man from the time of the signing of the contract until pregnancy has been confirmed in writing by a physician. The SURROGATE further agrees to and promises that she will not engage in any activity in which the possibility of semen other than that utilized in inseminations from the NATURAL FATHER could be introduced into her body such that the possibility of a pregnancy other than contemplated by this Agreement might occur.

XI
The SURROGATE agrees to assume all of the above- and below stated risks, and to indemnify for any cost of defense and/or liability incurred in conjunction with this Agreement and hold harmless against these risks, the NATURAL FATHER, XXXXX , XXXXXXX, XXXXXX and XXXXXXXXX, or any of their agents and employees,

including the professionals and others contemplated and/or involved in any aspect of the Agreement.

XII

The SURROGATE warrants that she has consulted with a physician and is aware of all medical risks, including death, which may result from the conduct contemplated by this Agreement. These risks involve medical examinations, artificial insemination, conception, pregnancy, childbirth and post-partum complications. Said risks have been explained to the SURROGATE by a physician following the thorough medical examination of the SURROGATE by said physician. The SURROGATE agrees to assume all of the above stated risks, and to indemnify and hold harmless against these risks, the NATURAL FATHER, XXXXXX , XXXXXXX, and XXXXXX and The Law Office of XXXXXXX, and any of their agents and employees, including the professionals and others contemplated and/or involved in any aspect of the Agreement.

XIII

In the event that the contemplated pregnancy has not occurred within a reasonable time, in the opinion of the NATURAL FATHER, or for any other reason of the NATURAL FATHER prior to an insemination, this Agreement shall terminate by written notice to the SURROGATE. Such notice shall be given by the NATURAL FATHER.

Notwithstanding the foregoing, all parties are aware that the average fertile man and fertile woman, having intercourse are able to conceive approximately 20% of the time. Thus it is not uncommon for a NATURAL FATHER and SURROGATE MOTHER to have to try inseminations over 5 - 8 ovulatory cycles. In addition, miscarriages may happen as frequently as 1 in 4 births, even for healthy fertile women. Accordingly, the parties being made aware of these facts, hereby commit to inseminating during at least 9 ovulatory cycles (which could mean 18 times if 2 inseminations are done per cycle.) While the parties still reserve their right to withdraw from this Agreement for other reasons, they agree to continue to try to inseminate if their only reason for terminating is their disappointment with the success of inseminations or their disappointment with a miscarriage. However, should a physician or psychologist inform either party that they have some impediment to getting pregnant or that it will affect them detrimentally psychologically to continue, then they may then withdraw their consent for further inseminations.

XIV

During the term of this Agreement, the SURROGATE agrees to immediately inform the NATURAL FATHER, in writing, of any material change in her circumstances which may reasonably affect this Agreement. These changes include, but are not limited to, change of address, illness or death of a party, loss of employment, change in insurance coverage, exposure to communicable illness, change in marital status or military status.

XV

During the term of this Agreement, and until the birth of the child/children contemplated herein, the SURROGATE agrees to adhere to all medical instructions given to her by her independent obstetrician, who must be approved by the NATURAL FATHER.

The SURROGATE agrees not to participate in dangerous sports or activities, not to knowingly allow herself to be exposed to radiation, toxic chemicals or communicable illness. The SURROGATE also agrees not to smoke cigarettes, drink alcoholic beverages or use any illegal drugs. She furthermore agrees not to use non-prescription medication, nor prescribed medication, without written consent from the above physician.

The SURROGATE further agrees to follow a prenatal examination schedule as prescribed by her independent obstetrician as well as adhere to all requirements regarding the taking of medicine and vitamins prescribed by her treating obstetrician. The SURROGATE further agrees to submit to any medical test or procedure deemed necessary or advisable by her obstetrician. Notwithstanding the foregoing, SURROGATE has the right to obtain a second opinion in the event her doctor recommends an extraordinary medical procedure.

XVI

The SURROGATE agrees to present to the NATURAL FATHER proper evidence, documentation or verifiable information that the SURROGATE has incurred or will incur the following kinds of expenses for which the NATURAL FATHER shall arrange prompt payment from NATURAL FATHER's trust funds: necessary living expenses and medical expenses relating to the pregnancy and delivery, including, but not limited to obstetrical, nursing, hospital, maternity, pharmaceutical and pediatric care for the child resulting from this contract. Payments for expenses not yet incurred by the SURROGATE shall be made only when advance payment is necessary. The SURROGATE agrees to submit all medical bills as described above to applicable insurance carriers prior to submission for payment to the NATURAL FATHER.

XVII

The SURROGATE agrees that she will not abort the CHILD once conceived, except if, in the opinion of her independent obstetrician, such action is necessary for the physical health of the SURROGATE, or the CHILD has been determined by the physician to be physiologically abnormal and an abortion is advisable in the opinion of the independent obstetrician. In the event of either of these two contingencies, the SURROGATE agrees to submit to said abortion. All parties understand that a pregnant woman has the absolute right to abort or not abort any fetus she is carrying. Any promise to the contrary is unenforceable. If the SURROGATE has an abortion, she is entitled to one more pregnancy related expense payment of $XXXXXXX as set forth in Exhibit A hereto.
Death of the CHILD, for any reason, terminates the Agreement immediately, with no

further obligation by either party, except that NATURAL FATHER will remain liable for medical costs incurred to date and for any deductible or any co-pay for any medical complications arising therefrom.

Financial arrangements pursuant to this Agreement are set forth in Exhibit A, attached hereto and incorporated herein by reference.

XVIII
On or about 14 weeks into the pregnancy, the SURROGATE shall submit to genetic testing to determine paternity of the CHILD. The cost of this testing will be paid by NATURAL FATHER and will include any or all of the following as designated by the physician:
(1) Blood Group (4) Serum Protein
(2) Red Cell Enzyme (5) White Cell~I.L.A.
(3) DNA genetic mapping

The NATURAL FATHER being excluded by one or more of the above mentioned tests would constitute an incurable, material breach of this agreement, unless the NATURAL FATHER, in his sole discretion, agrees to adopt the CHILD and the SURROGATE consents to this adoption. If NATURAL FATHER is excluded as set forth above, SURROGATE shall reimburse NATURAL FATHER for all expenses paid to her or on her behalf as of the date of the exclusion.

XIX
The NATURAL FATHER shall be responsible for the SURROGATE's telephone calls, transportation expenses (at $0.32 per mile), or any other pregnancy related expenses incurred by the SURROGATE in performing the obligations of this Agreement. In addition, the NATURAL FATHER shall be responsible for paying for up to 6 weeks of the cost of a housekeeper for the SURROGATE if the SURROGATE is unable to perform her normal household chores during her pregnancy as a result of her pregnancy (but not after the birth of the child) that she is unable to do as a result of her doctor advising her that for her health or the health of the baby, she must stay off her feet. To obtain coverage of these expenses, SURROGATE must provide a doctor's letter to the NATURAL FATHER or his representative, and a pay stub, W-2 or similar documentation showing the housekeeper's weekly wage, and this sum will be paid to her shortly after receipt.

XX
The NATURAL FATHER will make certain, either through the proceeds from a life insurance policy on his life or from a designation in his Will that the beneficiary of this policy will be the child contemplated by this Agreement.

XXI
SURROGATE warrants that she has full medical coverage covering surrogacy and covering complete pregnancy care and delivery, including C-sections and complications that may arise from pregnancy and birth. SURROGATE warrants that she is eligible for such coverage through XXXXXXXXXXX. SURROGATE'S health insurance coverage is primarily liable for medical costs. If SURROGATE is faced with losing her health insurance coverage because she chooses to withdraw from her job at XXXXXXXXXXXXXXX, the NATURAL FATHER shall pay the monthly premiums on the SURROGATE's health insurance policy through XX weeks after the birth of the child, or until the termination of this agreement, whichever is sooner.

The $XXXXXXXXXX total payment to the SURROGATE is inclusive of these health insurance premium payments. NATURAL FATHER shall also pay for all deductible and co-pay expenses associated with the normal anticipated doctor visits, ultrasounds, and hospital charges for the delivery anticipated with a pregnancy and delivery, as well as any necessary emergency medical care related to the pregnancy through XX weeks after the birth of the child, or until the termination of this agreement. SURROGATE will present all medical, hospital, prescription and other expenses to the insurance company for payment within XXX (XX) days of receipt. The NATURAL FATHER shall be immediately informed of any and all notices received by, or that come to the attention of, the SURROGATE, or any party, regarding said insurance coverage, including, but not limited to, cancellation notices, and changes in coverage.

XXII
NATURAL FATHER shall pay SURROGATE the pregnancy related expenses contemplated by this Agreement as set forth on Exhibit A.

XXIII
The SURROGATE agrees that after the delivery, she will take any and all necessary steps to effectuate and facilitate the signing of a surrender form after the birth of the child and to assist NATURAL FATHER in obtaining any court orders he desires to secure the permanent placement and custody of the child with him and the termination of any parental rights that she may have.

XXIV
The parties acknowledge that to effectuate the terms of this Agreement properly, the parties must disclose information of a personal and confidential nature to each other. The parties warrant that total information will be held by each in the utmost confidence as the best interests of the CHILD are served by strict protection of each other's privacy. The parties agree that they will not provide nor allow others to provide any information to the public, news media, or any other individual regarding his involvement in surrogate

parenting and/or conduct contemplated under this Agreement, or the involvement of any other party hereto without express written waiver and consent of all other parties.

XXV

In the event of the death of the NATURAL FATHER prior to the birth of the CHILD, all of the rights and obligations of the SURROGATE shall be of equal force and effect notwithstanding such event and all terms contained herein shall remain in effect. The CHILD shall be placed in the custody of the NATURAL FATHER's guardian or alternate guardian named in the NATURAL FATHER's Will, and in such case the SURROGATE agrees to consent to a single-parent adoption of the child/children by the guardian or alternate guardian, whichever is applicable.

XXVI

The SURROGATE agrees to inform the NATURAL FATHER, or his designated agents, of any change of current address for a period of eighteen (18) years following the birth of the CHILD. If, in the opinion of a physician, medical information must be obtained from any party, such party agrees to furnish such information.

XXVII

In the event of a material breach by SURROGATE for which NATURAL FATHER terminates this Agreement, pursuant to its terms, all obligations of NATURAL FATHER to make payments under this Agreement shall terminate. NATURAL FATHER shall give ten (10) days written notice to the SURROGATE of a breach. The parties to this Agreement agree that participation by the SURROGATE in the activities or use of the substances described in paragraph XVI shall be a material breach by SURROGATE and, and at the sole option of the NATURAL FATHER, NATURAL FATHER may immediately, upon notice as provided herein, terminate any and all of his obligations under this Agreement.

XXVIII

Should the NATURAL FATHER breach this agreement by failing to accept a CHILD that is biologically related to him, SURROGATE has the right to sue NATURAL FATHER to enforce the terms of this agreement. During the time of such breach, XXXXXXXXX shall be authorized to continue making all payments to the SURROGATE under this contract.

XXIX

The NATURAL FATHER and SURROGATE recognize and acknowledge that XXXXXXXXXXXXX , as mentioned in the RECITALS herein above, shall act as attorney for the NATURAL FATHER in only the negotiation of this Agreement, the administration of the trust, the obtaining of a paternity judgment, and the adoption of the child, if so requested. It is understood that while XXXXXXXXXXXXXX may act as attorneys, they are not parties to this Agreement. The NATURAL FATHER and SURROGATE recognize and acknowledge that XXXXXXXXXXXX and XXXXXXXXXXXX, shall act as attorney for the SURROGATE on only the negotiation of this Agreement and any representation of the SURROGATE necessary regarding the obtaining by the NATURAL FATHER of a paternity judgment and the adopting by the guardian or alternate guardian of the CHILD.

XXX

Notwithstanding the agency stated in the paragraph next above, no agency, partnership, employment or joint venture is created or intended to be created between the parties or agents herein.

XXXI

The SURROGATE warrants that all information prepared by the SURROGATE and submitted to the NATURAL FATHER for his review in connection with this Agreement, is true and correct. The SURROGATE further warrants that she has not knowingly falsified or omitted any material information, and understands that any knowing falsification or omission could constitute a breach of this Agreement. SURROGATE further warrants that she realizes the NATURAL FATHER has relied upon the information provided.

XXXII

This Agreement shall be amended only by a written Agreement signed by all the parties hereto.

XXXIII

This Agreement does not instruct the parties on immigration or taxation. It is the responsibility of any party receiving payment or other benefit pursuant to this Agreement to report receipt of said payments or benefits to the proper taxing authorities, State or Federal.

XXXIV

The parties expressly understand and agree that neither XXXXXXXXXXXXXX , or XXXXXXXXXXXXXXXXXXXX, or her agents or employees, nor the professionals whose services are contemplated herein, guarantee or warrant any of the representations made by SURROGATE, or: (1) that the SURROGATE will in fact carry to term a child after artificial insemination; (2) that the CHILD will be physically and mentally healthy and free of birth or congenital defects; (3) that the SURROGATE will comply with the terms and provisions of this Agreement, entered into between the parties; (4) that the NATURAL FATHER will comply with the terms and provisions of this Agreement

XXXV

LIMITATION OF REMEDIES: In order to maintain the confidentiality contemplated herein and in the event that litigation arises out of this Agreement, the parties to this Agreement, their legal counsel, their heirs and representatives agree to make all reasonable efforts to maintain such confidentiality as is intended by this Agreement as to the general public and as to each other, including, but not limited to, requesting that court records be sealed, requesting the court to invoke gag orders, requesting the court, in their procedures and in the conducting of hearings, to maintain confidential the identity of the parties.

XXXVI

This Agreement may be executed in two (2) or more counter- parts, each of which shall be an original, but all of which shall constitute one (1) and the same instrument. One original of the respective counterparts shall be maintained by the NATURAL FATHER's counsel and the other original shall be maintained by SURROGATE or her counsel.

XXXVII

This Agreement sets forth the entire Agreement between the parties with regard to the subject matter hereof. All Agreements, covenants, representations, and warranties expressed and implied, oral and written, of the parties, are contained herein. No other Agreement, covenants, representations, nor warranties, expressed or implied, oral or written, have been made by any party to the other with respect to the subject matter of this Agreement. All prior and contemporaneous conversations, negotiations, possible and alleged Agreements, representations, covenants and warranties, with respect to the subject matter hereof, are waived, merged herein and superseded hereby. This is an integrated Agreement.

XXXVIII

No provision of this Agreement is to be interpreted for or against any party because that party or that party's legal representative drafted the provisions.

XXXIX

In the event of any of the provisions, whether sentences, or entire paragraphs, of this Agreement are deemed to be invalid or unenforceable, the same shall be deemed severable from the remainder of this Agreement and shall not cause the invalidity or unenforceability of the remainder of this Agreement. If such provisions shall be deemed invalid due to its scope or breadth, such provision shall be deemed valid to the extent of the scope or breadth permitted by law.

XL

Each party acknowledges that they fully understand the Agreement and its legal effect, and that they are signing the same, freely and voluntarily, and that no party has any reason to believe that the other party did not freely and voluntarily execute this Agreement.

XLI
Any dispute arising under this Agreement will be adjudicated in XXXXXXXXX under XXXXXXXXXX law.

I have read this entire Agreement and fully understand all of its terms. I agree to be bound by all provisions, warranties and representations.

Executed this day of XXXXXXX , XXXX in XXXXX

____

XXXXXXX, NATURAL FATHER

I have read this entire Agreement and fully understand all of its terms. I agree to be bound by all provisions, warranties and representations.

____

XXXXXXX, SURROGATE

STATE OF XXXXXXXXXXXXX
XXXXX , XX , XXXX

Then personally appeared the above-named XXXXXXXXXX and acknowledged the foregoing to be his free act and deed. Before me,

____

Notary Public
My commission expires

____

STATE OF XXXXXXXXXXXXXX

XXXxX, XX , XXXX

Then personally appeared the above-named XXXXXXXX and acknowledged the foregoing to be her free act and deed. Before me,

____

Notary Public
My commission expires: _________________________

Used with permission from Everything Surrogacy, http://www.everythingsurrogacy.com.

INDEX